MAJOR HISTORICAL PLAYS OF STRINDBERG

THE HISTORICAL PLAYS OF AUGUST STRINDBERG
Translated by Walter Johnson

Queen Christina, Charles XII, Gustav III
The Last of the Knights, The Regent, Earl Birger of Bjälbo
Gustav Adolf
The Vasa Trilogy: Master Olof, Gustav Vasa, Erik XIV
The Saga of the Folkungs, Engelbrekt

THE VASA TRILOGY
Master Olof
Gustav Vasa
Erik XIV

THE VASA TRILOGY

Master Olof · *Gustav Vasa* · *Erik XIV*

By August Strindberg

TRANSLATIONS AND INTRODUCTIONS
BY WALTER JOHNSON

Seattle   University of Washington Press   *London*

Preface

IN THIS VOLUME are new translations of the three historical plays
that Strindberg called his Vasa trilogy. They have all been presented
on the Swedish stage in highly successful productions down through
the decades; some of the Swedish theater's most distinguished directors and greatest actors have found all three plays rewarding chal-
lenges that have usually brought them both critical approval and
the enthusiastic response of Swedish audiences. Such a statement
says a great deal, for in no other country, perhaps, can one find
critics more demanding or audiences more appreciative of sensitive
production, inspired acting, excellent theater, and great drama. Certainly, in our time no other country surpasses Sweden in its devotion
to the theater and to the practical as well as idealistic support of the
theater as a potent force in a dynamic and highly civilized society.

As in preceding volumes in this series, I have supplied introductions and notes that may be useful to those who do not know
Swedish history in great detail and even to those whose knowledge
of Strindberg may be confined to nonhistorical plays.

Strindberg's sources of historical detail were legion, but three popular and widely read works were, as he admitted on various occasions and in various places, major ones: A. A. Afzelius' *Svenska
folkets sagohäfder* (*The Legends and History of the Swedish People*) (Stockholm: Norstedt, 1881 edition); Anders Fryxell's *Berättelser ur svenska historien* (*Stories from Swedish History*) (Stockholm: Norstedt, 1900 edition); and C. Georg Starbäck and P. O.
Bäckström's *Berättelser ur svenska historien* (Stockholm: Beijers,
1885 edition; SB in the references). The dates indicate the editions

I have used; the first editions of these three works appeared in 1839–1870, 1822 ff., and 1860 ff., respectively. So far as possible, the historical material in the notes is presented from the point of view of Strindberg and his major sources.

WALTER JOHNSON

Contents

THE VASA TRILOGY

Master Olof
Gustav Vasa
Erik XIV

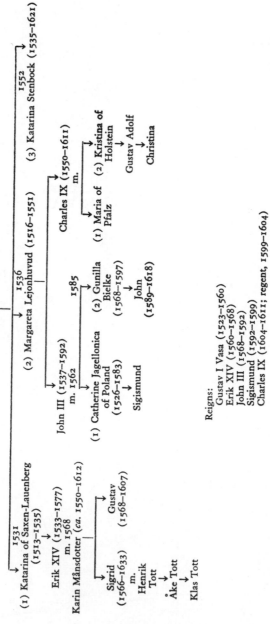

Gustav Vasa (*ca.* 1494–1560)
married

1531 (1) Katarina of Saxen-Lauenberg (1513–1535)

1536 (2) Margareta Lejonhuvud (1516–1551)

1552 (3) Katarina Stenbock (1535–1621)

From (1) Katarina of Saxen-Lauenberg:

Erik XIV (1533–1577)
m. 1568
Karin Månsdotter (*ca.* 1550–1612)

Gustav (1568–1607)

Sigrid (1566–1633)
m.
Henrik Tott
→ Åke Tott
→ Klas Tott

From (2) Margareta Lejonhuvud:

John III (1537–1592)
m. 1562

(1) Catherine Jagellonica of Poland (1526–1583)
→ Sigismund

1585 (2) Gunilla Bielke (1568–1597)
→ John (1589–1618)

Charles IX (1550–1611)
m.

(1) Maria of Pfalz

(2) Kristina of Holstein
→ Gustav Adolf
→ Christina

Reigns:
Gustav I Vasa (1523–1560)
Erik XIV (1560–1568)
John III (1568–1592)
Sigismund (1592–1599)
Charles IX (1604–1611; regent, 1599–1604)

Introduction to 'Master Olof'

No OTHER HISTORICAL play of Strindberg's has been subjected to closer or more frequent scrutiny or criticism either by Swedish scholars or, for that matter, by Strindberg himself than *Master Olof* (1872), his first dramatic masterpiece. It broke with the traditions of the Swedish theater by presenting great Swedes of the past as flesh-and-blood individuals instead of creatures out of a museum, by giving the historical play a new form, and by presenting dialogue that was startlingly realistic. The rejection of the play by the theater in 1872 and the advice that Strindberg rewrite it—as he did, partly in verse—kept him concerned with it directly over an appreciable number of years. In the middle 1880's when Strindberg was writing his four-volume autobiography, *Tjänstekvinnans son* (*The Son of a Servant*, 1886), he devoted a substantial portion of one of the four volumes, *I röda rummet* (*In the Red Room*), to a retrospective discussion and analysis of *Master Olof* and of its initial and subsequent receptions.

Swedish scholars have paid *Master Olof* the tribute of examining it in the study from almost every conceivable point of view, attempting to determine what influence such writers as Shakespeare, Goethe, Schiller, Kierkegaard, Ibsen, and various lesser predecessors and contemporaries may have had on *Master Olof;* investigating the sources of the historical details; and examining both the form and the content. The play has, moreover, become a textbook in the public schools, and there is little question that *Master Olof* is the historical play that most Swedes know best; it may even be said with some justification that Strindberg's concept of Master Olof has become a general Swedish one.

Since the prose version became a theatrical success when it was finally presented in 1881 and the poetic version made a similar record in 1890, *Master Olof* has held its position as the most frequently performed of all the historical plays, even though it has in recent decades had sharp and justified competition from, for example, the two other plays in this volume, *Gustav Vasa* and *Erik XIV.*

Of all that has been written about *Master Olof,* nothing deserves more sympathetic consideration than what Strindberg himself wrote in *In the Red Room,* some fourteen years after he completed his prose play. It is conceivable and even likely that during the intervening years Strindberg's recollections of his thinking and planning back in 1871 and 1872 had become somewhat inaccurate, but his comments on *Master Olof* are essentially sound nevertheless.

Strindberg says that *Master Olof* was planned as a drama of ideas (p. 280):

> The drama was the most suitable form through which one could say everything and then in the fifth act take back as much as one wanted to or leave it open for consideration. Back of the historical characters the author would conceal himself, and in Olaus Petri he would appear as the idealist, in Gustav Vasa as the realist, and in the anabaptist Gert as the communard, because he had now discovered that the men of the Paris commune had only applied what Buckle had taught. In his three major characters John would express his three thoughts from three points of view. To express everything he let Gert (Karl Moor) pretend to be insane, Olaus retract his ideas, and Gustav Vasa be right, and no one be wrong. The enemy from the old camp, Hans Brask, he treated with respect, too, as the person who has been right, but who with the passing of time had become wrong. For that reason, he had intended to call the play *What Is Truth?* But to get it played both of the tentative titles

[the other was *The Renegade*] were rejected for the more indifferent *Master Olof*.

And then began the attacks. First on truth as something always in the process of developing, which would become static every time anyone succeeded in persuading the masses he had found it. For that reason all useful truths had to be tentative.

Under the influence of extensive reading and the consideration of ideas from his own exceptionally fertile intellect, Strindberg set out in *Master Olof* to present and to examine the practical realism of the thinking of a Gustav Vasa, who has the very trying task of governing a nation he plans to free from all foreign control; the romantic idealism of an Olaus Petri, who plans to set his fellow Swedes free religiously from Rome; and the anarchical idealism of a Gert, who would set people free. To put it in still another way: Gert sees truth as something that can never really be fixed and static; Master Olof sees truth as fixed in the Holy Scriptures when stripped of the human impedimenta accumulated by the church over the centuries; King Gustav sees truth as something that a practical realist can come to grips with only relatively and incompletely in a specific environment. In sympathy with all three, Strindberg accepts Buckle's idea that truth is dynamic, not static.

Strindberg wrote his first major historical play as a drama of ideas and a drama of character, with the major emphasis placed on the character of the young enthusiastic reformer and his development in a harsh reality. What the historical setting for *Master Olof* was, according to the sources, is discussed briefly below.

II. The Historical Background

Modern Sweden was founded during the long reign of Gustav Vasa (1523–1560). After winning its independence from an unsatisfactory so-called union with its Scandinavian neighbors, Sweden was in a position to develop into one of the most powerful nations in

Europe. The reformation not only freed the Swedish king and the Swedish people from the control of foreign prelates and their Swedish servants, but at the same time provided Gustav Vasa ultimately with a large share of the means with which to make Sweden economically sound and politically free to develop in its own fashion. The two most important founders were Gustav Vasa, who saw his mission in life as the building of Sweden from "foundation to rafters," and Master Olof, who hoped to set his people free religiously from the Church of Rome.

In *Master Olof,* Strindberg has telescoped the major events that brought the two men into close cooperation or conflict during sixteen crucial years of Gustav's reign—from Master Olof's first appointment in 1524 as secretary to the city council of Stockholm and as preacher there until his reprieve from sentence of death in 1540. Since Strindberg emphasizes the different goals and methods of the king and the great reformer, it should be emphasized that the king worked realistically and practically toward the attainment of a broad, many-sided, and fundamentally idealistic goal, whereas Master Olof, as a young enthusiast, was primarily interested in the idealistic goal of religious freedom for his fellow Swedes.

The king welcomed Master Olof's Lutheran ideas largely because he saw in them useful justification for his seizure of church property and for nationalizing the church under his own control; in some degree, he may have welcomed the ideas because he believed in them. From the time King Gustav first heard the reformers, Lars Andersson and Master Olof, explain their ideas, he encouraged them to preach these ideas. In 1524, he made Lars Andersson his chancellor and Master Olof secretary and preacher—in Swedish—in Stockholm. The king encouraged Master Olof to teach the new doctrines through the printed word as well. Without breaking abruptly with the pope or the Catholic bishops, the king protected the reformers and supported their undertakings. For example, he stood by Master Olof when the people objected—violently on occasion—to the preaching in the native tongue, and, even more significantly, in 1525 when Master Olof broke the canonical law by getting married. Master Olof's numerous writings, which made him the outstanding literary man of his age, were printed largely because of the king's conviction that the reformer's word in print was useful propaganda. Only once did the king object to a major work by Master Olof— *The Swedish Chronicle* or *History of Sweden:* Master Olof was too competent a historian and had scholarly integrity. That work was not published in Gustav Vasa's time.

King Gustav had used Master Olof in 1524 by having him engage in public debate with the arch-Catholic Peder Galle, professor at Uppsala. Rarely, however, was the king willing to move as swiftly and finally as Master Olof would have liked to make Sweden Lutheran. Even at the important parliament of Västerås in 1527, King Gustav insisted that he had never wanted to introduce a new faith but had merely wanted to have the pure word of God preached and to curb the worldliness of the clergy. But, in spite of the opposition of Bishop Brask and others, he secured what he wanted: the confiscation by the crown of the bishops' castles, and the control and appreciable appropriation of the "superfluous" income of the bishops, the cathedral chapters, and the convents; the restoration to the aristocracy of landed estates that had come into the church's control since 1454; the acceptance of the preaching of God's pure word; the making of the clergy responsible in civil courts for civil offenses; and the substitution of the king for the pope as the head of the church.

Master Olof and his fellow reformers worked hard to realize the religious aspects of these decisions. Among other contributions Master Olof wrote and published a Swedish psalmbook, a Swedish handbook, and a Swedish catechism. In 1531, the reformers saw one very real reward: the election of the gentle but highly competent younger brother of Olof, Lars Petri, as the first Lutheran archbishop. The king did his share in destroying the old church by appropriating more and more of its property to the crown.

King Gustav found Master Olof an irritating as well as useful servant. Not only did Olof place religious life and religious ideals above all other considerations, but he also dared to criticize the king's behavior from the pulpit and, as the king suspected, in writing. By 1540, the king's resentment permitted him, apparently on the advice of his German officials, Georg Norman and Conrad von Pyhy, to bring charges of treason against both Master Olof and Lars Andersson. The charges, according to SB (III, 246-48), stated, among other things, that Master Olof in his *Swedish Chronicle* and in his sermons had spoken in a derogatory and false fashion about the king, that he had known about the conspiracy against the king's life in 1536, and that he had participated in the plundering and desecration of the churches in 1524. The judges included not only the two Germans but also Archbishop Lars Petri, the bishops of Strängnäs and Västerås, and ten members of the king's council. Little is known of the trial except that both reformers finally changed their plea to guilty, were sentenced to death, and, on the judges' recommendation of mercy and the payment of large sums of money, reprieved by the king. Gustav had further use for Master Olof. (See also the notes on characters at the end of the play.)

III. The Play

As Strindberg suggests, his major theme is that truth is relative. He applies his theme more emphatically to religious truth than he does to political and social truth since his central character, the Lutheran reformer, was primarily concerned with religious matters although he was forced to consider political and social ones as well. Strindberg emphasizes, then, his idea that no opinion or article of faith in either area or, by implication, in any other can be regarded as absolute or fixed, for each is, rather, tentative and transitory in humanity's slow and painfully irregular search for absolute truth. If truth is relative, it follows, as Gert suggests, that intellectual and spiritual leaders must accept freedom of thought and that doubt and questioning should be not only tolerated but cultivated as necessary virtues. It follows, too, that leaders must take into consideration such realistic factors as the people's unwillingness or unreadiness to accept new and (from Strindberg's point of view) tentative truths. Gustav Vasa does so regularly; Master Olof is forced to ultimately; Gert knows that it is inevitable.

Gert, the character Strindberg did not find in his sources, represents the eternal questioner and doubter. Of Lutheranism and the reformation that it represents, Gert says, "It's too little. Luther is dead. He started. We'll go farther." The advocate of freedom of the human spirit, Gert differs from Master Olof in understanding that the achievement of religious freedom from Rome is not enough; that there is no great advantage in religious freedom if it means merely the substitution of a book or another set of dogmas for the pope and the Church of Rome; that any form of what in our time would be called thought control must be opposed and eventually eliminated. In one ecstatic speech after the other, Gert pleads for the ultimate ideal: genuine spiritual and intellectual life and intellectual and political freedom in a millennium of freedom. For example:

> What we had planted was not ready for harvest. A lot of snow must fall if the seed planted in autumn shall grow; yes, centuries will pass before anyone will see even a sprout. The conspirators have been caught, they say, and they offer thanks to God; they're mistaken; the conspirators are everywhere, in the rooms of the royal palace, in the churches, and on the squares, but they don't dare to do what we dared. But the day will come! . . . The name of every new martyr will be a battle cry for a new host. Never believe that a lie has lighted a fire in a human soul; never doubt the emotions that have shaken you to the very core of your being when you have seen anyone suffer because of spiritual or physical oppression. Even if the whole world says you're wrong, believe your heart if you have the courage! The day you deny yourself, you're dead, and eternal damnation will be a favor to the one who has committed the sin against the Holy Ghost.

The twenty-three-year-old Strindberg expressed through Gert the ideals that he knew could be attained, if at all, only by such gradual advances as those represented primarily by two of his other characters—the idealist with limited goals (Master Olof) and the practical realist with reasonable and attainable ideals (Gustav Vasa).

It is Gustav Vasa who represents the realistic aspects of the idea that truth is relative. The king who has been called upon to make Sweden a strong and unified nation has one idea that dominates his thinking: to bring order out of chaos among his people without too fine a regard for the means. He has no illusions about human nature, certainly no faith in the equality of human endowments:

> KING: Will you be my man?
>
> OLOF: Your Majesty's secretary?
>
> KING: No. You'll be my right hand on the condition that the left doesn't know for the time being what the right is doing.

and

> KING: Oh, that's far off. I don't dare to think of it yet— Let them preach; it can't hurt the stupid fools to hear a new word even if it's crazy; but there must be no acts of violence; then the sword will join in the game.

He is not particularly interested in the reformation except in so far as it permits him to achieve his goal of national independence by ridding him of one kind of foreign control and, at the same time, supplying him with the means to make Sweden financially sound and independent. He is, to be sure, an idealist about the task he has to perform, but he is a practical, hard-headed realist about the means he uses to perform that task.

Yet *Master Olof* is not only a drama of ideas. It is also, as are all Strindberg's other major historical plays, a drama of character. By his own admission, both in *In the Red Room* and in *Open Letters to the Intimate Theater* (*Öppna brev till Intima teatern*), his principal model in characterization and in composition was Shakespeare. He says, for example, on page 123 of the *Letters* (1919 edition):

Shakespeare's manner of depicting in *Julius Caesar* historical figures and heroes intimately, at home, as well, became the decisive pattern for my first major historical drama, *Master Olof,* and with certain reservations, even for those written from 1899 on. This freedom from "the theatrical" or calculated effect which I took as my key, was long held against me until Josephson at the Swedish Theater discovered *Master Olof* in 1880.

What Shakespeare did for Strindberg was to give him the courage to break with the artificial conventions of the quantitatively rich Swedish historical drama and to suggest techniques that permitted him to bring the historic dead alive in his plays. But, it should be emphasized, Shakespeare stimulated Strindberg to write original plays, not imitations.

Although Strindberg's comments in the autobiographical volume on his characterization of Master Olof necessarily emphasize subjective elements, they nevertheless are helpful and extremely pertinent. For example:

> The author is impartial toward his hero Olaus. . . . He makes him a weak soul, who is driven ahead from below and who would prefer to be a follower. He makes him an idealist, who does not understand the realistic king's more rational methods for destroying the church by starving it to death. . . . [Strindberg presented Olaus] as he had found himself to be after years of self-examination: Ambitious and weak-willed; regardless of other people's feelings on crucial occasions; great self-confidence mixed with profound dejection; reasonable and unreasonable; hard and soft.

Even such a brief excerpt indicates that as early as the beginning of the 1870's Strindberg had already learned through literary sources such as Shakespeare, and particularly through his own observation and thinking, that characters in a play should not be simplified and typified.

Consequently, Master Olof is a complex character from the first curtain to the final one. In Act I, Strindberg presents the young reformer as an idealistic dreamer who is quite content to be putting on his *Comedy of Tobias* at the cathedral school of Strängnäs, as an idealistic dreamer who yearns to deliver his people from the Babylonian captivity of the Church of Rome, and as a youngster who is absolutely sure neither of what he wants to be nor of what he wants to do. The handsome young follower of Luther, who at Wittenberg has acquired the ideal of cleansing his church of the accumulation of human innovations in doctrines and practices over the centuries, has not yet come to the point of deciding what his role in the struggle is to be or what he can do to realize his dreams. Potentially, the qualities needed in a great religious leader are there—the keen intellect, the learning, the energy, the idealistic motivations, the sincerity, the enthusiasm and fervor, and the courage to fight against overwhelming odds. But the entrance into the struggle for a reformed church in which his ideal, "Each and every one by himself and with God," can be attained and the abuses of the church eliminated comes only through the stimulation of another man, the learned Lars Andersson, who sees clearly enough that the Lutheran goals cannot be achieved through the quiet labors in the classroom:

> OLOF: Why should I go first?
>
> LARS: You're the most daring.
>
> OLOF: Not the strongest?
>
> LARS: The strong will follow; and the strongest is at your side. He's the One who summons you to battle!
>
> OLOF: Help me, God! I go!
>
> LARS: Amen.
>
> OLOF: And you'll follow me.
>
> LARS: You're to go alone with God.
>
> OLOF: Why do you draw back?
>
> LARS: I wasn't born to be a fighter; I can only supply you with weapons. God's pure words shall be your weapons. You shall place them in the hands of the people; for the door of the papal armory has been broken open, and every human being must fight for the freedom of his own spirit.

OLOF: But where are my enemies? I'm eager for the struggle, but I
    see no enemies!
LARS: You don't have to summon them—they'll come!

Olof is an attractive young leader who has been stimulated into dangerous action in behalf of what he, from the Strindbergian point of
view, fails to see is a limited sort of goal for attaining spiritual life
and freedom—the setting up of the Bible as the one source of truth
by the elimination of the Roman priests as religious middlemen.

Aroused to action, Strindberg's Master Olof performs his first
act of courage—the ringing of the vesper bells and the conducting
of mass in defiance of the orders of the church. It is a daring blow
struck for freedom from oppression, but it is a limited blow for
Master Olof has as yet neither thought through the question of
freedom nor come to final decisions as to what spiritual life and
spiritual freedom mean. As Gert, the second man to drive him on to
thinking and to action, says, Master Olof wants to eliminate from
Swedish life the abuses the pope represents, but he still is bound by
his respect for temporal law and order in the person of the king.

In Act I, Strindberg presents Olof as a very human young man
romantically and physically in love with Kristina, as a young idealist who refuses to be bought by the wily Bishop Brask, and as a
gifted young man who, while he willingly enters the service of the
practical young king, nevertheless fails to see what the implications
of his royal appointment as secretary and preacher may be. It is
highly significant—from Strindberg's point of view—that Lars Andersson calls Master Olof a child. The two most important leaders
of their time have a working arrangement, in which the one foresees
no conflict. The other, however, speaks significantly of Master Olof
as "a pointer, who can raise the game; we'll see if he comes back
when I whistle."

The Master Olof of Act II is a dynamic figure who has developed
to the point where he can openly break with the Church of Rome,
denying the significance of its act of excommunication by tearing the

proclamation of excommunication to pieces, preaching the Lutheran doctrines in his specially constructed pulpit in the Great Church, and deciding to marry in spite of the popular and churchly point of view that even a canon is bound to celibacy. These three acts of courage are performed by a man who has daring and sincerity but who still compromises to a degree with the demands of the king and the pressure of popular prejudice about both religious practices and social conduct. As he is brought into open conflict with the established church and with his mother because of her devout Catholicism, many of Master Olof's human qualities of strength and weakness become evident.

The third act opens with the emphasis placed directly on the basic problem in Master Olof's attempt at securing religious freedom from Rome for his fellow Swedes:

> KING (*signals to* LARS *to leave; he exits*): Are you calm yet, Olof? (OLOF *does not answer*.) I gave you four days in which to think it over. How have you handled your assignment?
>
> OLOF (*violently*): I have spoken to the people—
>
> KING: So you're still running a temperature! You intend to defend the crazy fools they call Anabaptists?
>
> OLOF (*courageously*): Yes!
>
> KING: Easy! You got married in a hurry?
>
> OLOF: Yes!
>
> KING: You've been excommunicated?
>
> OLOF: Yes!
>
> KING: And you're just as daring anyway. And if you're sent to the gallows with the other agitators, what would you say?
>
> OLOF: I'd regret I didn't get to carry out my mission, but I'd thank God for what I've been allowed to do.
>
> KING: That's good. Do you dare to go up to the old owl's nest Uppsala and tell the professors that the pope isn't God and hasn't anything to do with Sweden?
>
> OLOF: Merely that?
>
> KING: Do you want to tell them the Bible alone is the word of God?
>
> OLOF: Nothing more?

KING: You may not mention Luther by name!

OLOF (*after consideration*): Then I don't want to.

KING: You'd rather go to your death?

OLOF: No. But my king needs me.

KING: It isn't noble of you, Olof, to make use of my misfortune. Say what you want; but you'll have to excuse me if I take back something later.

OLOF: One doesn't bargain about the truth.

KING: God's death! (*Changing his tone of voice*) Do as you want!

OLOF (*kneeling*): May I speak the whole truth?

KING: Yes!

OLOF: Then my life won't be wasted if I cast merely one spark of doubt into the souls of the sleeping people. So there's to be a reformation!

The practical realist still has use for his "pointer," but the pointer is only partially aware of what the king is doing. Master Olof does not understand that he is being used as an extremely important tool for the attainment of a very practical and very realistic goal that has little if anything to do with religious freedom and religious life.

In Act III, Strindberg also presents Master Olof as a husband and as a son. His work as a reformer and as a religious leader and his duties as husband and son lead to inner conflicts, which together with their outer manifestations are demonstrated in strikingly Strindbergian scenes foreshadowing the more universally known scenes of domestic conflict in the so-called naturalistic plays from *The Father* (1887) to *The Dance of Death* (1899). Both the revealing detail and the emotional tension which stamp those plays as Strindbergian are present in *Master Olof*.

As a fitting climax to Act III, Strindberg presents Master Olof as he receives the news of the parliamentary decisions that will mark his struggle for religious freedom as either a victory or a defeat. Significant is Olof's reaction to the letter from Bishop Brask congratulating him:

KRISTINA (*reads*): "You have won, young man! I, your enemy, am
the first to tell you this, and without humility I turn to you, for
you bore the weapons of the spirit when you spoke for the new
faith! I do not know if you are right, but I believe you deserve
a bit of advice from an old man. Stop now, for your enemies are
gone. Do not struggle with spirits of the air; that would cripple
your arm and you would die yourself. 'Do not rely on princes' is
the advice of a once powerful man, who now steps aside and
leaves in the hands of the Lord the fate of his ruined church.
Johannes Brask."

KRISTINA: You have won!

OLOF (*happy*): God, I thank thee for this hour! (*Pause*) No. I'm
afraid, Kristina. This good fortune is too great. I'm too young to
have reached my goal already. Nothing more to do: a dreadful
thought! No struggle any more: that's death itself!

KRISTINA: Rest for a moment, and be happy it's over.

OLOF: Can there be any end? An end to this beginning. No! No!
I'd like to begin again. It wasn't victory I wanted; it was the
struggle.

But Master Olof has not won, for the parliamentary decisions make
it clear to him that for a church controlled by Rome and its representatives in Sweden will be substituted a church controlled by the
king for his own purposes. The reformer realizes at last that the
king has not been really interested in religious and spiritual freedom but that he has merely used Master Olof and the reformation.

GERT (*comes up*): Well, Olof. The faith . . .

OLOF: The lack of faith, you mean!

GERT: But the pope's defeated! Shall we take on the emperor soon?

OLOF: We began at the wrong end.

GERT: Finally!

OLOF: You were right, Gert. I'm ready. War! But open and honest!

GERT: You've been living in childish dreams until today.

OLOF: I know. Now comes the flood. Let it come! Woe unto them
and us!

KRISTINA: Olof, for heaven's sake, stop!

OLOF: Go your way, child. Here you'll drown, or you'll drag me down.

GERT: My child! What were you doing out in the storm? (KRISTINA *goes. Ringing of bells. Cheering. Music. Beating of drums outside*)

OLOF (*goes to the window*): Why are the people cheering?

GERT: Because the king's treating them to a Maypole and music out beyond the North Gate.

OLOF: And they don't know he's given them the sword instead of birch branches!

GERT: Know? If they only knew!

OLOF: Poor children! They're dancing to his pipes and going to their deaths to the music of his drums—must all die that one may live?

GERT: One shall die that all may live!

(OLOF *makes a gesture of repugnance and amazement.*)

Aware at last that the king is his antagonist and not his ally, the Master Olof of Act IV has yielded to the demands of Gert, of whom Olof says, "Gert is a farsighted man—I'm very little compared to him":

LARS: As your brother and friend, Olof, I beg you not to rush on as you have.

OLOF: That's what you always say. But the person who puts the axe to the tree doesn't stop until the tree falls. The king has deserted our cause; now I'll take charge of it.

LARS: The king is wise.

OLOF: He's a miser, a traitor, and a patron of the lords! First he uses me like a dog; then he kicks me aside.

LARS: He sees farther than you do. If you were to go to three million people and say: "Your faith is false; believe what I say," do you think it would be possible for them to discard their deepest, profoundest convictions, which have sustained them both in sorrow and in joy? No, things would be badly arranged for the human spirit if it didn't take longer to throw the old faith overboard.

OLOF: That isn't so! All the people doubt; hardly one priest knows what to believe, even if he believes anything; everything is ready for the new faith, but you're to blame, you weaklings, who don't dare to take it on your consciences to cast out doubt where there's only a feeble faith.

LARS: Beware, Olof! You want to play the role of God!

OLOF: Yes, one has to, for He's not likely to descend among us again!

LARS: You tear down and tear down, Olof, so that soon there will be nothing, but when we ask, "What are you giving us instead?" you answer, "Not that, not that," but you never answer, "This"!

OLOF: Presumptuous! Do you think a person can give away faith? Has Luther given us anything new? No! He has simply knocked down the screens that stood in the way of light. What I want that's new is doubt of the old, not because it's old but because it's rotten.

(LARS *gestures toward his* MOTHER.)

At last he can say without qualification, "I'll cleanse the temple of the Lord even if the pope and the king don't want it!" He compromises with his convictions at his mother's death bed, however, by saying, "What is holy for you will be holy for me" and by proceeding to make the ceremonial arrangements that his devoutly Catholic mother had wanted.

Strindberg's Master Olof breaks openly with the king in Act V:

MÅRTEN: If you don't fear what's holy, fear your earthly king! You see, he still has so much respect left for the divine that he fears the wrath of the saints! (*Shows* OLOF *a document*)

OLOF: Do you know what the Lord did to the king of the Assyrians when he permitted the worship of idols? He struck him and his people; that's why the just must suffer with the unjust! In the name of the one almighty God, I abolish this worship of Baal, even if all the kings of this earth would permit it; the pope wanted to sell my soul to Satan, but I tore the contract to pieces, you remember! Should I now fear a king who wants to sell his people to Baal? (*He tears the order to pieces.*)

MÅRTEN (*to the monks and the nuns*): You are witnesses that he defames the king!

OLOF (*to the men with him*): You are my witnesses before God that I have led His people from an ungodly king!

MÅRTEN: Listen, men of faith! It's because of that heretic that the Lord has struck us with the plague; it was God's punishment that it struck his mother first!

OLOF: Listen, you papal unbelievers! It was the Lord's punishment of me because I served Sennacherib against Judah! I will atone for my sin; I will lead Judah against the King of Assyria and Egypt!

Hesitant at first about his fellow conspirators' intention of taking the life of his antagonist the king, he at last accepts their plan: "Let him die that all may live!" only to be taken prisoner by a highly practical and realistic antagonist.

The final scene is for the most part strikingly effective. Tried, condemned to death, in chains, and exposed in the Great Church to his congregation and, worst of all, to his pupils, Master Olof faces the most crucial test of his career as a reformer—the choice between martyrdom because of faithfulness to his idea of a church with a living faith and compromise with reality by retracting his criticism of the king and retreating from his struggle for religious life and freedom for his countrymen, between, one might say, the realistic pressures exerted by King Gustav's able and faithful servant, Lars Sparre, and faithfulness to his own spirit. As Vilhelm aptly puts it, "I've thought of you going to your death like that—with your face radiant and your eyes raised to the sky while the people shout: So dies a martyr!" Instead, the great reformer with his very human weakness of will retracts and thereby becomes not merely a servant of the king but an unfortunate figure in defeat.

Strindberg's characterization of Master Olof is worthy of comparison with the great creations in his later plays, for, like them, Master Olof is a highly complex and dynamic human being whom Strind-

berg has approached from a convincing psychological point of view.
The gifted Master Olof has been exposed to Luther and converted
by him into an enthusiastic disciple who becomes a leader in his
own right. He is torn by inner uncertainties and conflicts (his faith
in his own ability versus the fear that he will fail, the claims of the
ideal versus the demands of reality). In spite of his stubborn insistence that he is independent (Gert says, "To a man like you one says,
'Don't do that,' when one wants a thing done"), he is weak-willed
on occasion, and in need of the stimulation of others. Strindberg's
Master Olof is an idealistic human being who does not see far
enough and who does not have the courage and the strength of will
to go all the way. Presented by Strindberg in such typically human
roles as a son, a brother, a husband, a friend, a subject, a professional
man, and, above all, a man with a very special job to do, Master
Olof is revealed in the suggestive nuances of a particularly rich and
individualistic personality compounded of strength and weakness.

For those who are familiar with what Strindberg has to say about
dramatic characterization in the preface to *Lady Julie* (1888), *Master
Olof* must indicate that as early as 1872 Strindberg had pretty well
mastered the technique of making his characters live, having learned
the technique of dramatic composition not only from predecessors,
notably Shakespeare, but from himself. As he much later wrote in
Open Letters to the Intimate Theater (p. 298) about his last play
about historical Swedes (*Earl Birger of Bjälbo*), "I made the major
characters live by taking blood and nerves from my own life, so that
they became mine, and are my property." It is, of course, this fact
that he emphasized again and again in *In the Red Room*.

With the single exception of the fairly static Gert, Strindberg's
major, secondary, and more important minor characters are, from
the point of view of the stage, intensely alive. Note the secondary
characters, King Gustav I, Bishop Brask, Lars Andersson, the
mother, Master Olof's wife, and Mårten, and such minor characters
as Windrank, Lars Sparre, Bishop Måns, the *smålänning,* and the

nobleman. They are all presented in keeping with what Strindberg wrote in *Open Letters to the Intimate Theater* (p. 240):

> My purpose was as it was my teacher Shakespeare's to depict human beings both in their greatness and their triviality, not to avoid the right word; to let history be the background and to compress historical periods to fit the demands of the theater of our time by avoiding the undramatic form of the chronicle or the narrative.

Each of the secondary and minor characters is individualized to the degree necessary to make the characterization of the central character as complete as possible.

A Strindbergian element that has never detracted from interest in the play is the emphasis placed on such perennial problems as the relationships between man and woman, husband and wife, parent and child, and between in-laws. Not only were such matters already being debated in Scandinavia and elsewhere in Strindberg's own time, but they had already been subjects for debate in Sweden for several decades. C. J. L. Almquist's controversial *Det går an* (1839, translated by Professor Adolph B. Benson as *Sara Vidabeck* [New York: American-Scandinavian Foundation, 1919]) and Fredrika Bremer's internationally known novels of family life are the best known works that stimulated debate and discussion and prepared the way for Strindberg's own great interpretations of human relationships from the 1870's on.

Traces of the theatrical declamatory style of the Swedish stage in the 1860's and 1870's are obvious in occasional speeches, particularly in some of Gert's, Master Olof's and Kristina's. For example, consider the long declamatory exchanges between Olof and Kristina toward the end of Act II or some of Olof's longer speeches in the first scene of Act V. The final scene presents the most notable illustration of Strindberg's difficulty in 1872 in making a clean break with tradition. It is odd that the Gert who a few moments before should have accepted Master Olof's release as certain, who has learned from what Archbishop Lars has told Master Olof in Gert's presence that release is dependent on Olof's retraction of what he has said about the king, and has blessed Olof and urged him to take care of his daughter, should nevertheless shout "Renegade!"

Yet *Master Olof* was a remarkable achievement that ushered in a new era in Swedish drama and Swedish theater. In addition to an interesting plot, admirable characterizations, and a memorable interpretation of one of the most crucial periods in Swedish history, *Master Olof* was technically epoch-making. Note such matters as the superb first act, which in one richly colorful scene presents the basic exposition, the primary characters, the major theme, and the atmosphere; the tremendously effective interludes—the tavern scenes— which not only provide a measure of comic relief but also help make the moral, religious, political, and social settings clear; and the brilliant use of intimate domestic scenes. Because of all these factors, Sweden's greatest producers, directors, and actors have found *Master Olof* a highly rewarding challenge.

Master Olof · A Play in Five Acts

Characters

MASTER OLOF (*Olaus Petri*)

GERT BOOKPRINTER

KING GUSTAV I (*Gustav Vasa*)

BISHOP HANS BRASK of *Linköping*

BISHOP MÅNS SOMMAR of *Strängnäs*

LARS SIGGESSON SPARRE, *national marshal, lord high constable*

LARS ANDERSSON (*Laurentius Andreae*), *later chancellor*

LAURENTIUS PETRI (*Lars Pedersson*), *Master Olof's brother, later archbishop*

HANS WINDRANK, *a sea captain*

A SMÅLÄNNING (*native of Småland*)

A GERMAN

A DANE

BROTHER MÅRTEN and BROTHER NILS, *Dominicans or Black Friars*

KNIPPERDOLLINK

THE ABBESS

THE TAVERNKEEPER

AN UNDERTAKER'S ASSISTANT

PUPIL 1 and PUPIL 2

THE SEXTON and the SEXTON'S WIFE

THE SERVANT

THE OVERSEER

THE BURGHER and the BURGHER'S WIFE

KRISTINA, *Master Olof's mother*

A NOBLEMAN

KRISTINA, *Gert's daughter, Master Olof's wife*

THE PROSTITUTE

MINOR CHARACTERS

Settings

ACT I

IN STRÄNGNÄS

A crosswalk outside the study hall. Trees. At a distance the cloister church. At the back a wall above which can be seen fruit trees in bloom. OLOF *is sitting on a stone bench; in front of him stand pupils reading their parts in* The Comedy of Tobias.

PUPIL I: "Alas for us, poor children of Israel; we are caught in the toils of our enemies."

PUPIL II: "Dear brother, we should lament! The days of our tribulations have come—both our lands and our tithes are gone; never again can we look to the future with happy expectation. I have said and dreamt for a long time that the promise of Abraham was forgotten long ago." [1]

LARS ANDERSSON (*who has entered*): What are you doing?

OLOF: I'm playing.

LARS: You're playing!

25

OLOF: Yes. I'm playing a little comedy about the children of Israel and the Babylonian captivity.

LARS: Haven't you anything better to do? A greater task awaits you.

OLOF: I'm still too young.

LARS: Don't say you're too young.

OLOF: No, I suspect there are enough who do.

LARS (*unrolls a paper which he has taken out; observes* OLOF *for a while; then he reads*): And the Lord spoke to Jeremiah: "Before I formed thee in the belly, I knew thee; and before thou camest forth out of the womb, I sanctified thee, and I ordained thee a prophet unto the nations."

And Jeremiah said: "Ah, Lord God! behold, I cannot speak; for I am a child."

And the Lord said: "Say not I am a child; for thou shalt go to all that I shall send thee, and whatsoever I command thee thou shalt speak. . . .

"For, behold, I have made thee this day a defenced city, and an iron pillar, and brasen walls against the whole land, against the kings of Judah, against the princes thereof, against the priests thereof, and against the people of the land.

"And they shall fight against thee; but they shall not prevail against thee; for I am with thee . . . to deliver thee." [2]

OLOF (*jumps up*): Did the Lord say that?

LARS (*continues*): "Thou therefore gird up thy loins and arise, and speak unto them all that I command thee." [3]

OLOF: Why don't you go?

LARS: I'm too old.

OLOF: You're afraid!

LARS: Yes, for I don't have the strength; but you do—may God give you the faith.

OLOF: I once had the flame of faith, and it burned beautifully, but the gang of monks put it out with their holy water when they tried to drive the devil from my body.

LARS: That was a fire of straw that had to flicker out; now the Lord will make you a fire of logs, which will burn up the seed of the Philistines. Do you really know what you want to do, Olof?

OLOF: No, but I feel as if I were suffocating when I think about our poor people yearning for deliverance. They cry for water, living water, but no one has any to give them.

LARS: Tear down the rotten old house first—you can! The Lord Himself will build a new one!

OLOF: But they won't have a roof for a while.

LARS: They'll get fresh air, at least.

OLOF: But to rob a whole people of their faith! They'd despair!

LARS: Yes, they'll despair.

OLOF: They'll curse me and revile me and bring me before the authorities.

LARS: Are you afraid?

OLOF: No! But they'll be offended—

LARS: Olof! You were born to offend; you were born to strike. The Lord will heal.

OLOF: I feel how the current pulls; I still have hold of the sluice gate, but, if I let go, the current will carry me on.

LARS: Let go—those who hold back will come.

OLOF: If I get too far into the whirlpool, stretch out your hand to me, Lars.

LARS: That's beyond my power. You have to go into the whirlpool even if you perish.

OLOF: What storms you've stirred up in my soul; a little while ago I sat playing in the shadow of the trees, and it was Pentecost eve, and it was spring and there was peace. Now—why don't the trees tremble? Why doesn't the sky darken? Put your hand on my forehead; feel how my blood's throbbing! Don't leave me, Lars. I see an angel who comes to me with a cup; she walks on the evening sky over there; her path is blood red, and she has a cross in her hand.—No, I can't do it; I'll go back to the quiet valley; let others struggle; I'll look on.—No, I'll follow them and heal the wounded; I'll whisper words of peace in the ears of the dying.

Peace!—No, I want to fight, too, but in the last ranks. Why should I go first?

LARS: You're the most daring.

OLOF: Not the strongest?

LARS: The strong will follow; and the strongest is at your side. He's the One who summons you to battle!

OLOF: Help me, God! I go!

LARS: Amen.

OLOF: And you'll follow me.

LARS: You're to go alone with God.

OLOF: Why do you draw back?

LARS: I wasn't born to be a fighter; I can only supply you with weapons. God's pure words shall be your weapons. You shall place them in the hands of the people; for the door of the papal armory has been broken open, and every human being must fight for the freedom of his own spirit.

OLOF: But where are my enemies? I'm eager for the struggle, but I see no enemies!

LARS: You don't have to summon them—they'll come! Good-bye. You can begin when you please. God be with you.

OLOF: Don't go; I have to talk with you!

LARS: Here comes the vanguard—get your weapons ready! (LARS *exits.*)

(*A crowd of burghers—among them women and children—goes up to the church door to the right. They stop, remove their hats, and cross themselves.*)

GERT (*disguised as a burgher*): They haven't rung the bell for vespers on Pentecost eve—that's mighty strange.

BURGHER: And the church door's closed. Maybe the priest is sick.

GERT: Or hasn't got up.

BURGHER: What did you say?

GERT: I mean he's sick!

BURGHER: But he has so many acolytes that one of them could conduct mass.

GERT: They're too busy, I suspect.

BURGHER: Doing what?

GERT: That's hard to tell.

BURGHER: Take care, my good man. You seem to have a touch of Lutheranism.[4] Bishop Hans of Linköping's in town, and the king, too.

GERT: Is Brask in town?

BURGHER: He certainly is. But we'd better try the door first to see if the church is closed.

GERT (*runs up the steps and knocks on the door*): The house of God is closed on Pentecost eve. The most reverend priests don't grant an audience with God today, so you praiseworthy burghers will have to go home and go to bed without mass. Look, good people —here's a door, it's just a wooden door, but that makes no difference since it's lined with copper. Look at this door! If I tell you that God lives on the other side—for it is His house, if I tell you that the bishop's *diakonus* or *sekretarius* or *kanonikus* or any other man that ends in *-us,* for it's only men of the spirit who end in *-us,* if I tell you that a man like that has the key to this door hanging on a nail in his bedroom, I'm not saying that he has locked God away from us and hung the key on a nail in his bedroom, I'm simply saying that we can't get in to attend divine services tonight, we who have worked hard for six days making shoes and coats, and we who have brewed and baked and butchered all week long for the right worshipful priests so that on the seventh day they'd have the strength to conduct divine services for us. I don't blame the right worshipful chapter, for they're only human beings like us, and God alone could work for six days and rest on the seventh.

BURGHER: You're blaspheming God, master!

GERT: Oh well, He doesn't hear it when the door's shut.

A WOMAN: Mary, Mother of Jesus! He's an Antichrist!

GERT (*knocks on the door*): Hear how empty it sounds. The Bible says that the veil before the holy of holies was rent, and that must be true, but if the priests have sewn it together since, the Bible doesn't say, and it doesn't need to be a lie for all that.

(*The people rush toward* GERT; *the children scream.*)

BURGHER: Woe unto you, Luther, for you are one of them! We have sinned; so the Lord has closed His house. Unclean spirit, can't you hear how even the children scream at sight of you?

GERT: You're stepping on their toes, my friends.

WOMAN: Don't touch him; he's possessed by the devil!

BURGHER: Down with him! Down with him!

GERT: Don't touch me, for in this place I'm in God's sanctuary!

BURGHER: God doesn't protect the cast-out angel!

GERT: If God doesn't, the holy church does, and I'm within its consecrated walls.

BURGHER: Drag him outside the church walls!

GERT: If you don't fear God, at least fear the holy father's ban!

WOMAN: Drag him from the door; it's his unclean spirit that has bewitched the church!

BURGHER: Yes! Yes! God doesn't open His church to the devil!

(*They rush toward* GERT *just as the bishop's* SECRETARY *enters; he is preceded by a deacon who asks for their attention.*)

SECRETARY (*reads*): "Inasmuch as our cathedral city has not fulfilled its obligations to the bishop's chair and as the city continues to resist fulfillment of the same, the cathedral chapter has found it fitting, in accordance with its rights and with the approval of the curia, to close the doors of the church and to discontinue masses and offerings until the grievance named is corrected, reminding each and every one who does not conduct himself accordingly that he will have all our disfavor.

> "*Datum vigilia assumptionis Mariae*
> "The Chapter of Strängnäs."

(*Exits*)

GERT: What about that, good people?

BURGHER: No mass on Pentecost eve! That's a disgrace!

GERT: Watch out! Don't say anything against the priests—it's certainly not their fault.

BURGHER: Whose fault is it?

GERT: The church's! That invisible, almighty church! It's the church that has closed the church, you see.

(*The people express their displeasure.*)

OLOF (*has come up and now rings the vesper bell by means of a rope that hangs down from the tower*): If you're serious about your divine services, I'll celebrate mass for you!

BURGHER: Thank you, Master Olof, but don't you know what that may lead to?

OLOF: Let us fear God rather than man! (*The people kneel.*) "Dear friends, brothers and sisters in Jesus Christ! Since we are now gathered together . . ."

BURGHER: Master Olof . . .

OLOF: What?

BURGHER: We want our regular mass and not human innovations.

GERT: It will have to be in Latin, Master Olof. Otherwise, we won't understand what you're saying.

BURGHER: It has to be in the sacred language; otherwise, anyone at all could conduct mass.

OLOF: Yes, that's just how it's going to be. Each and every one by himself and with God.

PEOPLE: A Luther! A Luther! Antichrist!

BURGHER: Really, Master Olof. You, who are so young and enthusiastic, have been infected by that German devil. I'm an old man and have seen the world. For your own good turn back while you're still young. Grant us our wish and conduct the old mass.

OLOF: No, that trickery is done for. You should pray in spirit and in truth, not with words you don't understand.

BURGHER: Don't you think, my young friend, that our Lord understands Latin?

GERT: But He certainly doesn't understand Swedish at all!

BURGHER: Master Olof! Are you going to let the people go without a

word of edification? Don't you see how they long for their God?
Sacrifice your own sinful will, and don't let them go like sheep
without a shepherd.

OLOF: You call my will sinful?

BURGHER: You are a hard man.

OLOF: Don't say that! Do you know what the ringing of these bells
is going to cost me?

BURGHER: Your vanity!

GERT: And your peace! That was the signal bell that called to battle.
It's starting right now! Soon the bells of Stockholm will answer,
and then the blood of Huss, and of Ziska, and of the thousands
of German peasants will be on the heads of the princes and the
Catholics.[5]

WOMAN: God save us! Is he mad?

BURGHER: Do you know that man, Master Olof?

OLOF: No!

GERT: Olof! You know me! Don't deny me! Are you afraid of these
poor miserable people who don't want what's best for them—
people who have never heard the word freedom?

OLOF: Who are you?

GERT: If I were to tell you, you'd tremble! It's true, of course, you
have to tremble to awaken from your sleep. I'm the cast-out
angel, who will reappear ten thousand times; I'm the deliverer
who came too early; I'm called Satan because I loved you more
than my own life; I've been called Luther; I've been called Huss;
now I'm called Anabaptist! [6]

PEOPLE (*draw away from him and cross themselves*): Anabaptist!

GERT (*unmasks himself; is much older than he has seemed*): Now,
do you recognize me, Olof?

OLOF: Father Gert!

BURGHER: He calls him father!

PEOPLE (*draw away*): Anabaptist! Anabaptist!

WOMAN: Don't you see? He's the man who was excommunicated—

BURGHER: Gert Bookprinter. Brask's printer.[7]

ANOTHER BURGHER: The one who printed Luther!

WOMAN: Woe upon us and our city; woe upon our priests when they associate with Antichrist!

BURGHER: He denies baptism!

WOMAN: He denies God! (*The people leave.*)

OLOF: Father Gert, you said dangerous things.

GERT: Do you think *that* was dangerous, Olof? God bless you for that.

OLOF: Dangerous for you, I mean.

GERT: Not for anyone else?

OLOF: Let's hope not.

GERT: You have known Luther?

OLOF: Yes, I have. I want to do his work in my own country.

GERT: Is that all?

OLOF: What do you mean?

GERT: It's too little. Luther is dead. He started. We'll go farther.

OLOF: Where would you lead me?

GERT: Far. Far. Olof!

OLOF: I'm afraid of you, Father Gert!

GERT: Yes, yes! You'll be very much afraid, for I'll lead you up on a high mountain and from there you'll see the whole world. You see, Olof, it's Pentecost. That was the time the Holy Spirit descended and filled the Apostles with His Spirit, no, filled all mankind.[8] You can receive the Holy Spirit; I've received the Holy Spirit because I believed. The spirit of God came down to me, I feel it; and that's why they've locked me up as insane, but now I'm free; now I'll speak the word, for you see, Olof, now we're on the mountain top! Do you see how the people crawl on their knees up to the two men who sit on their thrones? The greater one has two keys in one hand, a thunderbolt in the other. That's the pope. Now he lifts the thunderbolt, and a thousand souls are damned, and the others kiss his foot and sing *Gloria Deo*—and the man on the throne turns and smiles. Now look at the other man! He has a sword and a scepter. Bow down before the scepter, or the sword will bite! He wrinkles his brows, and all the people tremble. Then he turns to his neighbor on the other throne, and they both smile. These are the two pillars of Baal.[9] But then there's a murmur in the air like the murmur of human voices. "Who murmurs?" cries the pope and shakes his thunderbolt. "Who murmurs?" and the emperor shakes his sword. No one answers. But there's still a murmur in the air, and it sighs and it calls: "Think!" And the pope is startled, and the emperor turns pale and asks: "Who cried 'think'? Bring him here, and I'll take his life," and the pope cries: "Bring him here, and I'll take his soul!" It was the air that cried; it was no one who cried; but the voice rises, and a storm wind rushes forward and crosses the Alps and roars over the Fichtel Mountains [10] and awakens the Baltic and echoes against the shores, and increased a thousandfold the cry goes out over the world: "Freedom! Freedom!" And the pope throws his keys into the sea, and the emperor sheathes his sword, for they can do nothing against that cry! Olof! You want to strike the pope, but you forget the emperor; the emperor who murders his people without counting them, because they dare to sigh when they're trodden underfoot. You want to strike the pope in Rome, but, like Luther, you want to give them a new pope in the Holy Scriptures. Listen to me! Don't bind the spirits with any bond! Don't forget the great day of Pentecost; don't forget your great goal: spiritual life and spiritual freedom. Don't listen to that death cry: "Lo, everything is good!" because then the millennium, the millennium of freedom, will never come into being, and that's just what is beginning now! (OLOF *remains silent.*)

GERT: Are you getting dizzy?

OLOF: You're going too far, Gert!

GERT: There'll come a day when people will call me a papist! Aim for the sky, and you'll hit the horizon.

OLOF: Back, Gert! You'll bring disaster on yourself and the kingdom. Don't you see how the country still trembles with fever from the wounds of recent wars? And you want to sow civil war.

That's godless!

GERT: No, now that the knife's in the flesh, cut away so you can save the body.

OLOF: I'll report you as a traitor.

GERT: You shouldn't—you've offended the church beyond help today, and besides—

OLOF: Speak out, Gert; just now you look like Satan.

GERT: I'll give you my secret; do with it as you wish. You see, the king's going to Malmö today; the day after tomorrow, let's say, Stockholm will be in revolt.

OLOF: What's that?

GERT: Do you know Rink and Knipperdollink? [11]

OLOF (*frightened*): The Anabaptists!

GERT: Yes! Why be so amazed? Why, they're just a couple of louts. A furrier and a shopkeeper who deny the value of baptism for an irresponsible child and are simple enough to oppose a deliberate false vow, extorted from an irresponsible being.

OLOF: There's something else.

GERT: What could that be?

OLOF: They're possessed!

GERT: By the spirit, yes! It's the storm that calls through them! Take care you don't get in their way!

OLOF: They must be stopped! I'll go to the king!

GERT: We ought to be friends, Olof. Doesn't your mother live in Stockholm?

OLOF: You know she does.

GERT: Do you know my daughter Kristina's living with your mother?

OLOF: Kristina?

GERT: Yes, for the time being. If we win, your mother will be safe because of my daughter. If the Catholics win, my daughter will be safe because of your mother. And you are concerned about Kristina, aren't you?

OLOF: Gert! Gert! Where did you get so wise?

GERT: In the insane asylum!

OLOF: Leave me. You'll lead me into misfortune.

GERT: Yes, if it's misfortune to be robbed of all earthly happiness, to be dragged to prison, to suffer poverty, to be ridiculed and reviled because of the truth. Then you're not worthy of such a great misfortune. I thought you'd understand me, I counted on your help, for you still have the fire, but the world's tempting you, I see. Follow the current and be happy.

OLOF: A man certainly can't reshape his time.

GERT: Luther did!

OLOF: One man can't set himself against the current.

GERT: Fool! Lead the current. For we are the current; the old people are stagnant puddles; you certainly won't have to struggle against them. Don't let them rot or dry up; give them outlets, and they'll follow the current.

OLOF: I understand; you've planted a thought in my soul, but I must strangle it at birth, or it will kill me.

GERT: Believe me, you shall be a Daniel,[12] who shall speak the truth to princes. They will try to destroy you, but the Lord will protect you. Now I can safely leave; I see the lightning flashing in your eye, and the tongue of fire flickering over your head. Happy Pentecost, Master Olof! (*As he goes*) Here comes the king of flies; don't let him sully your pure soul.

OLOF: Jesus help me!

(BISHOPS HANS BRASK *and* MÅNS SOMMAR [13] *enter.*)

MÅNS (*goes toward* OLOF; BRASK *remains behind, observing everything about him*): Canon! Who rang the bells for vespers?

OLOF (*gently and firmly*): I did.

MÅNS: Weren't you aware of the orders?

OLOF: I knew it was forbidden.

MÅNS: You dared to defy them?

OLOF: Yes, when the people were left as sheep without a shepherd, I wanted to gather them.

MÅNS: Why, you're reproaching us for our actions! You're really insolent.

OLOF: The truth is always insolent.

MÅNS: So you want to play the apostle of truth, young man; you'll get no thanks for that.

OLOF: I ask only ingratitude.

MÅNS: Save your truths; they're not much in demand.

OLOF (*violently*): Advice worthy of the father of lies! (*Gently*) Forgive me.

MÅNS: Do you know whom you're talking to?

OLOF (*heatedly*): To *servus servi servorum* Måns Sommar!

BRASK (*comes up to them*): Who is this man?

MÅNS: He's one of the servants of the church.

BRASK: What's his name?

MÅNS: Olaus Petri.

BRASK (*stares fixedly at* OLOF): Are you Master Olof?

(OLOF *bows and looks at* BRASK.)

BRASK: I like you! Will you be my secretary?

OLOF: Thank you, Your Grace, but I have no recommendation.

BRASK: Bishop Måns, what do you say?

MÅNS: They say Dr. Luther praised him highly.

BRASK: That's what I've heard. Merely youthful enthusiasm. We'll train him.

OLOF: I'm afraid it's too late.

BRASK: A young twig can be bent.

MÅNS: Your Grace should not foster serpents. Our canon is strongly inclined to the heresy and has dared to defy our orders today.

BRASK: Really?

MÅNS: We proclaimed the suspension of mass on entirely legal grounds, and he has dared to conduct mass, and what's worse a Lutheran mass, and thereby has stirred up the people.

BRASK: Be careful, young man! Do you know that excommunication strikes the man who preaches Luther's doctrines?

OLOF: I know. But I fear no god but God!

BRASK: Consider your words! I wanted to help you, but you push me away!

OLOF: You wanted to buy my talents to save your own sickly cause, and I was shameless enough not to sell myself!

BRASK: By St. George, I think you've lost your mind!

OLOF: If I have, don't use the same cure on me as on Gert Book-printer, the one you put in the insane asylum. He became too sane, I'm afraid.

BRASK (*to* MÅNS): Do you know Gert?

MÅNS: No, Your Grace.

BRASK: He's a mad fellow who used my press to print Lutheran documents when I put anti-Lutheran ones in his hands. And then he raved about the Apocalypse and the millennium. (*To* OLOF) Have you seen him?

OLOF: He was just here, and you can expect little good from him.

BRASK: Has he been let out?

OLOF: He'll soon be in Stockholm, and then you'll certainly hear about him. Be careful, Lord Bishop!

BRASK: Huh! There's no danger yet.

OLOF: The Anabaptists are in Stockholm!

BRASK: What's that?

OLOF: The Anabaptists are in Stockholm!

BRASK: The Anabaptists?

KING GUSTAV (*enters hastily*): What's going on? The city's stirred up. The people are rushing along the streets demanding mass. What's the meaning of this?

BRASK: Mischief, Your Majesty!

KING: Bishop Måns!

MÅNS: The city has not paid its tithes.

KING: So you refuse to conduct divine services. God's death!

BRASK: Your Majesty should consider . . .

KING: Bishop Måns! Answer me!

MÅNS: Your Majesty should consider that matters like these which fall under the jurisdiction of the church . . .

KING: I command you to do your job!

BRASK: The bishops of Sweden take orders only from their superiors, the pope and the canonical law.

KING (*subdued*): I know, but if the pope can't keep his eye on you all the time?

BRASK: That's our business.

KING (*flares up, but calms down*): You're right, Your Reverence. It shall be your business.

BRASK: To change the subject. They say Stockholm's on the verge of revolt.

KING: Who says so?

MÅNS: Our canon.

KING: Your schoolmaster? Where is he? (*To* OLOF) Are you the one? What's your name?

OLOF: Olaus Petri.

KING: Master Olof! You're a heretic, aren't you? And have plans against the holy church? That's dangerous business!

BRASK: He tore off his mask today. He was audacious enough to break the chapter's prohibition of mass openly. Because of that we demand Your Majesty's approval of his being duly punished.

KING: That's a matter for the cathedral chapter and does not concern me. But what did you say about a revolt in Stockholm?

OLOF: The Anabaptists!

KING: Is that all?

BRASK: Your Majesty, don't you know how those mad fools have behaved in Germany? We suggest that Your Majesty return with your soldiers yourself.

KING: That's my affair!

BRASK: But civil war!

KING: That will be my business! Olof, I appoint you secretary to the Council of Stockholm. Go there at once. Speak to the people. I'll rely on you.

BRASK: For the sake of our country, I beg Your Majesty to consider how foolish it is to talk to fools.

KING: You can't subdue the spirit by swords. Consider that, my lords!

BRASK: The church has never . . .

KING: Yes, not with keys, either. (*To* OLOF) Go to my chancellor and you'll get your official appointment.

BRASK: You'd better wait a moment, canon.

KING: Our secretary doesn't obey your orders ahead of mine.

BRASK: The rights of the church shall be satisfied first—Olaus Petri!

KING (*corrects him*): Secretary . . .

BRASK: Secretary Olaus Petri, don't leave the city before the chapter has handed down its judgment.

KING: The chapter doesn't hand down judgment before it has investigated!

BRASK: That's our affair!

KING: It won't be your affair, Bishop Brask! The bishop of Linköping does not judge a canon in Strängnäs. Bishop Måns, speak up!

MÅNS: After what has happened . . . hm!

BRASK: Further arguments should be superfluous.

KING: Bishop Brask, be silent or step aside when I speak privately to Bishop Måns—privately! Speak up, Lord Måns!

MÅNS: I can't see anything else—but—since His Reverence Bishop Brask—

KING: Now it's a question of Master Olof. You can postpone the investigation, my lords. Please leave us.

(*The* BISHOPS *go.*)

KING: Will you be my man?

OLOF: Your Majesty's secretary?

KING: No. You'll be my right hand on the condition that the left doesn't know for the time being what the right is doing. Go to Stockholm.

OLOF: The chapter will demand my return and excommunicate me.

KING: Before they've had time to go that far, you may blame me. Until then, stand on your own feet as well as you can.

OLOF: What does Your Majesty wish?

KING: Talk to the fanatics in Stockholm.

OLOF: And then?

KING: Oh, that's far off. I don't dare to think of it yet—let them preach; it can't hurt the stupid fools to hear a new word even if it's crazy; but there must be no acts of violence; then the sword will join in the game. Farewell, Olof. (*Exits*)

OLOF: The emperor doesn't want to agree with the pope!

(PUPILS, *who have been on a walk at the back, come forward.*)

PUPIL I: May we go on with the play now, Master Olof?

OLOF: There'll be no more playing, children.

PUPIL I: Are you leaving us, Master Olof?

OLOF: Yes, and apparently for always.

PUPIL I: You could stay over Pentecost so we could put on our comedy.

PUPIL II: And so I may play the angel Gabriel.

PUPIL I: Do as we wish, Master Olof. You were the only one who was kind to us and let us get out of the terrible fasts.

PUPIL II: Master Olof, don't leave us!

OLOF: Children, you don't know what you ask. The day will come when you'll thank God that I left you. No. May that day never come! Let's make our parting brief. Good-bye, Nils; good-bye, Vilhelm. (*He embraces them; they kiss his hand.*)

(LARS *has entered; observes them closely.*)

PUPIL I: Won't you ever come back, Master Olof?

LARS (*steps forward*): Are you ready to leave?

OLOF (*to the boys*): No, I'll never come back.

PUPILS (*as they exit*): Good-bye, Master Olof; don't forget us!

(OLOF *looks after them.*)

LARS: I have met the king.

OLOF (*absent-mindedly*): Have you?

LARS: Do you know what he said?

OLOF: No.

LARS: "I've acquired a pointer, who can raise the game; we'll see if he comes back when I whistle."

OLOF: Look! They're sitting among the graves, playing and picking flowers and singing Pentecost songs.

LARS (*takes him by the arm*): Child!

OLOF (*startled*): What did you say?

LARS: I thought you had taken such a firm grip on the plow today that it was too late to look back.

(OLOF *waves to the* PUPILS.)

LARS: Are you still dreaming?

OLOF: That was the last fair morning dream that went; forgive me— now I am awake!

(*They go to the right. When* OLOF *comes to the wing, he turns once more to look at the* PUPILS. *The* BLACK FRIARS MÅRTEN *and* NILS *have stepped forward from the very wing through which the* PUPILS *have made their exit.*)

(OLOF *gives a cry of involuntary amazement and draws his hand across his forehead.*)

(LARS *takes him by the arm, and they go.*)

CURTAIN

ACT II

STOCKHOLM

SCENE I

*A beer tavern in the wall of the Great Church. At the back a counter with beer cans and stoups, etc. To the right of the counter a table, behind which can be seen an iron door. At this table are sitting two disguised monks—*MÅRTEN *and* NILS—*drinking beer. At the rest of the tables are sitting farmers, sailors, and Ger-*

*man soldiers. The street door is to the right. A fiddler is sitting on
a barrel. The soldiers are shaking dice. Everyone is intoxicated
and noisy.* HANS WINDRANK, *a native of Småland, a* GERMAN
BURGHER, *and a* DANE *are sitting at one table.*

GERMAN (*to the* DANE): So you're defending that bloody scoundrel
Christian! [14]

DANE: Good gracious! He's a human being.

GERMAN: No, he's a monster! A bloodhound! A cowardly, false
Dane!

DANE: Heavens! You mustn't talk about blood! Do you remember
the Käpplinge murders when the German [15]—

WINDRANK: Listen, gentlemen. We should get together and have
fun; so I'll talk about America.

GERMAN: Do you blame us Lübeckers for what the Germans did?

DANE: Good gracious! I only said the Germans—

WINDRANK: Listen, you gentlemen shouldn't quarrel. (*Calls to the
tavern keeper*) Four mugs of brandy. Now we'll be agreeable and
peaceful, and I'll talk about America . . .

(*The brandy is put on the table.*)

GERMAN (*tastes the brandy*): A marvelous drink. Just think, gentlemen, how civilization has progressed. Today the grain's growing
in the field . . .

WINDRANK: And tomorrow it's changed to liquor. I wonder who
made that discovery.

GERMAN: I beg your pardon—it's a German invention—I say invention—because they discover America.

WINDRANK: And Germans never make discoveries.

GERMAN: God's death!

WINDRANK: There, there. You're surely not German.

DANE (*to the* GERMAN): Can you tell me who invented the idea that
the Germans gave Sweden its present king? [16] (*Laughter*)

GERMAN: The Lübeckers gave Sweden its liberator when it stood on
the verge of destruction.

WINDRANK: A toast to the king!

DANE: A toast to Lübeck!

GERMAN (*flattered*): I can't find words really . . .

WINDRANK: You're certainly not the king.

GERMAN: I beg of you, it was my Danish brother's . . .

DANE: You're not a Lübecker when you're a burgher in Stockholm, are you?

WINDRANK (*to the* SMÅLÄNNING): Why aren't you drinking, our silent brother?

SMÅLÄNNING: I'll drink your liquor, but I'll do this to the toast.

(*Crushes the tin mug and throws it on the floor*)

WINDRANK (*reaches for his knife*): You refuse to drink a toast to the king?

SMÅLÄNNING: I have drunk from his cup so long I haven't the slightest desire to drink his toast.

WINDRANK: God's blood!

GERMAN (*in a lively fashion*): Quiet! Quiet! Let's hear the man!

DANE (*in the same fashion*): Good gracious!

SMÅLÄNNING: God help me when I get home!

WINDRANK (*touched*): What is it, poor fellow? You look sad. Don't you have any money? Look here, and we'll see. (*Takes up his purse*) I have half my wages left. What's wrong with you?

SMÅLÄNNING: Let's not talk about it. More brandy! Brandy! I have money, too! Look! Gold! (*The brandy is brought.*) But it isn't mine. But I'm going to drink up every penny! And you're going to be decent and help me!

WINDRANK: But it's not your money—how come?

GERMAN: Who has wronged you, my good fellow? I can see it's something bad.

SMÅLÄNNING: I'm ruined! You see, I bought two hundred oxen on credit, and when I got to Stockholm, the king's bailiff took charge and said I couldn't sell them at a price higher than his! [17] The king fixes the price. The king's the one who has ruined me.

GERMAN: Oh, no!

SMÅLÄNNING: Oh, I know a lot more. They say he'll take the monks and priests away from us soon just to give everything to the lords.

DANE: The lords?

SMÅLÄNNING: Yes, indeed! King Christian should have clipped a little closer! [18] God bless him!

WINDRANK: Goodness, is the king like that? I thought he had the lords by the ear.

SMÅLÄNNING: He? No, he lets them hatch with the right to cut oaks on my land—if I had any left! You see, I did have a bit of land once, but then a lord came along and said my great-grandmother had borrowed it from his great-grandfather, and that was that.

GERMAN: Can the king be like that? I certainly didn't think that.

SMÅLÄNNING: Oh, yes, indeed! And the lords' boys run around with their guns in our woods shooting wild game just for the hell of it; but if we farmers were starving to death and should shoot an animal, we wouldn't have to die of hunger—they'd hang us—not in an oak, God save us; that would disgrace the royal tree—no, in a pine! You see, the pine isn't born with a crown, so it isn't royal . . . That's why the ballad goes:

> *"And we hanged the farmers up*
> *In the pine trees' highest top"*

It doesn't say crown—you notice.

GERMAN: But the pine raises its head all the same, and is as straight as can be.

SMÅLÄNNING: Drink, gentlemen. I mean it sincerely. That's a blessed drink! If I only didn't have a wife and children at home! Oh, well. That doesn't matter. Oh, I know a lot more, but I won't say anything.

WINDRANK: What do you know?

GERMAN: Maybe it's something funny?

SMÅLÄNNING: You see—if you'd count all the pine trees in Småland, they'd outnumber the oaks, I think.

GERMAN: You think so?

WINDRANK: I don't like it when anyone says anything against the king. Of course, I don't know what he does and says, and it's none of my business, either. But I do know this: he's all in favor of shipping.[19] Yes, he's the one who's equipped ships for trade with Spain, and he made me a sea captain, so I certainly haven't anything to complain about.

GERMAN: And he's done that out of spite just to ruin Lübeck's commerce, Lübeck's—to which he owes so much.

SMÅLÄNNING: He'll get to enjoy it. The oxen still have their horns even if they've been cut. Thanks for your company.—I have to go.

GERMAN: Oh, no. Another little mug, so we can talk.

SMÅLÄNNING: No thanks, though it's good of you; I don't dare to drink any more for then I'm afraid I'd be in for it. You see, I have a wife and children at home, and now I'm going home to tell them we're ruined—no—I don't dare to. (*Changes his mind*) Thank you, Mr. German—we'll have some more.

GERMAN: Fine, that's right. (*They drink.*)

SMÅLÄNNING (*empties his mug and jumps up*): The devil, how bitter it is! (*Staggers out*)

GERMAN (*to the* DANE): Well! Wait till that fellow wakes up!
(DANE *nods in agreement. The noise has increased; the fiddler plays. Then the organ can be heard from the church.*)

WINDRANK: Strange all the same that the king lets them have a tavern in the church wall.

GERMAN: So you have scruples, captain! The king doesn't know about this.

WINDRANK: Well, it doesn't sound good, that organ music with this singing. You see I've always been religious; I got that from home.

GERMAN (*ironically*): Lucky the man who's been brought up like that! You had a mother—

WINDRANK (*touched*): Yes—yes!

GERMAN: Who tucked you into bed at night and taught you: "There went an angel 'round our house."

WINDRANK: Yes, yes!

GERMAN: She was a splendid woman.

WINDRANK (*is getting drunk*): Oh, if you only knew!

GERMAN: God has heard her prayers. You're crying. You are a good man.

DANE: Good gracious!

GERMAN: If your mother could see you now! With tears in your eyes!

WINDRANK: Oh, I'm a weak sinner, I know, but you see—I have a heart—the devil take me. If a poor soul would come along and he were hungry, I'd take the shirt off my back.

GERMAN: Shouldn't we have one more mug?

WINDRANK: No, I don't think so.

(*Sharp blows can be heard on the iron door. General excitement*)

WINDRANK: Oh, oh!

GERMAN: You're surely not afraid! That's not the door to heaven.

WINDRANK: I'll never drink again. I promise. (*Dozes off*)

GERMAN (*to the* DANE): Isn't brandy a blessed drink that can move a rascal like that to enthusiasm, even to thoughts of temperance?

DANE: You're right. There just isn't another drink like it.

GERMAN: It opens the heart wide and closes the head tight; that is to say, it makes us good people, for the good people are the ones who have a big heart and a little head.

DANE: Yes, I go still further; brandy makes us religious, because it kills reason, and reason's the rock that keeps religion from entering the heart.

GERMAN: Brandy's a sacred drink! Strange that . . .

DANE: Enough said!

(*Blows on the iron door can again be heard.*)

WINDRANK (*who has been asleep, wakes up*): Help! I'm dying!

GERMAN: Too bad about such a beautiful soul.

(*The door is opened violently, overturning the table with the stoups and mugs, at which* MÅRTEN *and* NILS *are sitting. A woman dressed in a black and red skirt with a nun's veil over her head rushes in; for a moment* GERT *can be seen in the doorway behind her. Then the door is closed violently.*)

PROSTITUTE (*looks about in amazement*): Save me! The people want to kill me!

A GERMAN SOLDIER: A prostitute with a nun's veil! (*Laughs*)

(*Laughter*)

MÅRTEN (*crosses himself*): A prostitute! Who brought her into this respectable company? Keeper, take her out if you don't want to hurt the reputation of your place and the sanctity of the church.

PROSTITUTE: Isn't there anyone who'll help me? (*The* KEEPER *has taken her by the arm to lead her out to the street.*) Don't drive me out among the raging people! I wanted to steal into the Lord's house to get a crumb of His mercy; I wanted to start a new life—but the monks drove me away and set the people on me; then Father Gert came along and saved me by bringing me here.

MÅRTEN: You can all hear she has desecrated the sanctuary of God. She wants to conceal her garb of shame with the veil of holiness.

GERMAN: And the veil wasn't long enough!

MÅRTEN (*goes up to her to tear off her veil*): Tear off your mask, and show your vileness! (*He recoils when he sees her face.*)

PROSTITUTE: It's you, Mårten, is it? You murderer!

GERMAN: Old acquaintances!

MÅRTEN: A shameful lie! I've never seen her before! I'm Brother Mårten, and Brother Nils is my witness!

NILS (*drunk*): I can testify—that Brother Mårten has never seen that woman.

PROSTITUTE: And still, Nils, you were the one who showed me Mårten's letter of absolution when I was driven out of the cloister and they let him stay.

NILS: Yes, that's the truth, that is.

MÅRTEN (*beside himself with fury, pulls* NILS *by the arm*): You're lying, you, too! You can all see he's drunk!

GERMAN: Good people, I testify that the holy brother's drunk and therefore he's lying.

PEOPLE (*with disgust*): A drunken priest!

GERMAN: Oh, well! The binge gives absolution to the lie. Isn't that right, Father Mårten?

KEEPER: I have to say this: you'll have to behave here; if this goes on, I'll lose my customers and probably be dragged before the chapter. So please take out the miserable creature who's causing all this commotion.

MÅRTEN: Take her out, or I'll have you excommunicated! Don't you know we're within the walls of the holy church even if the chapter has opened this room for the bodily refreshment of travelers?

GERMAN: Good people, this is a holy room, and God obviously lives here.

(PEOPLE *drag the* PROSTITUTE *toward the door.*)

PROSTITUTE: Christ, help me!

OLOF (*has appeared in the door, now forces his way forward, takes the* PROSTITUTE *by the hands, and draws her away from the drunken people*): Tell me. Who is this woman?

MÅRTEN: She's not a woman—

OLOF: What's that?

MÅRTEN: She's not a man—though she's disguised!

OLOF: You say *she*. Isn't she a woman?

MÅRTEN: She's a prostitute!

OLOF (*startled; lets go her hand*): A prostitute!

GERMAN: Don't let go of her, Master Olof, or she'll run away!

OLOF: Why do you lay hands on her? What is her crime?

GERMAN: She goes to church!

OLOF: I see. (*Looks about*)

MÅRTEN: What are you looking for?

OLOF (*becomes aware of* MÅRTEN): A priest.

MÅRTEN: I'm a black friar.

OLOF: So! I guessed that! You're the one who set the people on her!

MÅRTEN: I'm the one who protects the church from vileness and wants to keep it pure from vice. She's an excommunicated woman who sells her body, which should be the temple of God. (*The woman falls to her knees before* olof.)

olof (*takes her hand*) : You see, black friar, I dare to take her hand and match her against you! She has sold her body, you say! How many souls have you bought? I, too, am a priest! No, I'm a human being, for I'm still not so presumptuous that I've locked the house of God, and, as a sinful man, I give my hand to a fellow human being who can't be without sin. Let him who is without sin come forward to cast the first stone. Come here, Brother Mårten, you angel of light, who have clad yourself in the black garb of innocence and have shaved your head so no one will see how you've grown gray in sin. Maybe you don't have a stone ready? Woe unto you! What have you done with the stones you were going to give to the people when they asked for bread? Have you already given all of them away? Come here, respectable burgher. (*To* windrank, *who's sleeping on the floor*) You, who sleep the sleep of beasts, why don't you wake up so you can throw your knife? See how he blushes? Because of shame over the bad company you've given him or because of sensual pleasure? (*The* people *murmur disapprovingly.*) You murmur! From shame because of what I've said or because you're ashamed of yourselves? Why don't you cast stones? True, you haven't any. Oh, well. Open the door. Call the people and drag the woman out. If you don't believe fifty men can tear her to pieces, be assured that five hundred women can! Well! You don't say anything! Woman! Rise! They have acquitted you. Go and sin no more, but don't show yourself to the priests, for they'd throw you to the women.

mårten (*who has tried to interrupt* olof *several times but has been held back by the* german, *takes out a paper*) : The man to whom you're listening is a heretic. You heard that in what he said, but he has been excommunicated, too. Look here! Read it yourselves! (*He takes a candle from one of the tables and throws it into the middle of the floor.*) "As that light is extinguished which we here

cast out, so may joy and comfort and all the good he may have
from God be extinguished for him."

PEOPLE (*cross themselves and draw back;* OLOF *stands alone with the*
PROSTITUTE *in the middle of the stage*): Anathema!

MÅRTEN (*to the* PROSTITUTE): Now you hear what Master Olof's absolution is worth.

OLOF (*who has been reticent*): Woman, do you still dare to rely on
my words? Aren't you afraid of me? Don't you hear the lightning
of excommunication hissing about our heads? Why don't you go
over to these twenty righteous men who are still within the protection of the holy church? Answer me! Do you believe God has
cast me out as these have?

PROSTITUTE: No!

OLOF (*takes the proclamation of excommunication*): Well, then!
The great bishop of the little city of Linköping has sold my soul
to Satan for my lifetime—his power doesn't extend beyond that—
because I urged the people to turn to God at a forbidden time.
Here's the contract; since the church as bound me to Hell by this,
I release myself from the same (*he tears the parchment to pieces*),
and from the ban of the church! God help me, amen!

PEOPLE (*howl*): Anathema!

MÅRTEN: Pull him down! Strike him! He's excommunicated!

OLOF (*places himself in front of the* PROSTITUTE): Listen to the devils
crying for their sacrifice! (*To the* PEOPLE) Don't touch me!

MÅRTEN: Down with him!

(*A soldier lifts his weapon; the iron door is opened, and the
Anabaptists, led by* KNIPPERDOLLINK, *rush in shouting; they are
carrying smashed crucifixes, saints' images, and rent choir robes.
All the people in the tavern are crowded toward the exit.*) [20]

KNIPPERDOLLINK (*who has been in the lead, as he opens the door
wide*): In here, people; here's another holy house. What's this? A
tavern in the temple! Look! The abomination has gone so far
that they desecrate the sanctuary. But I'll cleanse it with fire! Set
fire to the church and put the saints on the fire!

OLOF (*steps forward*) : Consider what you're about to do!

KNIPPERDOLLINK: Are you afraid the heat will make the beer kegs burst, you Belial? Are you the papal tavern keeper, who doesn't hesitate to erect a chapel for vice in the church wall?

OLOF: I'm the secretary of the city council; in the name of the king I command you to observe law and order!

KNIPPERDOLLINK: So you're the man the king has sent out to fight against our sacred cause! Forward, forward, men of God, and seize him first. After that we'll cleanse the house of God from idolatry.

MÅRTEN: Go on, good people! He's a heretic and has been excommunicated.

KNIPPERDOLLINK (*to* OLOF) : Heretic! So you're not one of the Catholics?

OLOF: Since I've been excommunicated, I don't belong to the church any more.

KNIPPERDOLLINK: Then you're on our side. (OLOF *remains silent.*) Answer me! Are you for or against us?

MÅRTEN: He's Olaus Petri—the king has sent him.

KNIPPERDOLLINK: Are you Olaus Petri?

OLOF: Yes.

KNIPPERDOLLINK: But you're a heretic!

OLOF: I'm proud that I am.

KNIPPERDOLLINK: And are in the king's service!

OLOF: Yes. (*The Anabaptists shout and surround* OLOF.)

GERT (*rushes in*) : Stop it! What are you doing?

KNIPPERDOLLINK: Gert! Who is this man?

GERT: He's ours! Let go of him, friends. There are the devil's messengers!

　　(GERT *points at* MÅRTEN *and* NILS, *who steal out through the door. The Anabaptists run after them, raining blows on them.* GERT *turns by the door to* OLOF. *The* PROSTITUTE *has withdrawn into a corner.* WINDRANK *is still sleeping under the table.* OLOF *stops thoughtfully in the center of the room.*)

GERT (*throws himself on a bench, exhausted*): It's heavy work, Olof.

OLOF: What have you done?

GERT: We've done some cleaning, to start with.

OLOF: That will cost you dearly.

GERT: We still have the upper hand. The whole city's on the move. Rink's at work up in St. George's chapel. Listen, has the king sent you against us?

OLOF: Yes.

GERT: That was very sensible.

OLOF: Tomorrow I'll preach in the new pulpit.[21]

GERT: Well! How are you attending to your royal job? You're still standing here with your arms folded!

OLOF: Bring your friends with you to church tomorrow.

GERT: Will it be a Catholic sermon?

OLOF: I was excommunicated today.

GERT (*jumps up and embraces* OLOF): God bless you, Olof! That was the baptism of your rebirth!

OLOF: I still don't understand you. Why do you behave like wild animals? Why, you desecrate everything holy!

GERT (*picks up a broken saint's image*): Is this fellow holy? A St. Nicholas,[22] I think. Has Jesus Christ come and lived in vain when people still worship pieces of wood? Is what I can smash a god? Look at it!

OLOF: But the people consider him holy.

GERT: So was the golden calf, so was Zeus, and Thor and Odin, too! And still they were struck down. (*Catches sight of the* PROSTITUTE) Who's that woman? Oh, yes, the one I tried to get into your safekeeping. Olof! Tell me one thing! Has the king bought you?

OLOF: Leave me, Gert! I hate you!

GERT: Who's that pig sleeping over there?

OLOF: When I stand before you, I become very small. Leave me. I want to do my work and not yours.

GERT: Listen . . .

OLOF: You want to confuse our destinies.

GERT: Listen . . .

OLOF: You've thrown an invisible net about me; you proclaim that I'm an Anabaptist. How can I defend myself to the king?

GERT: Which king?

OLOF: King Gustav.

GERT: Oh! That one! Good-bye, Olof . . . So you're going to preach tomorrow . . . Why doesn't the woman go? . . . Good-bye. (*Goes*)

OLOF: Is he doing the errands of God or of the devil?

PROSTITUTE (*approaches* OLOF; *kneels*): Let me thank you.

OLOF: Thank God alone for having saved your soul, and don't believe that you have atoned for your sins today. Get strength to bear the curse for your lifetime. God has forgiven you—people never will. (OLOF *takes her by the hand and leads her out through the door.*)

MÅRTEN (*appears in the doorway and after him* OLOF'S MOTHER *and* KRISTINA, GERT'S *daughter*): We've come to the wrong place, I think.

MOTHER (*when she becomes aware of* OLOF *and the* PROSTITUTE, *is beside herself*): Olof! Olof!

KRISTINA: Who is that woman? She looks so unhappy.

MÅRTEN: Let's leave this dreadful den.

OLOF (*turns and runs toward the door, which is slammed shut by* MÅRTEN): Mother! Mother! (*He runs out through the other doorway; the stage becomes dark.*)

CURTAIN

Interlude

(*The door to the church is opened again carefully and the* ORGANBLOWER-SEXTON *with a lantern and his* WIFE *climb in carefully.*)

SEXTON: Katrina, darling! Hold the lantern while I padlock the door.

WIFE: Bengt, dear, we ought to take a look at this mess first. I never could have believed we were so close to the tavern. Why, it's terrible! See, large barrels with beer in them!

SEXTON: And brandy, too. How it smells! I'll get a headache if I stay any longer.

WIFE: Merciful God, what a godless life they've led in here!

SEXTON: Katrina, darling!

WIFE: Yes, dear.

SEXTON: You know, I feel sick already. It's so cold and damp down here!

WIFE: Maybe we ought to go home.

SEXTON: I think I'll have to sit down and rest on this bench.

WIFE: Don't sit here in the damp and cold; let's go into the church.

SEXTON: No, you know, I think it was still colder there.

WIFE: Maybe you have a fever.

SEXTON: Yes, I almost think so. I'm so hot.

WIFE: Maybe you want something to drink.

SEXTON: Maybe that wouldn't be so bad.

WIFE: I'll see if there's any water.

SEXTON: There's not likely to be any in a hole like this.

WIFE: You certainly can't drink beer when you have a fever.

SEXTON: You know, I think the fever's gone; I feel frozen.

WIFE: I'll look for some mild beer.

SEXTON: If it's going to do any good, it had better be strong. Look: there's a keg of Rostock Number 4 stamped A.W.

WIFE (*searching*): I don't see any. Here's an Amsterdam Number 3.

SEXTON: Can't you see the fourth shelf from the top to the right?

(WIFE *searching*)

SEXTON: There's a metal tap to the left, right next to the funnel.

WIFE: I can't see any.

SEXTON: Well, I ought to know!

WIFE: I found it!

(SEXTON *gets up to help her but happens to step on* WINDRANK.)

WINDRANK (*awakens*): Oh, oh! Jesus Christ! St. Peter and St. Paul

and Ferdinand and Isabella and St. George and the dragon [23] and
all the rest, and in came the doom in *dejom pote potentum ernos
ternon* Jesus Christ, the great dipper certainly is, an angel went
'round our house, the fellow was a great singer, in came Nils *in
puttri*. Amen! Amen! Who's stepping on my stomach?

SEXTON: Please be merciful enough to say if you're a man or an evil
spirit!

WINDRANK: I used to be a spirit, but at the moment I'm a pig!

SEXTON: What sort of spirit are you if I may ask?

WINDRANK: I'm a sea spirit! But you don't have to tramp on my
bellows for all that.

SEXTON: Look, sir; my bread and butter is tramping the bellows . . .
of the great organs.

WINDRANK: So it's the organ-tramper I have the honor—

SEXTON: Sexton, really, but I have a little clothing shop in the church
wall, too.

WINDRANK: So you're an organ-tramper, a sexton, and a dealer in
clothes—

SEXTON: In one person. Without confusion or transformation . . .

WINDRANK: That's a respectable trinity!

SEXTON: One doesn't joke about things like that.

WINDRANK: Oh! Oh! I'm drowning. Help!

SEXTON: What in God's name?

WINDRANK: There's a flood—ugh!

SEXTON: Katrina, darling! Where are you, angel? (*Runs up*) Christ,
you've given my wife heart failure! She has run away from the
beer keg . . . and taken the tap with her! Get up, get up, and let's
get out of this godless den!

WINDRANK: My friend, now that I've just got into my proper element, I'll most likely stay.

SEXTON: By all means; the clock's striking twelve, and the ghostly
hour begins.

WINDRANK (*jumps up*): That's another matter! (*The* SEXTON *is lead-*

ing WINDRANK.) Listen, sexton. I'm beginning to be attacked by strong doubts of the trinity.

SEXTON: Well, I declare!

WINDRANK: I mean your trinity!

SEXTON: What do you mean by that, captain . . .

WINDRANK: There are four of you all the same!

SEXTON: Four? Which?

WINDRANK: What about the tapster? Mayn't he be along?

SEXTON: Sh! Sh! That's only at night! (*They both fall down on the smashed St. Nicholas.*)

WINDRANK: Oh! Oh! Ghosts! Help, Mary, Mother of God!

SEXTON (*gets up and lifts up the image*): By my soul, it's so one's hair could stand straight on end. Here lies St. Nicholas smashed and swimming in beer. That's going pretty far, when they drag sacred things down into the dirt—the world won't last long, I guess; when the like of that happens to dry wood—

WINDRANK (*who has recovered*): To wet, you mean!

SEXTON: Silence, blasphemer! St. Nicholas is my patron saint. I was born on his day.

WINDRANK: That's why the two of you both like beer, I suppose.

SEXTON: It's the fashion to be a heretic now.

WINDRANK: Yes, it must be in the air, for I'm a very religious man otherwise. But don't be sad; I'll glue St. Nicholas together for you.

SEXTON (*calls into the church*): Katrina!

WINDRANK: Sh, sh! What the hell, don't call up the ghosts!

SEXTON: Shame! (*They leave.*)

CURTAIN

Scene 2

A door. A smaller one leading into the pulpit. Stoles and choir robes on the walls. Prayer stools and some small chests. The sun is shining in through a window. The bells are ringing. An uninterrupted murmur can be heard at the left wall. The sexton *and his* wife *come in, stop by the door, and pray silently.*

sexton: There. Hurry up and dust a little, Katrina, darling.

wife: Oh, well. It doesn't have to be so particular; it's only that Master Olof who's preaching today. I can't understand how the chapter can permit anything like that.

sexton: He has the king's permission, you see.

wife: Yes! Yes!

sexton: And he's had a basket put on the wall! Just new-fangled notions. I declare, that Luther! [24]

wife: There'll be the same trouble as yesterday, I suppose. I thought they'd tear down the whole church.

sexton (*carries a glass of water up into the pulpit*): He'll most likely need something to wet his throat today, the poor fellow.

wife: I don't think it matters in the least.

sexton (*up in the pulpit*): Katrina! Here comes Master Olof!

wife: That's terrible; they haven't rung the sermon bell yet. No, no, they probably won't ring it for that fellow.

(olof *enters, serious and solemn—goes to a prayer stool and kneels.* sexton *comes down and brings a robe which he holds out to* olof.)

olof (*gets up*): God's peace.

(wife *curtseys and goes.* sexton *holds out the robe.*)

olof: Let it hang.

sexton: Aren't you going to wear a robe, master?

OLOF: No.

SEXTON: But it's always done. What about the cloth?

OLOF: I don't need it.

SEXTON: Well, I declare!

OLOF: Please leave me, my friend.

SEXTON: Shall I leave? I usually . . .

OLOF: Do me that favor.

SEXTON: Well! Yes, indeed! But first I'll tell you I've put the missal to the right as you come up, and I've put a marker where you're to stop, and I've put the water right next to it. Don't forget to turn the hourglass, master, for things could drag on too long . . .

OLOF: Don't worry. There'll be those who'll tell me when to stop!

SEXTON: Yes, Lord preserve us! Beg your pardon. We have our customs here, see.

OLOF: Tell me, what's that mournful murmur?

SEXTON: A devout brother's praying for a poor soul. (*Goes*)

OLOF: "Thou therefore gird up thy loins, and arise, and speak unto them all that I command thee"—God help me! (*Throws himself onto a prayer stool; finds a piece of paper on it. Reads*) "Don't appear in the pulpit today; they're after your life!"—the tempter wrote that! (*Tears the paper to pieces*)

MOTHER (*enters*): You've gone astray, my son!

OLOF: Who knows?

MOTHER: *I* know! But, as your mother, I give you my hand. Turn back!

OLOF: Where would you lead me?

MOTHER: To the fear of God and virtue.

OLOF: If the decision of the pope's chancery is fear of God and virtue, it's too late.

MOTHER: It's not merely the doctrine; it's the life you're leading, too.

OLOF: I know you mean the company I had last night, but I'm too proud to answer you. It wouldn't do any good, anyway.

MOTHER: Oh, that I should get this reward for sacrificing so you could go away to study.

OLOF: Your sacrifice won't be in vain, God willing. You're the one I have to thank for this day when I at last can step forward openly to speak the words of truth!

MOTHER: Do you talk about truth, you, who have made yourself the prophet of lies?

OLOF: That was a harsh word, mother!

MOTHER: Have I and my people before me lived and believed and died in a lie?

OLOF: It *wasn't* a lie, but it has become a lie. When you were young, mother, you were right. When I get old, well, then I may be wrong. One doesn't grow with time.

MOTHER: I don't understand you.

OLOF: That's my only great sorrow. Everything I do and say from the purest of motives must seem like sin and ungodliness to you.

MOTHER: Olof! I know you've made up your mind, I know you've gone astray—I can't do anything about that, for you know more than I do. God will surely bring you back, but I beg you not to rush into damnation today. Don't cut your life short!

OLOF: What do you mean? Surely they won't kill me in the pulpit!

MOTHER: Haven't you heard that Bishop Brask is negotiating with the pope for the introduction of the law that condemns heretics to the stake?

OLOF: The inquisition?

MOTHER: Yes! That's it!

OLOF: Leave me, mother; I have to preach today!

MOTHER: You mustn't!

OLOF: Nothing will prevent me!

MOTHER: I have prayed that God would change your heart—I'll tell you something, but you may not repeat it—I was weak with age, and my knees wouldn't support me—I sought out a servant of the Lord and asked him, who's closer to God, to read masses for your soul. He refused, because you've been excommunicated! Oh, it's terrible! God forgive me; I bribed his clear conscience with gold, with devil's gold, just to save you!

OLOF: What are you saying, mother? It's not possible!

MOTHER (*takes* OLOF *by the hand and leads him to the left wall*):
Listen! He's praying for you in the chapel!

OLOF: So that was the mumbling! Who is he?

MOTHER: Friar Mårten—

OLOF: You're having that devil pray for me! Forgive me, mother—
thank you, for you meant well, but—

MOTHER (*weeps; on her knees*): Olof! Olof!

OLOF: Don't ask me! A mother's prayers can tempt the angels in
heaven to desert their cause. The psalm's almost ended; I have to
go. The people are waiting.

MOTHER: You'll be the death of me, Olof!

OLOF (*violently*): The Lord will awaken you! (*Kisses her hand*)
Don't say any more; I don't know what I'd answer.

MOTHER: Listen! The people are murmuring.

OLOF: I'm coming! I'm coming! The God who held His hand over
Daniel in the lion's den will protect me, too. (OLOF *goes. During
the following scenes in the sacristy a powerful speaking voice can
be heard, but the words cannot be made out. When the sermon
has proceeded for a while, there is murmuring which quickly
becomes shouts.*)

KRISTINA (*enters*): Did you see him, mother?

MOTHER: Did you come, child? Why, I asked you to stay at home.

KRISTINA: Why mayn't I go into the house of the Lord? You're con-
cealing something from me.

MOTHER: Go home, Kristina!

KRISTINA: Mayn't I hear Olof preach? Why, they're the words of
God, aren't they, mother?

(MOTHER *remains silent.*)

KRISTINA: You don't answer! Why? Didn't Olof have permission to
preach? Why do the people out there look so strange? They were
muttering when I came.

MOTHER: Don't ask me. Go home, and thank God for your ignorance.

KRISTINA: Am I a child, that I mustn't be told . . .

MOTHER: Your soul is still pure and mustn't be sullied. You haven't anything to do with this struggle.

KRISTINA: Struggle? I felt there was something like that.

MOTHER: Yes, there's a struggle here, so go, go. You know what our lot is when men wage war.

KRISTINA: Tell me what it's about. Ignorance makes me unhappy. I can see a terrifying darkness and moving shadows. Give me light so that I may really know. Perhaps I know these ghosts.

MOTHER: You'll tremble when you see who they are.

KRISTINA: Let me tremble, then, rather than be tormented by this horrible calm!

MOTHER: Don't call the lightning from the clouds—it would crush you!

KRISTINA: You frighten me! But tell me the truth; I must know—or I'll ask someone else!

MOTHER: Have you decided to enter the convent?

KRISTINA: Father wants me to.

MOTHER: You're hesitating.

(KRISTINA *remains silent.*)

MOTHER: There's a bond that holds you?

KRISTINA: You know that.

MOTHER: I know, and you have to break it.

KRISTINA: That will soon be impossible.

MOTHER: I'll save you, child—you still can be saved; I'll give the Lord my greatest sacrifice if only one soul can be saved from damnation. My son!

KRISTINA: Olof?

MOTHER: Olof's lost, and I, his mother, have to tell you that.

KRISTINA: Lost?

MOTHER: He's a prophet of lies! The devil has captured his soul.

KRISTINA (*violently*): That isn't true!

MOTHER: Would to God it weren't!

KRISTINA: Why, why do you tell me this now for the first time?—but that's right, it's a lie! (*Goes to the door and opens it slightly*) See, mother; there he stands. Is it the evil spirit who speaks through his mouth? Is it a fire from Hell that glows in his eyes? Does one utter lies with trembling lips? Can darkness radiate light? Don't you see the radiance about his head? You're wrong! I know that! I don't know what he's preaching, I don't know what he's denying, but he *is* right! He's right, and God is with him!

MOTHER: You don't know the world, child; you don't know the tricks of the devil. Watch out! (*She draws* KRISTINA *away from the door.*) You mayn't listen to him; your soul's weak; he's the apostle of Antichrist!

KRISTINA: Who is Antichrist?

MOTHER: He's Luther!

KRISTINA: You've never told me who Luther is, but if Olof is his apostle, Luther is great.

MOTHER: Luther is possessed by the devil!

KRISTINA: Why didn't anyone tell me that before? Now I don't believe it!

MOTHER: I'm telling you now—I wanted to protect you from the evil of the world, so I kept you in ignorance . . .

KRISTINA: I don't believe you! Let me go; I have to see him; I have to hear him; because he doesn't talk like the others.

MOTHER: Jesus, my Saviour! You, too, are possessed by the unclean spirit!

KRISTINA (*at the door*): "You should not bind the souls of men," he said. "You are free, because God has made you free!" Look, the people tremble at his words; they're getting up; they're murmuring. "You don't want freedom; woe unto you; that is a sin against the Holy Ghost."

SEXTON (*enters*): I don't think it's wise for you ladies to stay here; the people are getting restless. This won't end well for Master Olof.

MOTHER: Mary, Mother of God! What are you saying?

KRISTINA: Don't be afraid; the spirit of God is with him!

SEXTON: Well, I don't know about that, but he certainly can preach. As old a sinner as I am, I couldn't keep from weeping up where I was sitting in the organ loft. I don't understand how a heretic and an Antichrist can preach like that. Well, I'll say this, that Luther! (*Shouts out in the church*) There! Now there'll be something terrible again, and the king had to be away, too.

MOTHER: Let's leave. If God is with him, they can't hurt him. If it's the devil—then Thy will be done, Lord, but forgive him.

> (*Shouts outside. They leave. The stage is empty for a moment and only* OLOF's *voice* [*now stronger than ever*] *can be heard— interrupted by shouts and throwing of stones.* KRISTINA *comes back alone and shuts the door from the inside and throws herself onto a prayer stool. Heavy blows on the door can be heard; there is a tumult in the church. Then it becomes quiet, and* OLOF *comes down with a bloody forehead and disheveled appearance.*)

OLOF (*without seeing* KRISTINA, *throws himself in a chair*): In vain! They don't want to! I loosen the prisoner's bonds, and he strikes me; I tell him, "You're free!" and he doesn't believe me. Is that word so great that there isn't room for it in a human brain? If there were only one who believed—but now I'm alone—a fool, whom no one understands . . .

KRISTINA (*goes up to him*): Olof! I believe in you!

OLOF: Kristina!

KRISTINA: You are right!

OLOF: How do you know?

KRISTINA: I don't know, but I believe. I heard you just now.

OLOF: And you don't curse me?

KRISTINA: You're preaching the word of God, aren't you?

OLOF: Yes!

KRISTINA: Why hasn't anyone told us this before? Why do they speak a language we don't understand?

OLOF: Girl, who put those words on your tongue?

KRISTINA: Who? I hadn't thought about that.

OLOF: Your father?

KRISTINA: He wants me to enter a convent.

OLOF: Has it gone that far? And what do you want to do?

KRISTINA (*looks at* OLOF's *injured forehead*): They've hurt you, Olof; for goodness' sake, let me bandage your forehead.

OLOF (*sits down*): Kristina, have I destroyed your faith?

KRISTINA (*takes her handkerchief, tears it, and bandages* OLOF *during the following speech*): My faith? I don't understand—tell me, who is Luther?

OLOF: I mustn't say.

KRISTINA: Always the same answer! That's what my father says, your mother says it, and you, too! Don't people dare to tell me the truth? Is truth dangerous?

OLOF: Look! (*Pointing at his forehead*) Truth is dangerous!

KRISTINA: So you want to have me shut up in a convent cell to a living death in ignorance.

(OLOF *remains silent.*)

KRISTINA: You want me to weep my life away, my youth, and pray the long eternal prayers until my soul falls asleep. No—I don't want that, now that I've awakened; people are struggling around me, they're suffering and are in despair; I have seen that, but I mayn't have a part in it, not even look on, not even know what they're struggling about; people have kept me in a beastlike sleep. Don't you think I have a soul, which can't be satisfied with bread or empty prayers that have been put into my mouth? "Don't bind the spirits," you said. If you only knew how those words struck me—they brought daylight, and the wild shouts out there sounded like the morning songs of the birds . . .

OLOF: Kristina! You're a woman; you weren't born to fight.

KRISTINA: But at least let me suffer—just so I don't have to stay asleep. You see, God awakened me all the same. You'd never have dared to tell me who Antichrist is, you'd never have let me know who Luther is, and when your mother frightened me by saying you were a Luther, I blessed Luther! Whether he's a heretic or a believer, I don't know, I don't care, for neither Luther nor the pope nor Antichrist can bring peace to my immortal soul when I don't have faith in the eternal God!

OLOF: Kristina! If you want to, you can be by my side and help me, for you are the one I love.

KRISTINA: Now I can say yes to you, because I know what I want, and without appealing to my father, for I am free! I *am* free!

OLOF: Do you know what lies ahead of you, too?

KRISTINA: Now I do. And you won't have to destroy any false dreams—they're gone; I've dreamt about the knight who'd come to offer me a kingdom and who'd talk about flowers and love— Olof, I want to be your wife. Here's my hand. I'll tell you, though, that you were never the knight of my dreams. Thank God he never came—he'd have gone, too—like a dream.

OLOF: You'll be mine, Kristina, and you'll be happy, for you were the one who was always with me when I was in trouble and temptation, and now you'll be by my side. You were the fair maiden of my dreams, imprisoned in the tower by the stern lord of the castle. Now you're mine!

KRISTINA: Beware of dreams, Olof! (*Blows on the door*)

OLOF: Who is it?

GERT (*outside*): Gert!

OLOF: What will he say? My promise!

KRISTINA: Are you afraid? Shall I open?

    (OLOF *opens the door.*)

GERT (*startled*): Kristina? Olof! You've broken your promise!

OLOF: No.

GERT: You're lying! You've stolen my child, my only comfort!

KRISTINA: Olof isn't lying!

GERT: You were in church, Kristina?

KRISTINA: I've heard what you didn't want me to hear.

GERT: The Lord begrudged me my only joy.

OLOF: The current you wanted to free takes its sacrifices where it will.

GERT: You have stolen my child!

OLOF: Give her to me, Father Gert.

GERT: Never!

OLOF: Isn't she free?

GERT: She's my child!

OLOF: Don't you preach freedom? She's mine! God has given her to me, and you can't take her from me!

GERT: God be praised, you're a—priest!

OLOF AND KRISTINA: A priest!

GERT: So—you can't marry! [25]

OLOF: If I do anyway?

GERT: Do you dare?

OLOF: Yes!

GERT: Do you want a husband who has been excommunicated, Kristina?

KRISTINA: I don't know what that means.

OLOF: You see, Gert.

GERT: God, Thy punishment is heavy.

OLOF: The truth is for everyone.

GERT: Your love is greater than mine. That was only selfishness. God bless you! Now I'm alone. (*Embraces them both*) There, there. Go home, Kristina, and calm them. I want to talk with Olof. (KRISTINA *goes*.) Now you're mine!

OLOF: What's that?

GERT: My kinsman!—did you get my letter?

OLOF: So you were the one who advised me not to preach!

GERT: The very opposite, though I did express myself a little strangely.

OLOF: I don't understand.

GERT: No, no. You're still too young, so you need a Providence. To a man like you one has to say, "Don't do that," when one wants to get something done.

OLOF: Why weren't you in church with your followers?

GERT: Only the sick need doctors; we were at work elsewhere.

You've done good work today, and I see you got your wages. I've set you free today, Olof.

OLOF: You?

GERT: The king ordered you to calm the rebels, and look at what you've done.

OLOF: I'm beginning to understand, Father Gert.

GERT: I'm glad. Yes, you've really stirred things up.

OLOF: Yes, I have.

GERT: What do you think the king will say about that?

OLOF: I'll answer for that!

GERT: Good!

OLOF: And the king will approve what I've done, because he wants a reformation, but doesn't dare to do it himself yet.

GERT: Fool!

OLOF: I see you want to set me against the lawful king.

GERT: Listen, how many masters do you think you can serve?
    (OLOF *remains silent.*)

GERT: The king's here!

OLOF: What's that?

GERT: He just got back.

OLOF: And the Anabaptists!

GERT: In jail, of course.

OLOF: And you stand here absolutely calm.

GERT: I'm old, I've raged like you, too, but I only got tired. Rink and Knipperdollink were my vanguard. They had to fall, that's plain; now my work begins. (*Drums are beaten out on the street.*)

OLOF: What was that?

GERT: The royal drums accompanying the prisoners to jail. Come over here and see.

OLOF (*gets up on a bench and looks out through the window*): What in the world! Women and children dragged off by soldiers!

GERT: Oh, well, they threw stones at the king's guards. That certainly won't do.

OLOF: Are they going to take fools or sick people to prison?

GERT: There are two kinds of fools: you put one kind into insane asylums and give them pills and cold baths; you cut off the heads of the other kind. That's a radical cure, but then that kind's dangerous.

OLOF: I'll go to the king; he can't want these atrocities.

GERT: Watch out for your head, Olof!

OLOF: Watch out for yourself, Father Gert!

GERT: I'm in no danger. I'm certified to the insane asylum.

OLOF: I can't bear to see this; I'll go to the king, even if it costs my life! (*Goes toward the door*)

GERT: This is a matter the king doesn't decide. Turn to the law.

OLOF: The king is the law.

GERT: Yes, unfortunately! If the horse knew his strength, he wouldn't be crazy enough to wear the harness—someday when he gets wise, he'll run away from his oppressor—then they'll say he's crazy . . . Let's pray to God to save the minds of these poor people.

CURTAIN

ACT III

SCENE I

A room in Stockholm Castle. In the background a gallery, which is later divided by means of a curtain. An old SERVANT *is walking in the gallery.*

OLOF (*enters*): Is the king receiving today?

SERVANT: Yes.

OLOF: Do you know why they've let me wait in vain four days in a row?

SERVANT: No, I don't. I don't know anything about that.

OLOF: It seems strange I haven't been received.

SERVANT: What did you want?

OLOF: That doesn't concern you.

SERVANT: No, no. I understand that, but I thought I perhaps could throw some light on it.

OLOF: Are you usually in charge of the king's audiences?

SERVANT: No, not at all, but you see anyone who hears as much as I do knows a little about everything. (*Pause*)

OLOF: Will it be long?

(SERVANT *pretends that he doesn't hear.*)

OLOF: Do you know if the king is coming soon?

SERVANT (*with his back to* OLOF): What?

OLOF: Don't you know whom you're talking to?

SERVANT: No, I don't.

OLOF: I'm the king's secretary.

SERVANT: Goodness, are you Master Olof? I knew your father, Peter Smith—you see, I'm from Örebro, too.[26]

OLOF: Can't you be polite anyway?

SERVANT: Oh, yes. That's how it goes when a person gets up in the world—he forgets his poor ancestors.

OLOF: If my father actually honored you with his acquaintance—maybe he did—but I don't believe he put you in his place as father when he died.

SERVANT: Well, well. There you see. Your poor mother! (*Goes to the left. Pause. Then* LARS SIGGESON SPARRE *enters from the right.*)

SPARRE (*throws his coat to* OLOF *without looking at him*): Is the king coming soon?

OLOF (*takes the coat and throws it on the floor*): I don't know!

SPARRE: Get me a chair.

OLOF: That's not my job!

SPARRE: I haven't any idea what the doorkeeper's duties are.

OLOF: I'm not the doorkeeper!

SPARRE: It doesn't concern me what you are; I don't carry a list of the servants. But be polite!

(OLOF *says nothing.*)

SPARRE: Are you going to do anything? I think the devil's got you!

OLOF: Excuse me! It isn't part of my job as secretary to wait on people!

SPARRE: So! Master Olof! So it amuses you to sit by the door acting like a servant to reveal yourself later as God! I thought you were a proud man. (*He picks up the coat and puts it on the bench.*)

OLOF: Lord Marshal!

SPARRE: No! You're a vain upstart! Please come here and sit down, Mr. Secretary. (*Shows him a place; then goes into a side room. OLOF sits down. A young NOBLEMAN greets OLOF from the gallery.*)

NOBLEMAN: Good morning, Mr. Secretary. No one here yet? Well, how are things in Stockholm? I've come directly from Malmö.

OLOF: Things are pretty bad here.

NOBLEMAN: Yes, so I've heard. The mob's cutting up as usual when the king turns his back. And those stupid priests! Forgive me, you're a freethinker, aren't you, Mr. Secretary?

OLOF: I don't understand.

NOBLEMAN: Don't be embarrassed. You see, I've had my training in Paris.[27] Francis I, oh *Saint-Sauver!* He's a man who'll go far! Do you know what he said to me at a *bal masqué* at the carnival recently? (OLOF *says nothing.*) *"Monsieur,"* he said, *"la religion est morte, est morte,"* said he; but that doesn't keep him from attending mass!

OLOF: So-o!

NOBLEMAN: And do you know what he said when I asked him why he did? *"Poésie! Poésie!"* he said. Isn't he divine?

OLOF: What did you say then?

NOBLEMAN: "Your Majesty," I said, in French, of course, "happy the country which has a king who can look beyond the narrowness of his time so that he sees what the spirit of the time demands, but who all the same doesn't force the sleeping masses to accept a

higher point of view for which they'd need centuries to get ready."
Wasn't that nicely said?

OLOF: Yes, indeed. But I suspect it lost something in translation.
Things like that ought to be said in French.

NOBLEMAN (*not paying attention*): You're absolutely right! You
know, you ought to make your fortune. You're so far ahead of
your time.

OLOF: I don't think I'll get that far. Unfortunately, my training was
neglected; I got it in Germany, you know, and the Germans
haven't got beyond religion yet.

NOBLEMAN: Yes, yes. Can you tell me why they're making all that
fuss about that reformation in Germany? Luther's an enlightened
man, I know, I believe it, but he could keep it to himself or at
least not throw out sparks among the crude masses, which will always be like casting pearls before swine. If one looks at the time,
if one absorbs the great movements of thought a little, one can
easily see the causes of the disturbances in balance that now are
dominant in the great civilized countries. I'm not talking about
Sweden, for it isn't civilized. Do you know what the center of
gravity is, the one whose destruction leads to the dissolution of
everything, and without whose stabilizing force everything's
turned upside down? It's the aristocracy! The aristocracy is the
intelligentsia! The feudal system's on its way out—*hoc est* the
world, education's on the decline, culture's dying! Yes, yes! So
you don't believe that! But if you had the slightest historical sense,
you'd see it. The aristocracy did the crusades, the aristocracy did
this, the aristocracy did that. Why is Germany torn to pieces?
Well, the peasants revolt against the aristocracy. Cut off their own
heads. Why is France strong? *La France,* well, because France is
the aristocracy and the aristocracy is France; they're identical con-
cepts; they're inseparable. Why, I ask again, is Sweden just now
shaken to its very foundations? Well, the aristocracy is crushed.
Christian II was a man of genius, he knew how to conquer a
country, he sawed off not a leg or an arm; no, he knocked off the

head! Oh, well! Sweden will be saved; the king knows how. The aristocracy will be restored, and the church crushed. What do you say to that?

OLOF (*gets up*): Nothing! (*Pause*) Are you a freethinker?

NOBLEMAN: Of course.

OLOF: So you don't believe Balaam's ass could talk? [28]

NOBLEMAN: Good heavens, no!

OLOF: But I do!

NOBLEMAN: Really!

LARS ANDERSSON (*enters*): God's peace, Olof.

OLOF (*embraces him*): Welcome, Lars.

NOBLEMAN (*goes*): Rabble!

LARS: How do you like it here?

OLOF: It's stuffy.

LARS: Well, yes.

OLOF: And the ceiling's so low.

LARS: That's why they have a hard time walking upright.

OLOF: During the last ten minutes I've become such a courtier that I've learned to keep still when an ass talks.

LARS: That doesn't do any harm.

OLOF: What does the king think?

LARS: He doesn't say. (*People have begun to gather.*)

OLOF: How does he look?

LARS: Like a question mark with several exclamation points after it.

(BRASK *enters; everyone gives way to him.* LARS SPARRE *has returned, goes up to the* BISHOP, *and greets him.* OLOF *greets* BRASK, *who looks amazed.*)

BRASK (*to* SPARRE): Is this the clerks' room?

SPARRE: It shouldn't be, but our king is so infinitely gracious.

BRASK: Condescending, you mean.

SPARRE: Exactly!

BRASK: Many audiences today.

SPARRE: Mostly formal calls after His Majesty's happy return.

BRASK: It's a pleasure, Lord Marshal, to express my sincere felicitations to the king on the happy solution to the problem.

SPARRE: You're much too courteous, Lord Bishop, to take the trouble to make such a long journey at your age.

BRASK: Yes, yes. And I can't always rely on my health.

SPARRE: So your health isn't too good, my lord. It's always sad not to have one's full strength, especially when one occupies such a high and responsible position.

BRASK: You're looking well, Lord Marshal.

SPARRE: Yes, God be praised! (*Pause*)

BRASK (*sits down*): Isn't there a draft, Lord Marshal?

SPARRE: Yes—there is. Perhaps we should have the doors closed.

BRASK: No, no, thank you; I don't think that's necessary. (*Pause*)

SPARRE: The king certainly is taking his time.

BRASK: Yes.

SPARRE: Probably it isn't worth waiting.

BRASK: Probably.

SPARRE: May I call your servants, my lord?

BRASK: Since I've waited this long, I think I'll stay. (*Pause*)

SERVANT: His Majesty!

KING (*enters*): Welcome, my lords. (*Sits down at a table*) If you'll step out into the antechamber, my lords, I'll receive you one at a time. (*All go except* BRASK.) Our marshal will stay.

BRASK: Your Majesty!

KING (*with raised voice*): Lord Sparre! (BRASK *goes*. SPARRE *stays*. *Pause*) Speak up. What shall I do?

SPARRE: Your Majesty! The state has lost its main support, so it's tottering; the state has an enemy that has become more powerful than it is. Raise the support, the aristocracy, and crush the enemy, the church.

KING: I don't dare!

SPARRE: Your Majesty has to!

KING: What's that?

SPARRE: In the first place: Brask's negotiating with the pope for the

introduction of the inquisition; Lübeck's insisting on its shameless
demands, and threatens war; the treasury's empty; there are rebellions in every part of the country . . .

KING: Enough! But the people are with me!

SPARRE: Excuse me, no! The Dalesmen, for example: a spoiled tribe,
who argue with the Lübeckers over the honor of having given
Sweden a king; they're ready to revolt at the first chance and
come up with demands like these: "No foreign fashions with
fancifully cut multicolored clothes such as those which have just
been introduced at the king's court may be used!"

KING: God's death!

SPARRE: "Everyone who eats meat on Fridays or Saturdays shall be
burned alive or otherwise killed." Further: "No new faith or
Lutheran doctrine may be forced upon us." What a faithless,
spoiled people!

KING: They showed they were men once, all the same!

SPARRE: When fire was threatening them, it wasn't strange that they
carried water themselves. And how often haven't they broken
faith and promise! No! They've heard their praises sung so often
they call their crude insolence old-fashioned Swedish honesty.

KING: You're a nobleman!

SPARRE: Yes, and I'm convinced the yeomen have finished playing
their part: the expulsion of the enemy by crude strength. Your
Majesty! Crush the church, for it keeps the people in bondage;
take the church's gold and pay the kingdom's debt—and return
to the ruined aristocracy what the church has got from the lords
through trickery.

KING: Call Brask!

SPARRE: Your Majesty!

KING: Bishop Brask! (SPARRE goes. BRASK enters.)

KING: Please speak out, Lord Bishop.

BRASK: I want to extend our congratulations for . . .

KING: Thanks, Lord Bishop. Go on.

BRASK: Unfortunately, there have been rumors of complaints from various parts of the kingdom about the unpaid loans of silver from the church that Your Majesty has made.[29]

KING: And you're demanding payment now! Are all the chalices really needed for communion?

BRASK: Yes.

KING: Let them drink out of pewter, then!

BRASK: Your Majesty!

KING: Is there anything else?

BRASK: The worst of all—heresy.

KING: That doesn't concern me; I'm not the pope.

BRASK: I'll tell Your Majesty this: the church will insist on what's coming to it, even if it should get into conflict—

KING: With whom?

BRASK: With the state!

KING: The devil take your church! Now it's said!

BRASK: I know!

KING: And you waited only to hear it directly from me?

BRASK: Yes!

KING: Watch out! You travel with two hundred men in your retinue and dine on silver while the people eat bark.

BRASK: You take too narrow a view of the matter, Your Majesty.

KING: Do you know Luther, then? You're an enlightened man. What sort of phenomenon is he? What do you say about the movements under way throughout Europe?

BRASK: A step forward in reverse! Luther's role is simply to purge what is old, centuries-old, and tried, so that it may be purified and through conflict go forward in victory.

KING: I'm not interested in your learned arguments.

BRASK: But Your Majesty takes criminals under his protection and interferes with the rights of the church! Master Olof has seriously offended the church.

KING: Well, excommunicate him.

BRASK: We have, but he's in Your Majesty's service anyway.

KING: What else do you want to do to him? Tell me that. (*Pause*)

BRASK: Moreover, he's said to have gone so far as to have married secretly against canonical law.[30]

KING: Well! That has gone fast!

BRASK: It doesn't concern Your Majesty, perhaps; but what if he stirs up the people?

KING: Then I'll take charge! Anything else?

BRASK (*after a pause*): For the sake of Heaven, don't plunge the country into ruin! It's not yet ready for a new faith. We are frail reeds that can be bent, but the faith, the church, never!

KING (*gives him his hand*): You're probably right. Let's be enemies, Bishop Hans, rather than false friends!

BRASK: Fine! But never do what you'll regret. Every stone you tear from the church the people will throw at you!

KING: Don't force me to extremes, bishop, for then we'll get the same terrible spectacles as in Germany.[31] For the last time: Will you make concessions if the welfare of the country is at stake?

BRASK: The church—

KING: The church first, I see. Farewell! (BRASK *leaves.* SPARRE *enters.*)

KING: The bishop confirmed what you said. Yes, that was the idea. Get masons that can tear down; the walls may stand, the crosses may remain on the roofs and the bells in the towers, but I'll smash the cellars; one starts with the foundation, you see.

SPARRE: But the people will be convinced they're being robbed of their faith; they must be enlightened.

KING: We'll let Master Olof preach.

SPARRE: Master Olof's a dangerous fellow.

KING: He's needed now.

SPARRE: He has been behaving like an Anabaptist instead of fighting them.

KING: I know. That will come later. Send him in!

SPARRE: Chancellor Lars is better.

KING: Bring in both of them.

SPARRE: Or Olof's brother, Lars Petri.

KING: Won't do yet. He's too faint-hearted to fight. His time will come.

(SPARRE *brings in* OLOF *and* CHANCELLOR LARS [ANDERSSON].)

KING (*to the* CHANCELLOR): Do you want to help me, Lars?

LARS: With the church?

KING: Yes! It's to be torn down!

LARS: I'm not the man for that. But if Your Majesty turns to Master Olof!

KING: So you don't want to?

LARS: I can't. But I can give you a weapon! (*Hands the* KING *a copy of the new translation of the Bible*) [32]

KING: The Holy Scriptures! That's a good weapon! Do you want to handle this, Olof?

OLOF: Yes, with God's help!

KING (*signals to* LARS *to leave; he exits*): Are you calm yet, Olof? (OLOF *does not answer.*) I gave you four days in which to think it over. How have you handled your assignment?

OLOF (*violently*): I have spoken to the people—

KING: So you're still running a temperature! You intend to defend the crazy fools they call Anabaptists?

OLOF (*courageously*): Yes!

KING: Easy! You got married in a hurry?

OLOF: Yes!

KING: You've been excommunicated?

OLOF: Yes!

KING: And you're just as daring anyway. And if you're sent to the gallows with the other agitators, what would you say?

OLOF: I'd regret I didn't get to carry out my mission, but I'd thank God for what I've been allowed to do.

KING: That's good. Do you dare to go up to the old owl's nest Uppsala and tell the professors that the pope isn't God and hasn't anything to do with Sweden? [33]

OLOF: Merely that?

KING: Do you want to tell them the Bible alone is the word of God?

OLOF: Nothing more?

KING: You may not mention Luther by name!

OLOF (*after consideration*): Then I don't want to.

KING: You'd rather go to your death?

OLOF: No. But my king needs me.

KING: It isn't noble of you, Olof, to make use of my misfortune. Say what you want; but you'll have to excuse me if I take back something later.

OLOF: One doesn't bargain about the truth.

KING: God's death! (*Changing his tone of voice*) Do as you want!

OLOF (*kneeling*): May I speak the whole truth?

KING: Yes!

OLOF: Then my life won't be wasted if I cast merely one spark of doubt into the souls of the sleeping people. So there's to be a reformation!

KING (*after a pause*): Yes! (*Pause*)

OLOF (*frightened*): What will happen to the Anabaptists?

KING: You're asking me? They're going to die!

OLOF: Would Your Majesty permit one question?

KING: Tell me, what do these crazy fools want?

OLOF: The tragedy is that they themselves don't really know. And if I were to say it . . .

KING: Speak up! (GERT *enters suddenly, acting as if he were insane.*) Who are you that dare to force your way in?

GERT: I ask most humbly that Your Majesty certify the correctness of this statement.

KING: Wait till you're called!

GERT: Yes, I can, but the guards don't want to wait for me! See, I ran away from prison because I didn't belong there.

KING: Were you with the Anabaptists?

GERT: Yes, I happened to be with them, but I have a certificate that I belong in the insane asylum, Department 3 for Incurables, Cell 7.

KING (*to* OLOF): Call the guards!

GERT: No, that's unnecessary; all I ask is justice, and the guards don't handle that.

KING (*stares fixedly at* GERT): Didn't you take part in the outrage committed in the city churches?

GERT: Of course. A sane person surely can't behave in such a crazy way. We merely wanted to make a few minor changes in the style, you see; the ceiling was too low, we thought.

KING: What did you really want?

GERT: Oh! We want so much, though we haven't had time for half of it yet; yes, we want so much and so fast that one's thoughts don't keep up with it, and that's why we're a little behind. Yes, and we wanted to repaper a little in the church and take out the windows because it smelled musty. Yes, and we wanted still more, but we'll have to let it go just now.

KING (*to* OLOF): That's a dangerous disease; it can't be anything else.

OLOF: Who knows?

KING: Now I am tired. I'll give you fourteen days to prepare yourself. Your hand on helping me.

OLOF: I'll do my share.

KING: Order that they take Rink and Knipperdollink to Malmö.[34]

OLOF: And then?

KING: They may escape! Have that fool taken to the insane asylum. Farewell. (*Exits*)

GERT (*shakes his fist at the* KING): Shall we go?

OLOF: Where?

GERT: Home! (OLOF *doesn't say anything.*) Do you want to take your father-in-law to the insane asylum, Olof?

OLOF: Want to? It's my duty!

GERT: Aren't there higher duties than obeying an order?

OLOF: Are you starting that again?

GERT: What will Kristina say when you've put her father away with madmen?

OLOF: Don't tempt me.

GERT: Do you see how hard it is to serve the king? (OLOF *says nothing*.) Poor boy, I won't trouble you. Here's absolution for your conscience. (*Shows* OLOF *a paper*)

OLOF: What is it?

GERT: A health certificate. You see, one has to be a madman among the sane and sane among the madmen.

OLOF: How did you get it?

GERT: Don't you think I deserve it?

OLOF: I don't know.

GERT: That's true; you don't dare yet.

SERVANT (*enters*): Please go; we have to sweep in here.

GERT: Probably it ought to be aired out, too?

SERVANT: Yes, indeed.

GERT: Don't forget to open the windows.

SERVANT: No, indeed. That's certainly needed; we don't usually have such company.

GERT: Listen, man, I have greetings from your father.

SERVANT: Really!

GERT: Maybe you don't know him.

SERVANT: Yes, indeed!

GERT: You know what he said?

SERVANT: No.

GERT: You should wet your broom, he said; otherwise you'll get dust on you.

SERVANT: I don't understand.

GERT: That's your excuse. (*Exits*)

SERVANT: Riffraff!

CURTAIN

SCENE 2

OLOF's *study. The sunlight is streaming through the windows
at the back. Trees outside.* KRISTINA *is standing by a window
watering flowers; she chats with the birds in a cage as she does so.*
OLOF *is sitting writing; with an expression of impatience he looks
up from the papers toward* KRISTINA *as if he wanted her to be
quiet. This is repeated several times until* KRISTINA *knocks down a
flower pot.* OLOF *stamps gently on the floor.*

KRISTINA: Poor plant! See, Olof, four buds broke off!

OLOF: I see.

KRISTINA: No, you don't. Come over here.

OLOF: Dear, I haven't time.

KRISTINA: You haven't even looked at the goldfinches I bought you
this morning. Don't you think they sing beautifully?

OLOF: Oh, yes.

KRISTINA: Oh, yes?

OLOF: I have such a hard time working when they screech!

KRISTINA: They certainly don't screech, Olof, but apparently you prefer a screaming night owl! What does the owl on your signet
ring mean?

OLOF: The owl's an old symbol of wisdom.

KRISTINA: That's stupid, I think—the wise man certainly doesn't love
the dark.

OLOF: The wise man hates the dark and the night, but he makes
night day with his sharp eyes.

KRISTINA: Why are you always right, Olof? Can you tell me why?

OLOF: Because I know it pleases you to admit I'm right, dear.

KRISTINA: Now you're right again. What are you writing?

OLOF: I'm translating.

KRISTINA: Read a little of it to me.

OLOF: I don't think you'd understand this.

KRISTINA: Understand! Isn't it Swedish?

OLOF: Yes, but it's too abstract for you.

KRISTINA: Abstract? What does that mean?

OLOF: You wouldn't understand me if I told you, but if you don't understand what I'm going to read, you'll know what abstract means.

KRISTINA (*picks up a half-finished piece of knitting*): Read while I knit.

OLOF: Listen carefully, and forgive me if it bores you.

KRISTINA: I'll understand you; I want to.

OLOF (*reads*): "Matter conceived in its abstraction from form is completely without predictability, undefined, and indistinguishable. Because not from pure nonbeing but only from reality's nonbeing, that is to say, out of being as a possibility, can anything originate. The possible being is just as little nonbeing as reality. Every existence is therefore a realized possibility. Matter is thus for Aristotle a far more positive substratum than for Plato, who explains matter as a pure nonbeing. From this one can see how Aristotle could conceive matter in contrast to form as a positive negative."

KRISTINA (*throws her knitting aside*): Stop! Why can't I grasp that? Don't I have the same mental faculties as you? I'm ashamed, Olof, that you have such a poor wife she can't understand what you're saying; no, I'll stay with my knitting; I'll clean and dust your study; I'll learn to read the wishes in your eyes at least. I'll be your slave, but I'll never, never, understand you! Oh, Olof, I'm not worthy of you! Why did you marry me? You overestimated me in a moment of infatuation. You'll regret it, and we'll both be unhappy!

OLOF: Kristina! Calm yourself, dear. Sit down by me. (*Picks up her knitting*) Will you believe me if I tell you it's impossible for me to do work like this? I'll never be able to. So aren't you more skillful than I, and I less than you?

KRISTINA: Why can't you?

OLOF: For the same reason you didn't understand what I read; I've never learned. Will you be happy again if I tell you that you can learn to understand this book—which you ought to distinguish very carefully from me—while I never can learn your work?

KRISTINA: Why not?

OLOF: I'm not made for it, and I don't want to.

KRISTINA: But if you wanted to?

OLOF: You see, dear, that's just my weakness—I never can want to. Believe me, you're stronger than I; you control your will; I can't control mine.

KRISTINA: Could I learn to understand that book?

OLOF: I'm sure of it. But you mustn't.

KRISTINA: Am I still to be kept in ignorance?

OLOF: No, no, don't misunderstand me. The minute you understand what I understand, you'd lose your respect for me . . .

KRISTINA: As a god . . .

OLOF: If you wish! But, believe me, you'd lose what makes you greater than I: the strength to subdue your will, and then you'd be less than I, and I wouldn't respect you. Believe me: our happiness lies in overestimating each other; let's keep that illusion.

KRISTINA: Now I can't understand you, but I'll have to believe in you, Olof. You're right.

OLOF: Please, Kristina, I need to be alone.

KRISTINA: Do I disturb you?

OLOF: I'm busy with very serious matters. I'm expecting the decision today, you know. The king has abdicated because they don't want to accept his proposals.[35] I'll either have reached my goal today or have to begin the struggle over again.

KRISTINA: Mayn't I be happy today, Olof, on midsummer eve?

OLOF: Why are you so happy today?

KRISTINA: Shouldn't I be happy when I've been released from bondage, when I've become your wife?

OLOF: Forgive me, if my joy is heavier to bear, for my happiness has cost me—a mother.

KRISTINA: I know; I feel it keenly, too. When she finds out we're married, your mother will forgive you but curse me. Who'll have the heavier burden? But that doesn't matter; it's for your sake! I know this: great struggles lie before you, daring thoughts are born in your brain, and I can never take part in the struggle, can never help you with advice, never defend you against those who defame you, but I have to look on anyway, and the whole time live in my little world, busy myself with these little things, which I think you don't appreciate, but which you'd miss. Olof, I can't weep with you; help me by smiling with me; step down from your heights which I can't attain; turn home now and then from the struggles you wage up on the mountains; I can't come up to you; come down to me for a moment. Olof, forgive me if I'm talking childishly. You're a man sent by God, I know, and I've felt the blessing of your words, but you're more than that; you're a human being—you're my husband or should be! You won't fall from your heights if you put away your solemn talk and let the clouds disappear from your forehead for once. Are you too great to look at a flower or to listen to a bird? I put the flowers on your table to rest your eyes; you let the maid carry them out, because you get a headache; I wanted to interrupt the lonely silence of your studies so I gave you the song of the birds; you call it screeching; I asked you to come to dinner a while ago; you didn't have time; I want to talk with you; you don't have time; you despise this little reality, and still you've given it to me. You don't want to raise me; at least don't trample me down! I'll take away everything that disturbs you. You won't be disturbed by me—or my rubbish. (*She throws the flowers out of the window, takes the bird cage, and is going.*)

OLOF: Kristina, dear child, forgive me! You don't understand me!

KRISTINA: Always the same; you don't understand me! Oh, now I know! That moment in the sacristy made me old—so old I became a child again.

OLOF: Dear, I'll look at your birds and babble with your flowers.

KRISTINA (*carries the cage away*): Oh, no! I'm done with babbling now—it'll be serious here; don't be afraid of my noisy happiness. I just pretended for your sake, but since it doesn't suit you and your serious calling . . . (*She bursts into tears.*)

OLOF (*embraces and kisses her*): Kristina! Kristina! Now you're right. Forgive me.

KRISTINA: Olof, you gave an unfortunate gift when you gave me freedom. I can't manage it. I have to have someone to obey.

OLOF: You will, but let's not say anything more about this. We'll go to dinner; I'm quite hungry.

KRISTINA (*happily*): Can you really be hungry? (*Looks out through the window and makes a movement of amazement*) Go ahead, Olof. I'll come right away; I want to straighten up a little first.

OLOF (*goes*): Don't make me wait for you as long as you've had to for me.

(KRISTINA *extends her hands as if in prayer and stations herself to wait for someone who will come through the street door. Pause*)

MOTHER (*enters, goes past* KRISTINA *without turning to her*): Is Master Olof at home?

KRISTINA (*who has gone up to her in a friendly fashion, stops with amazement and then assumes the same tone as the* MOTHER): No. Won't you sit down? He'll soon be here.

MOTHER: Thank you. (*Sits down. Pause*) Bring me a glass of water. (KRISTINA *does.*) Leave me.

KRISTINA: As his wife it's my duty to keep you company.

MOTHER: I didn't know a priest's housekeeper calls herself wife.

KRISTINA: I'm Master Olof's wife in the sight of God. So you don't know we're married!

MOTHER: You're a prostitute! That I do know.

KRISTINA: I don't understand that word.

MOTHER: You're the kind of woman that Master Olof talked to that evening in the tavern.

KRISTINA: The one who looked so unhappy. Well, I'm not happy!

MOTHER: No, I should think not! Get out of my sight; your presence is an insult to me!

KRISTINA (*kneels*): For your son's sake, don't abuse me!

MOTHER: With a mother's power I order you to leave my son's house, whose threshold you've desecrated.

KRISTINA: As his wife I'll open my door to anyone I please. I would have closed it to you if I could have guessed what you'd say.

MOTHER: Big words, indeed! I order you to go!

KRISTINA: With what right do you dare to force your way into this house and drive me out of my home? You bore a child, you brought him up; that was your duty, your destiny, and you can thank God that you've been permitted to fulfill it so well, for not everyone is that fortunate; you're approaching your grave; step aside before it's over; or have you brought up your son so badly that he's still a child and still needs your guidance? If you want gratitude, look for it, but in another way. Do you think it's the child's lot to sacrifice his life simply to show you gratitude? His calling says, "Go there!" You call, "Ungrateful boy, come here!" Is he to go astray, is he to sacrifice his powers, which belong to the community, to humanity, simply to satisfy your personal little selfishness, or do you think your having given him life and upbringing even deserves gratitude? Wasn't that the purpose and function of your life? Shouldn't you thank God that you've had such a great mission? Or did you do it simply to demand gratitude for half a lifetime? Don't you know that by the word gratitude you tear down what you once built up? And what right do you have to interfere with me? Is marriage the mortgaging of my free will to the one whom nature has made the mother or father of my husband, who unfortunately couldn't exist without both? You're not my mother, and I never vowed to be faithful to you when I married Olof, and I have enough respect for my husband so that I won't let anyone insult him, even his mother! That's why I've said all this!

MOTHER: Now I see the fruits of the doctrines my son is spreading!

KRISTINA: If you want to abuse your son, you'll do it in his presence! (*She goes to the door and calls.*) Olof!

MOTHER: So you're already that sly!

KRISTINA: Already? I've always been, I think, even if I didn't know it until I needed it.

OLOF (*enters*): Mother! Welcome!

MOTHER: Thank you, my son; farewell!

OLOF: Are you going? What does this mean? I'd like to talk to you.

MOTHER: That won't be necessary. She has said everything. You don't need to show me the door.

OLOF: Mother, what in God's name are you saying? Kristina, what is this?

MOTHER (*wants to leave*): Farewell, Olof, I'll never forgive you for this!

OLOF (*wants to have her stay*): Stay and give me an explanation at least!

MOTHER: It's shameful! You send her to tell me you don't owe me anything, that you don't need me any more! That's hard to take! (*She goes.*)

OLOF: What did you say to her, Kristina?

KRISTINA: I don't remember, but there were a lot of things I had never dared to think, but that I must have dreamed while my father kept me in bondage.

OLOF: You're like a different person, Kristina!

KRISTINA: You know, I'm beginning to find myself a little strange.

OLOF: You were unfriendly to my mother!

KRISTINA: Yes, I must have been. Don't you think I've become hard, Olof?

OLOF: Did you tell her to leave?

KRISTINA: Forgive me, Olof; I wasn't polite to her.

OLOF: For my sake you could have spoken a little more gently. Why didn't you call me right away?

KRISTINA: I wanted to see if I could manage by myself. Olof, will you sacrifice me for your mother if she asks you to?

OLOF: I won't answer a question like that offhand!

KRISTINA: I'll answer! It pleases you to bend before your mother's will and wishes because you're strong; but it humiliates me, because I'm weak. I'll never do it!

OLOF: If I ask you to?

KRISTINA: You can't ask that! Do you want me to hate her? . . . Tell me, Olof, what does prostitute mean?

OLOF: You certainly ask strange questions.

KRISTINA: Would you stoop to answering it?

OLOF: Will you forgive me if I don't?

KRISTINA: Always this eternal silence! Don't you dare to tell me everything yet? Am I still a child? Put me in the nursery, then, and talk to me as if I were an infant.

OLOF: It's an unfortunate woman.

KRISTINA: No. It's something else.

OLOF: Has anyone dared to call you that?

KRISTINA (*after a pause*): No.

OLOF: You're not telling the truth, are you, Kristina?

KRISTINA: I'm lying, I know. Oh, I've become bad since yesterday.

OLOF: Something happened yesterday that you haven't told me.

KRISTINA: Yes. I thought I could bear it all by myself, but I can't any more.

OLOF: Tell me! Please!

KRISTINA: But you mustn't call me weak. A mob pursued me to the door and shouted this terrible word that I don't understand. People don't laugh at an unfortunate woman!

OLOF: Yes, dear, that's exactly what they do.

KRISTINA: I didn't understand their word, but I understood enough of their gestures to get angry!

OLOF: And you've been so considerate, anyway! Forgive me if I've been unkind to you . . . It's the name that brute strength gives to its victims. You'll soon hear more about this, but never come to the defense of an "unfortunate woman," for people will throw dirt at you! (*A messenger with a letter enters.*) At last! (*Reads the letter hastily*) Read it, Kristina; I want to hear the happy news from your lips.

KRISTINA (*reads*): "You have won, young man! I, your enemy, am the first to tell you this, and without humility I turn to you, for you bore the weapons of the spirit when you spoke for the new faith! I do not know if you are right, but I believe you deserve a bit of advice from an old man. Stop now, for your enemies are gone. Do not struggle with spirits of the air; that would cripple your arm and you would die yourself. 'Do not rely on princes' is the advice of a once powerful man, who now steps aside and leaves in the hands of the Lord the fate of His ruined church. Johannes Brask." [36]

KRISTINA: You have won!

OLOF (*happy*): God, I thank Thee for this hour! (*Pause*) No. I'm afraid, Kristina. This good fortune is too great. I'm too young to have reached my goal already. Nothing more to do: a dreadful thought! No struggle any more: that's death itself!

KRISTINA: Rest for a moment, and be happy it's over.

OLOF: Can there be any end? An end to this beginning. No! No! I'd like to begin again. It wasn't victory I wanted; it was the struggle.

KRISTINA: Don't tempt God, Olof. I've a feeling there's a lot left to do, a lot.

NOBLEMAN (*enters with a document*): Good day, Mr. Secretary. Pleasant news! (KRISTINA *goes.*)

OLOF: Welcome! I've already heard something.

NOBLEMAN: Thanks for the excellent defense against that stupid Galle.[37] You crushed him like a man—only a little too much; not so much fire; a little poison doesn't hurt.

OLOF: You have news from the king?

NOBLEMAN: Yes. I'll give you the decisions most briefly. (*Unfolds the document, reads*) Number one: Mutual agreement to resist and punish all rebellions.

OLOF: Go on, please.

NOBLEMAN: Number two: The right of the king to take possession of the bishops' castles and strongholds, to determine their incomes . . .

OLOF: Number three.

NOBLEMAN: This is the best of all, the very kernel of the whole business. Number three: The right of the lords to repossess their estates that have come into the control of churches and cloisters since King Charles VIII's confiscations in 1454 . . .[38]

OLOF: Number four.

NOBLEMAN: . . . in so far as the heir can support his claim through right of birth by means of twelve men's oaths at the *Thing*. (*Folds the paper*)

OLOF: Is that all?

NOBLEMAN: Yes. Isn't this fine?

OLOF: Nothing more?

NOBLEMAN: Oh, yes, then there are a few minor matters, but they're not particularly important.

OLOF: What are they?

NOBLEMAN (*reads*): There's a fifth provision about the right of preachers to preach the word of God, but they had that before.

OLOF: Nothing else?

NOBLEMAN: Yes, there's this ordinance: "That lists shall be made of the income of all bishops, cathedrals, and canons, and that the king shall determine . . ."

OLOF: That's beside the point.

NOBLEMAN: ". . . how much thereof they may retain and how much they shall give him for the needs of the crown; that priestly offices"—this ought to interest you—"priestly offices, not only higher but lower as well shall henceforth be filled only with the king's approval so that . . ."

OLOF: Be so good as to read what it says about the faith . . .

NOBLEMAN: The faith—it's not mentioned. Yes, let me see—"The Bible shall after this day be studied in all schools."

OLOF: Is that all?

NOBLEMAN: All! No, that's true. I have special orders from the king to you, very sensible, that as long as the people are stirred up about these new matters, you may not in any way disturb the old, not do away with mass, holy water, or other customary uses as well as in general not undertake any new liberties, because the king will not close his eyes to your future undertakings as he did in the past when he didn't have the power to do anything else.

OLOF: Oh! What about the new faith he let me preach!

NOBLEMAN: Let it mature slowly. It'll come. It'll come.

OLOF: Is there anything else?

NOBLEMAN (*gets up*): No. Now just take it calmly, and you'll go far. Oh! I almost forgot the best news! Rector, I have the honor to congratulate you. Here is your letter of appointment. Rector in the Great Church with 3,000 *dalers* at your age! [39] My word, you can really take it easy and enjoy life even if you never get any higher. It's fine to have reached one's goal when one's so young. Congratulations. (*Goes*)

OLOF (*throws his letter of appointment on the floor*): This was what I've struggled and suffered for. An appointment! A royal appointment! I served Belial instead of God! Woe unto you, false king, who sold your Lord and God! Woe unto me who sold my life and my work to Mammon! God in Heaven, forgive me! (*Throws himself on a bench and weeps.* KRISTINA *and* GERT *enter.* KRISTINA *comes forward.* GERT *remains in the background.*)

KRISTINA (*picks up the letter of appointment, reads it, and then goes joyously up to* OLOF): Olof! Now I want to congratulate you with a happy heart! (*She wants to caress him, but he jumps up and pushes her aside.*)

OLOF: Leave me! You, too!

GERT (*comes up*): Well, Olof. The faith . . .

OLOF: The lack of faith, you mean!

GERT: But the pope's defeated! Shall we take on the emperor soon?

OLOF: We began at the wrong end.

GERT: Finally!

OLOF: You were right, Gert. I'm ready. War! But open and honest!

GERT: You've been living in childish dreams until today.

OLOF: I know. Now comes the flood. Let it come! Woe unto them and us!

KRISTINA: Olof, for heaven's sake, stop!

OLOF: Go your way, child. Here you'll drown, or you'll drag me down.

GERT: My child! What were you doing out in the storm? (KRISTINA *goes. Ringing of bells. Cheering. Music. Beating of drums outside*)

OLOF (*goes to the window*): Why are the people cheering?

GERT: Because the king's treating them to a Maypole and music out beyond North Gate.

OLOF: And they don't know he's given them the sword instead of birch branches!

GERT: Know? If they only knew!

OLOF: Poor children! They're dancing to his pipes and going to their deaths to the music of his drums—must all die that one may live?

GERT: One shall die that all may live!

(OLOF *makes a gesture of repugnance and amazement.*)

CURTAIN

ACT IV

A room in OLOF's MOTHER's *home. To the right a four-poster bed in which the* MOTHER *is lying, ill.* KRISTINA *is sitting on a chair sleeping.* LARS PETRI *fills the night lamp with oil and turns the hourglass.*

LARS (*to himself*): Midnight! It's to be decided now. (*He goes up to his* MOTHER's *bed and listens.* KRISTINA *moans in her sleep.* LARS *goes up to her, awakens her, and says*) Kristina!

(KRISTINA *startled*)

LARS: Go to bed, child. I'll keep watch.

KRISTINA: No, I want to! I have to talk with her before she dies . . . Olof ought to be here soon!

LARS: So you're keeping watch for Olof's sake.

KRISTINA: Yes. You mustn't tell him I fell asleep. Promise!

LARS: Poor child . . . You're not happy.

KRISTINA: Who said I should be happy?

LARS: Does Olof know you're here?

KRISTINA: No. He'd never have let me come. He wants me to be like a saint on a pedestal. The smaller and weaker I am, the greater his pleasure in placing his strength at my feet . . .

MOTHER (*awakens*): Lars!

(KRISTINA *holds* LARS *back and goes up to the bed.*)

MOTHER: Who are you?

KRISTINA: Your nurse.

MOTHER: Kristina! . . .

KRISTINA: Is there something you want?

MOTHER: From you, nothing!

KRISTINA: Madame!

MOTHER: Don't embitter my last moments. Go.

LARS (*steps up*): What is it, mother?

MOTHER: Take that woman away. Bring my father confessor; I'm dying.

LARS: Isn't your son worthy of your last confession?

MOTHER: He doesn't deserve to be! Has Mårten come?

LARS: Mårten's an evil person!

MOTHER: God, Thy punishment is too great! My children come between Thee and me. Are they going to deny me the comfort of religion in my last moments? You've taken my life. Do you want to destroy my soul—your mother's soul? (*She becomes unconscious.*)

LARS: You heard, Kristina. What am I going to do? Is she to die, deceived by a scoundrel like Mårten, and probably thank us for it? Or is her last prayer to be a curse? No! Let them come! What do you think, Kristina?

KRISTINA: I don't dare to think anything.

LARS (*goes out, but comes back immediately*): It's terrible! They've fallen asleep playing dice and drinking. And they are to prepare mother for death!

KRISTINA: Tell her the truth.

LARS: She doesn't believe the truth; it would be like a lie on our heads.

MOTHER: My son! Grant your mother's last request!

LARS (*goes*): God forgive me!

KRISTINA: Olof would never do this!

(LARS *comes in with* MÅRTEN *and* NILS *and then takes* KRISTINA *out with him.*)

MÅRTEN (*goes up to the bed*): She's asleep.

NILS (*places a box on the floor, opens it, and takes out a vessel of holy water, an incense burner, a container of oil, palms, and candles*): So we can't start the job yet.

MÅRTEN: If we've waited this long, we can wait a little longer, just so that devil of a priest doesn't come.

NILS: Master Olof, you mean . . . Do you think his brother noticed anything out there?

MÅRTEN: I don't care—just so the old lady hands over the money. Then I'm free!

NILS: You're a pretty big rascal all the same.

MÅRTEN: Yes, but I'm tired of it. I'd like to get a little peace and quiet. Do you know what life is?

NILS: No.

MÅRTEN: Pleasure! The flesh is God! Doesn't it say so somewhere?

NILS: The word became flesh, you mean.

MÅRTEN: Oh, is that it? Yes!

NILS: You could've been a mighty able fellow, with your brains.

MÅRTEN: Yes, I certainly could. That's what they were afraid of, and that's why they whipped the spirit out of my body in the monastery, for I did have a spirit just the same. But now I'm only a body, and now it's to have its day.

NILS: Well, they must have whipped the conscience out of you at the same time.

MÅRTEN: Yes, almost . . . But give me that recipe for spiced Rochelle that you started before we fell asleep out there.

NILS: Did I say Rochelle? I meant claret. That is, it could be either. Well, for every half gallon of wine, you add half a pound of cardamom, well cured—

MÅRTEN: Shut up—she's stirring! Get the book!

NILS (*reads softly during the following speeches*):
Aufer immensam, Deus aufer iram;
Et cruentatum cohibe flagellum:
Nec scelus nostrum proferes ad aequam
          Pendere lancem.

MOTHER: Is it you, Mårten?

MÅRTEN: It's Brother Nils invoking the holy Virgin.
     (NILS *lights up the incense burner while he reads.*)

MOTHER: What a wonderful comfort to hear the word of God in the sacred language!

MÅRTEN: No more acceptable sacrifice is ever given to God than the prayers of pious souls.

MOTHER: My heart is lighted like incense by holy reverence.

MÅRTEN (*sprinkles her with holy water*): Thy God purifies thee of the mire of sin.

MOTHER: Amen ... Mårten, I'm dying; our king's ungodliness forbids me to strengthen the power of the holy church to save souls by giving it earthly gifts; take my property, pious man, and pray for me and my children. Pray that the Almighty will turn their hearts from falsehood so that we may meet again in heaven.

MÅRTEN (*accepts the bag of money*): Madame, your sacrifice is pleasing to the Lord, and for your sake God will hear my prayers.

MOTHER: I'd like to sleep a little so I'll be strong enough to receive the last sacrament.

MÅRTEN: No one shall disturb your last moments; not even those who used to be your children.

MOTHER: That's hard, Father Mårten, but that's how God wants it. (*Dozes*)

MÅRTEN (*opens the bag and kisses the money*): What treasures of joy are hidden in these hard pieces of gold! Ah!

NILS: Shall we go?

MÅRTEN: I certainly could, since I've done my job, but it's a shame to let the old woman die unsaved.

NILS: Unsaved?

MÅRTEN: Yes.

NILS: Do you believe that?

MÅRTEN: I don't know what to believe. The one dies saved through this, the other through that. They all insist they've found the truth.

NILS: What if you were to die right now, Mårten?

MÅRTEN: That isn't possible!

NILS: But if?

MÅRTEN: I'd go to Heaven like all the rest. Only, I'd like to settle a few little matters with Master Olof first! You see, there's one pleasure that's greater than all the others. That's revenge!

NILS: What harm has he done you?

MÅRTEN: He dared to look right through me, he stripped me, he sees what I think!

NILS: So you hate him!

MÅRTEN: Isn't that reason enough? (*Someone knocks on the outer door.*) Somebody's coming! Go on, read for Hell's sake! (NILS *rattles off the verses above. The door is opened from outside; a key can be heard inserted into the lock.*)

(OLOF *enters, looking bewildered and upset.*)

MOTHER (*awakens*): Father Mårten!

OLOF (*goes up to the bed*): Here's your son, mother. You didn't let me know you were sick!

MOTHER: Farewell, Olof! I'll forgive you the evil you've done to me if you don't disturb me while I'm preparing for heaven. Father Mårten! Give me the extreme unction so I may die in peace.

OLOF: So that's why you didn't call me! (*Sees the money bag* MÅRTEN *has neglected to conceal; snatches it from him*) You're dealing in souls here. And this is the price. Leave this room and this death bed; it's my place to be here, not yours!

MÅRTEN: You intend to keep us from performing our duties!

OLOF: I'm showing you the door!

MÅRTEN: We're here professionally, not with papal but with royal authority, as long as we haven't been suspended.

OLOF: I'll cleanse the temple of the Lord even if the pope and the king don't want it!

MOTHER: Olof! You want to plunge my soul into damnation; you want to let me die with a curse!

OLOF: Be calm, mother; you shall not die in a lie; seek your God through prayer. He isn't as far away as you think.

MÅRTEN: A man has to be a prophet of the devil if he doesn't want to spare his own mother the agonies of purgatory!

MOTHER: Christ, help my soul!

OLOF: Get out of this room or I'll use force! Take this nonsense away! (*Kicks the accessories aside*)

MÅRTEN: If you give me the money your mother has given the church, I'll go.

MOTHER: Was that why you came, Olof—you want my gold? Give it to him, Mårten. Olof, you may have all of it if you'll only let me be in peace—you'll get still more! You'll get everything!

OLOF (*in despair*): In God's name, take the money and go! Please!

MÅRTEN (*snatches the bag and goes out with* NILS): Madame Kristina! Where the devil is, we have no power! (*To* OLOF) Heretic, you're damned for all eternity. Lawbreaker, you'll get your punishment even in this life! Watch out for the king! (*They go.*)

OLOF (*kneels at his* MOTHER's *bed*): Mother, listen to me before you die!

(MOTHER *has become unconscious.*)

OLOF: Mother, mother, if you're still alive, talk to your son! Forgive me, for I cannot do otherwise! I know that you've suffered for a lifetime for my sake; you've prayed God that I would walk His paths; the Lord has heard your prayer. Would you want me to make your whole life pointless, do you want me to destroy what has cost you so much effort and so many tears by obeying you? Forgive me!

MOTHER: Olof! My soul doesn't belong to this world any more—it's from the other side I'm speaking to you—turn back, break the unclean bond your body has made, take up again the faith I gave you, and I'll forgive you.

OLOF (*with tears of despair*): Mother! Mother!

MOTHER: Swear you'll do it!

OLOF (*after a pause*): No!

MOTHER: God's curse rests on you! I see Him. I see God with His eyes filled with wrath! Help me, holy Virgin!

OLOF: That isn't the God who is love!

MOTHER: It's the avenging God! You are the one who has enraged

Him, you are the one who casts me into the fire of His wrath—
cursed be the hour I gave you birth! (*Dies*)

OLOF: Mother! Mother! (*He takes her hand.*) She's dead! Without
forgiving me! If your soul still lingers in this room, look down
on your son; I want to do as you wished; what is holy for you
will be holy for me. (*He lights the large wax candles, which the
monks have left, and places them about the bed.*) You shall have
the consecrated candles to light you on the way (*he places a palm
in her hand*), and with the palm of peace you shall forget the last
struggle with what is earthly. Mother, if you see me, you will
forgive me. (*The sun has begun to rise and throws a reddish glow
on the curtains.*)

OLOF (*jumps up*): Morning sun, you make my candles pale. You
have more of love than I. (*He goes up to the window and opens
it.*)

LARS (*enters slowly; is amazed*): Olof!

OLOF (*embraces him*): Brother! It's over!

LARS (*goes up to the bed, kneels, rises*): She's dead. (*Prays silently*)
You were alone with her!

OLOF: You were the one who let in the monks.

LARS: You drove them out!

OLOF: Yes; you should have.

LARS: Did she forgive you?

OLOF: She died with a curse! (*Pause*)

LARS (*points at the candles*): Who arranged these? (*Pause*)

OLOF (*irritated and ashamed*): I was weak for a moment.

LARS: So you're a human being all the same. Thank you for that.

OLOF: Are you sneering at my weakness?

LARS: I'm praising it.

OLOF: I curse it! God in Heaven, am I not right?

LARS: You're wrong!

KRISTINA (*who has just entered*): You're all too right!

OLOF: Kristina! What are you doing here?

KRISTINA: It was so quiet and lonely at home.

OLOF: I asked you not to come here.

KRISTINA: I thought I could be of some use, but I understand . . . I'll stay home another time.

OLOF: You've been up all night!

KRISTINA: That isn't hard. I'll go now if you tell me to.

OLOF: Go in and rest, while Lars and I talk.

(KRISTINA *walks absent-mindedly about extinguishing the candles.*)

OLOF: What are you doing, dear?

KRISTINA: Why, it's broad daylight. (LARS *gives* OLOF *a look.*)

OLOF: My mother's dead, Kristina.

KRISTINA (*goes up to* OLOF *with mild but cold sympathy to receive a kiss on her forehead*): I'm sorry for your sake. (*Goes. Pause.* LARS *and* OLOF *look first after* KRISTINA, *then at each other.*)

LARS: As your brother and friend, Olof, I beg you not to rush on as you have.

OLOF: That's what you always say. But the person who puts the axe to the tree doesn't stop until the tree falls. The king has deserted our cause; now I'll take charge of it.

LARS: The king is wise.

OLOF: He's a miser, a traitor, and a patron of the lords! First he uses me like a dog; then he kicks me aside.

LARS: He sees farther than you do. If you were to go to three million people and say: "Your faith is false; believe what I say," do you think it would be possible for them to discard their deepest, profoundest convictions, which have sustained them both in sorrow and in joy? No, things would be badly arranged for the human spirit if it didn't take longer to throw the old faith overboard.

OLOF: That isn't so! All the people doubt; hardly one priest knows what to believe, even if he believes anything; everything is ready for the new faith, but you're to blame, you weaklings, who don't dare to take it on your consciences to cast out doubt where there's only a feeble faith.

LARS: Beware, Olof! You want to play the role of God!

OLOF: Yes, one has to, for He's not likely to descend among us again!

LARS: You tear down and tear down, Olof, so that there soon will be nothing, but when we ask, "What are you giving us instead?" you answer, "Not that, not that," but you never answer, "This"!

OLOF: Presumptuous! Do you think a person can give away faith? Has Luther given us anything new? No! He has simply knocked down the screens that stood in the way of light. What I want that's new is doubt of the old, not because it's old but because it's rotten.

(LARS *gestures toward his* MOTHER.)

OLOF: I know what you mean. She was too old, and I thank God she died. Now I'm free, now for the first time; so it was the will of God.

LARS: You're either out of your mind or you're a wicked person.

OLOF: Don't reproach me for that. I respect my mother's memory as much as you do, but, if she hadn't died now, I don't know how far I'd have gone in my compromises. Brother, have you seen in the spring how last year's fallen leaves cover the ground and want to smother the young plants that should come up? What do they do? They either shove the dry leaves aside or go straight through them because they *have to* come up.

LARS: You're right in a way . . . Olof, you've broken the laws of the church during a time of lawlessness and unrest; what was then forgiven must be punished now; don't force the king to appear worse than he is; don't let your unlawful acts and your willfulness force him to punish a man whom he admits he is grateful to.

OLOF: He reigns willfully; he has to learn to bear it in others. Tell me, you're in the king's service. You intend to work against me?

LARS: Yes!

OLOF: So we're enemies! I need them, for the old ones have gone.

LARS: Olof, our blood ties!

OLOF: I don't recognize them except in their very source, the heart.

LARS: You did weep over mother!

OLOF: Weakness, perhaps old affection and gratitude, but not blood ties. What are they?

LARS: You're exhausted, Olof.

OLOF: Yes, I'm weary. I've been up all night.

LARS: You came very late.

OLOF: I was out.

LARS: Your work shuns daylight.

OLOF: Daylight shuns my work.

LARS: Beware of false apostles of freedom.

OLOF (*struggling against sleep and weariness*): That's a contradiction! Don't talk with me; I haven't the strength any more. I talked so much at the meeting—that's true, you don't know about our group ... *Concordia res parvae crescunt* ... We're going to complete the reformation—Gert is a farsighted man—I'm very little compared to him. Good night, Lars. (*He falls asleep in a chair.*)

LARS (*looks at him with sympathy*): Poor brother! God protect you! (*Knocks on the house entrance can be heard.*) What is it? (*He goes to the window.*)

GERT (*outside*): Open for God's sake!

LARS (*goes out*): I hope it's not a matter of life and death, Father Gert.

GERT (*outside*): Let me in, in the name of the Lord!

KRISTINA (*comes in with a blanket*): Olof! Why are they knocking? He's asleep. (*Tucks the blanket about* OLOF) Why am I not sleep so that you would flee to me when you're tired of the struggle? (*The rumbling of a heavy cart, which stops outside the house, can be heard.*)

OLOF (*startled out of his sleep*): Is it five o'clock already?

KRISTINA: It's only three.

OLOF: Wasn't that a baker's cart I heard?

KRISTINA: I don't know. But it doesn't sound that heavy. (*Goes to the window*) Look, Olof, what is it?

OLOF (*goes to the window*): The hangman's cart! No! It isn't the hangman's cart.

KRISTINA: A hearse!

LARS: The plague! [40]

ALL: The plague!

GERT (*who has entered*): The plague has broken out! Kristina, my child, leave this house. The angel of death has placed his mark on its gate!

OLOF: Who sent the cart over here?

GERT: The one who drew the black cross on the gate. The dead may not remain in the houses for a minute.

OLOF: It's Mårten, who's the angel of death. So the whole thing's a lie.

GERT: If you look out of the window, you'll see the cart's filled. (*Blows on the entrance*) Listen! They're waiting.

OLOF: Without a funeral! That shan't be!

LARS: Without ceremonies, Olof!

GERT: Kristina, leave this terrible house with me; I'll take you out of town to a healthier place.

KRISTINA: I go with Olof. If you had loved me a little less, father, you'd have harmed me less.

GERT: Olof, you have the right; tell her to go with me.

OLOF: I freed her from your selfish tyranny once; I won't return her to it.

GERT: Kristina, leave this house, at least.

KRISTINA: Not one step before Olof tells me to.

OLOF: I don't order you to do anything, Kristina; remember that. (*The* UNDERTAKER'S ASSISTANTS *enter.*)

UNDERTAKER'S ASSISTANT: I was to fetch a body. Quickly!

OLOF: Be on your way!

UNDERTAKER'S ASSISTANT: The king's orders!

LARS: Olof! Think it over. The law demands it.

GERT: Delay won't do. The crazy people have been stirred up

against you, Olof. This was the first house to be marked. "God's punishment on the heretic!" they're shouting.

OLOF (*kneels by his* MOTHER's *bed*): Forgive me, mother! (*Gets up*) Do your duty. (*The* UNDERTAKER's ASSISTANTS *go up and begin to get their ropes ready.*)

GERT (*aside to* OLOF): We shout, "God's punishment on the king!"

CURTAIN

ACT V

Scene i

The churchyard of St. Clara's convent. At the back a half-razed convent building out of which workmen are carrying lumber and debris. To the left a burial chapel; lights can be seen through the windows; when the door is opened later, a strongly lighted figure of Christ can be seen above the sarcophagus in the chapel. Graves here and there have been opened. The moon is beginning to come up behind the convent ruins. WINDRANK *is sitting on watch at the chapel door. Singing can be heard from the chapel.*

NILS (*enters and goes up to* WINDRANK): Good evening, Windrank.

WINDRANK: Please don't talk to me.

NILS: What's up?

WINDRANK: Didn't you hear what I said?

NILS: So your embarrassing dismissal from the ship hit you so hard you're thinking of entering a cloister!

WINDRANK: 52, 53, 54, 55, 56, 57 · · ·

NILS: Are you crazy?

WINDRANK: 58, 59, 60. Please leave, for Christ's sake!

NILS: Have a little nightcap with me.

WINDRANK: 64, 65. I thought so! Go away, tempter! I'm not drinking any more—not before the day after tomorrow.

NILS: It's medicine for the plague. You want to watch out for the smell of corpses here.

WINDRANK: 70. Is it really good for the plague?

NILS: Excellent!

WINDRANK (*takes a drink*): Well, just a little.

NILS: Just a little. But tell me, don't you get dizzy after you count to a hundred?

WINDRANK: Sh-h! sh-h! A new era's to start!

NILS: Era?

WINDRANK: Yes, the day after tomorrow.

NILS: And that's why you're counting!

WINDRANK: No, that's only because I have such a hard time keeping my mouth shut. Don't say anything, for God's sake! Please leave, or I'll be ruined! 71, 72, 73.

NILS: Who's in there?

WINDRANK: 74, 75.

NILS: Is it a funeral?

WINDRANK: 76, 77. Please go to Hell!

NILS: Another little drink and it'll be easier to count.

WINDRANK: Another little drink. All right. (*Drinks. Singing can be heard.*)

NILS: The nuns of St. Clara are coming to celebrate the memory of the saint for the last time.

WINDRANK: What sort of nonsense is that in our enlightened times?

NILS: They have the king's permission. You see, the plague broke out in St. Clara's parish, and they think it comes from the ungodly tearing down of St. Clara's convent.

WINDRANK: And now they're going to sing the plague away! It must hate music; it wouldn't amaze me if it fled from their screeching.

NILS: Who's invading this last sanctuary? The saint's remains were to be interred here before the building's torn down.

WINDRANK: Then there'll most likely be a fight! (*The singing has*

come nearer; a procession of Dominican monks and Franciscan nuns enters; at the head of the procession is MÅRTEN. *They stop but continue singing. Workmen are making noise at the back.*)
Cur super vermes luteos furorem
Sumis, O magni fabricator orbis!
Quid sumus quam fex, putris, umbra, pulvis
Glebaque terrae!

MÅRTEN (*to the* ABBESS): You see, sister, how they've laid waste the dwelling place of the Lord.

ABBESS: The Lord who delivered us into the hands of the Egyptians will redeem us in due time.

MÅRTEN (*to the workmen*): Stop your work, and don't disturb our holy task.

FOREMAN: Our orders are to work day and night until this den has been torn down.

ABBESS: Alas, disbelief has made its way so far down among the people.

MÅRTEN: We're celebrating this festival with the king's permission.

FOREMAN: Fine, go ahead.

MÅRTEN: On that basis I order you to stop all this noise. I'll turn to your workmen whom you've forced to undertake this infamous thing; I'll appeal to them if they still have enough respect for what's holy . . .

FOREMAN: You shouldn't, for I'm the one who gives orders here; besides, I'll tell you: they're happy enough to tear down these old hornets' nests that they themselves have had to pay for, and they're grateful, too, I think, to earn a little in this time of famine. (*Goes away*)

MÅRTEN: Let's forget the evil and tumult of this world, and go into the sanctuary to pray for them.

ABBESS: Lord, Lord, Thy holy places are laid waste; Zion is laid waste! Jerusalem is in ruins!

WINDRANK: 100! No one's to come in!

CONSPIRATORS (*in the burial chapel*): We swear!

MÅRTEN: Who has invaded the chapel?

WINDRANK: It isn't a chapel any more; it's the king's storehouse.

ABBESS: So that was why that godless man permitted our festival!

(*The chapel door is opened; the conspirators* [41]—OLOF, LARS ANDERSSON, GERT, *the* GERMAN, *the* DANE, *the* SMÅLÄNNING, *and others come out.*)

OLOF (*heatedly*): What sort of buffoonery is this?

MÅRTEN: Make way for the servants of St. Clara!

OLOF: Do you believe your idols can ward off the plague God has sent you by way of punishment? Do you believe the Lord finds those pieces of bone you carry in that box so pleasing that He'll forgive your horrible sins? Away with the abomination! (*He snatches the box from the* ABBESS *and throws it into a grave.*) From dust you came and dust you shall be even if your name was St. Clara da Spoleto and you only ate an ounce and half of bread a day and slept among the swine at night! [42] (*The nuns scream.*)

MÅRTEN: If you don't fear what's holy, fear your earthly king! You see, he still has so much respect left for the divine that he fears the wrath of the saints! (*Shows* OLOF *a document*)

OLOF: Do you know what the Lord did to the king of the Assyrians [43] when he permitted the worship of idols? He struck him and his people; that's why the just must suffer with the unjust! In the name of the one almighty God, I abolish this worship of Baal, even if all the kings of this earth would permit it; the pope wanted to sell my soul to Satan, but I tore the contract to pieces, you remember! Should I now fear a king who wants to sell his people to Baal? (*He tears the order to pieces.*)

MÅRTEN (*to the monks and the nuns*): You are witnesses that he defames the king!

OLOF (*to the men with him*): You are my witnesses before God that I have led His people from an ungodly king!

MÅRTEN: Listen, men of faith! It's because of that heretic that the Lord has struck us with the plague; it was God's punishment that it struck his mother first!

OLOF: Listen, you papal unbelievers! It was the Lord's punishment of me because I served Sennacherib against Judah! I will atone for my sin; I will lead Judah against the king of Assyria and Egypt! (*The moon has risen, it is red, and a red glow falls on the stage. The people are frightened.*)

OLOF (*steps up on a grave*): Heaven is weeping blood over your sins and your worship of idols! Punishment will come, for those in power have sinned! Don't you see how the graves open their jaws for prey . . .

(GERT *takes* OLOF *by the arm, whispers to him, and is leading him away. General panic*)

ABBESS: Give us back our box so we may leave this place of desolation!

MÅRTEN: Rather let the remains of the saint rest in this consecrated earth than expose them to the desecrating hands of the heretic!

OLOF: You're afraid of the plague, you cowards! Wasn't your faith in the holy relics greater than that? (GERT *whispers to* OLOF *again. The procession has dispersed so that only a few of its participants are on stage.*)

OLOF (*to* MÅRTEN): Now you can be satisfied, you hypocrite! Go and tell the one you serve they're burying a silver box, and he'll tear it out of the ground with his nails; tell him the moon which otherwise is silver is changed to gold so that for once your master may turn his eyes to heaven; tell him that your blasphemous acts have succeeded in arousing an honest man's indignation . . . (*as* MÅRTEN *and the procession go*)

GERT: Enough, Olof! (*To all the conspirators except* OLOF *and* LARS) Leave us! (*They whisper among themselves and leave.*)

GERT (*to* OLOF *and* LARS ANDERSSON): It's too late to turn back!

OLOF: What is it, Gert? Speak up!

GERT (*takes out a book*): To both of you, servants of God, a whole people come forward to make their confession. Do you acknowledge your oaths?

OLOF AND LARS: We have sworn!

GERT: This book is the fruit of my quiet labor! On every page you'll read a cry of distress, the sighs of thousands who have been blind enough to believe it was God's will that they should suffer the oppression of one man; they have thought it their duty not to dare to believe in their deliverance.

(OLOF *is reading.*)

GERT: You will hear cries of distress from farthest Norrland to the sound—from the ruins of the church the aristocrats are building new castles for themselves and new prisons for the people—you will read how the king sells law and justice when he lets murderers escape punishment if they'll work at the salt boilers; [44] you will read how he taxes vice when he lets prostitutes pay for the privilege of plying their trade; yes, even the fish in the rivers, even the sea water he has brought under his control, but it's over now; the eyes of the people have been opened; it's fermenting, and soon the oppression will be crushed, and they will be free.

OLOF: Who has written this book?

GERT: The people! They're folk songs, you see; this is how they sing when they're under the yoke. I've traveled about in the cities and out in the country; I have asked them: Are you happy? Here are recorded the answers. I have held court! Here are the decisions! Do you think that the will of millions depends on one person? Do you think that God has given this country with its human souls and possessions to one person so that he can deal with them as he wishes? Don't you rather believe that he should carry out what all the people want? You don't answer! Oh, well, you tremble at the thought that it can end. Listen to my confession! To-morrow the oppressor shall die, and you will all be free!

OLOF AND LARS: What are you saying?

GERT: You didn't understand what I said at our meetings.

OLOF: You have deceived us!

GERT: Not at all. You're free. Two voices less make no difference. Everything's ready!

LARS: Have you considered the consequences?

GERT: Fool, it was just because of the consequences I did this!

OLOF: If you were right, Gert? What do you say, Lars?

LARS: I wasn't born to be in the vanguard.

OLOF: Everyone's born to be in the vanguard, but it isn't everyone who's willing to sacrifice his life!

GERT: Only the one who has the courage to be laughed at and ridiculed goes foremost. What is their hate compared to their deadly ridicule?

OLOF: If we don't succeed?

GERT: Risk even that! You don't know that Thomas Münster has set up a new spiritual kingdom in Mühlhausen.[45] You don't know that all Europe is in revolt. Who was Dacke [46] if not a defender of the oppressed? What have the Dalesmen done in their revolts but defend their freedom against the one who has broken both faith and promise? He breaks them without being punished, but, when they want to defend themselves, others shout about treason and revolt!

OLOF: So that's where you wanted to lead me, Gert!

GERT: Hasn't the current led you this far? You want to, but you don't dare. Tomorrow the bomb will explode in the Great Church. That will be the signal for the people to rise and elect a ruler to their liking!

OLOF (*puts his fist to the book*): If that is what everyone wants, no one can prevent it! Gert, let me go to the king with this book and show him what his people want, and he'll give them justice.

GERT: Child! He'd be frightened for a moment, maybe he'd return a silver stoup to some church; then he'd point to Heaven and say: It's not my will that makes me sit here dealing with you unjustly; it's God's.

OLOF: Let the will of God be done!

GERT: How?

OLOF: Let him die that all may live! They may call me murderer, ungrateful, traitor—well, let them! I sacrificed everything, even

honor and conscience and faith—could I give more to these poor
souls who cry for deliverance? Let's go before I regret it!

GERT: Even if you did, it's too late. You don't know Mårten's a spy;
the sentence over the agitator has probably been handed down.

OLOF: Well, then, I shan't! And why should I regret an action that
carries out the judgment of God? Forward in the name of the
Lord! (*They go.*)

PROSTITUTE (*has entered, kneels beside a grave which she strews
with flowers*): Hast Thou punished me enough now, Lord, so
that Thou canst forgive me?

KRISTINA (*comes in hastily*): Tell me, ma'am, have you seen Master
Olof?

PROSTITUTE: Are you his friend or enemy?

KRISTINA: You're insulting me . . .

PROSTITUTE: Forgive me. I haven't seen him since I last prayed.

KRISTINA: You look troubled. I recognize you! You were the one
Olof talked to one evening in the Great Church.

PROSTITUTE: You shouldn't talk to me so anyone sees it. Don't you
know who I am?

KRISTINA: Yes, I do.

PROSTITUTE: You do! They've told you?

KRISTINA: Olof did.

PROSTITUTE: My God! And you don't despise me?

KRISTINA: You're an unhappy mistreated woman, Olof said. Why
should I despise misfortune?

PROSTITUTE: Then you're not happy yourself.

KRISTINA: No. We share the same fate.

PROSTITUTE: Then I'm not the only one! Tell me, to what unworthy
man did you give your love?

KRISTINA: Unworthy?

PROSTITUTE: Forgive me, no one a person loves is unworthy. To
whom did you give your love?

KRISTINA: You know Master Olof?

PROSTITUTE: Say that it isn't true! Don't rob me even of my faith in him; that's the only thing I have left since God took my child.

KRISTINA: You had a child! Then you have been happy!

PROSTITUTE: I thank God He never let my son know how unworthy his mother was.

KRISTINA: Have you committed a crime that you talk like that?

PROSTITUTE: I have just buried it.

KRISTINA: Your child? What are you saying? And I who pray to God every day that He will give me a being, just one, that I may love.

PROSTITUTE: Poor child! Pray to God He will protect you.

KRISTINA: I don't understand you, madame.

PROSTITUTE: Don't call me that; you know who I am.

KRISTINA: Don't people pray in the churches for those who are expecting?

PROSTITUTE: Not for us!

KRISTINA: Us?

PROSTITUTE: They pray for the others—they curse us!

KRISTINA: What do you mean by the others? I don't understand.

PROSTITUTE: Do you know Master Olof's wife?

KRISTINA: Why, I'm his wife!

PROSTITUTE: You! Why didn't I see that? Can you forgive me for a moment's doubt? Would sin look like you and him? Go! You're a child who doesn't know about evil. You oughtn't to talk with me any more. God bless you! Farewell! (*She wants to go.*)

KRISTINA: Don't leave me. Whoever you are, stay, for God's sake. They've broken into our house, and I can't find my husband. Go with me, to your home, anywhere. You're a good woman; you can't be a criminal . . .

PROSTITUTE (*interrupts*): If I tell you that the vulgarity of the mob can't hurt you half as much as my company, you'll forgive me for leaving . . .

KRISTINA: Who are you?

PROSTITUTE: I'm an outcast, in whom the curse God hurled at woman when Eve fell has been fulfilled. Don't ask me any more, for, if I told you more, your contempt would tempt me to self-defense, which would be still more contemptible. Here comes someone who probably would be noble enough to escort you if you promised him your honor and eternal peace for his trouble, for he's not likely to ask for less for his protection at such a late hour. Forgive me, I don't want my bitterness to hurt you.

WINDRANK (*comes in, drunk*): It's a hell of a thing one can't be left alone even when he's among the dead. Listen, women, please don't ask me anything, for I don't guarantee that I'll answer. I'm going to tell everything the day after tomorrow, because it'll be too late then. Maybe you're nuns who've lost your home. Yes, yes! Although you women are only women, I don't think I have the right to be impolite even though the sun has set; there's an old law, of course, that no one may be seized after sunset, but the law's a tramp, who doesn't, out of politeness, want to be applied to women. Hush! Hush, my tongue; why, you're going like a spinning wheel; but that's because of that damned brandy! But why should they drag me into things like that? It's certainly true I'll be well paid and will be a wealthy man, but you mustn't think I'm doing it for the sake of money. But it's done now! But I don't want to; I don't want to! I want to sleep at night and not be disturbed by ghosts. If I should go and tell? No, then they'll seize me! If anyone else should go and tell? Maybe one of you nuns would!

KRISTINA (*who has conferred with the* PROSTITUTE): If you have something on your conscience that's troubling you, go ahead and tell us.

WINDRANK: Should I tell? That's just what I want to get out of. But it's terrible; I can't stand it any longer. And I'm the one who has to do it. Why should I be the one? I don't want to!

KRISTINA: My friend, you intend to commit . . .

WINDRANK: A murder? Who told you? Thank God you know! By all means, go ahead and tell—right now; otherwise, I'll get no peace, no peace in eternity.

KRISTINA (*who has been amazed, recovers her self-control*): Why are you going to murder him?

WINDRANK: Oh, there's a lot, a lot! Just look at how he's tearing down your convents!

KRISTINA: The king!

WINDRANK: Yes, exactly, the liberator and father of our country. Of course, he's an oppressor, but he certainly shouldn't be murdered for that.

KRISTINA: When is it going to happen?

WINDRANK: Tomorrow, mind you, in the Great Church, in the church itself.

(*The* PROSTITUTE *goes at a silent signal from* KRISTINA.)

KRISTINA: Why did they select you to commit an act like that?

WINDRANK: Well, see, I have a few connections with some of the servants in the church, and I am so poor. But it doesn't matter who fires the gun, just so some sensible person aims it, and besides we have several ideas in reserve though I'm to start firing. But why don't you go and tell?

KRISTINA: That has already been done.

WINDRANK: Well, God be praised! Good-bye, my money!

KRISTINA: Tell me: who are you, you conspirators?

WINDRANK: No, that I simply won't tell.

(NILS, *soldiers, and people cross the stage.*)

KRISTINA: You see, they're already searching for you.

WINDRANK: I wash my hands!

NILS (*goes up to* WINDRANK *without seeing* KRISTINA): Have you seen Olaus Petri?

WINDRANK: Why?

NILS: We're looking for him.

WINDRANK: No, I haven't seen him. Are there others you're looking for?

NILS: Oh, yes, several.

WINDRANK: No, I haven't seen anyone at all.

NILS: We'll be right back for you. (*Goes*)

KRISTINA: Is it the conspirators they're looking for?

WINDRANK: Yes, that's it. I'll be going. Good-bye.

KRISTINA: Tell me before you go . . .

WINDRANK: Haven't time.

KRISTINA: Is Master Olof one of you?

WINDRANK: Of course!

(KRISTINA *falls, unconscious, on a grave.*)

WINDRANK (*becomes sober and is genuinely moved*): God in Heaven, she's his wife! (*Goes up to* KRISTINA) I think I've killed her! Hans! Hans! Now you can go and hang yourself! Why did you get mixed up with the big shots? (*Calls*) Come here and help a poor woman!

OLOF (*is brought in by soldiers who carry torches, sees* KRISTINA, *tears himself loose and falls to his knees beside her*): Kristina!

KRISTINA: Olof! You're alive! Let's leave this place and go home!

OLOF (*crushed*): It's too late!

CURTAIN

Scene 2

A part of the Great Church. OLOF *and* GERT *in prison garb in pillories by the door. The organ is playing. The church bells are ringing. The divine services are over, and the people are leaving. The* SEXTON *and his* WIFE *are standing to one side downstage.*

SEXTON: Chancellor Lars got mercy, but not Master Olof! [47]

WIFE: The chancellor has always been a peaceful man, who hasn't stirred up much fuss; I can't understand how he could want to be in on such a horrible thing.

SEXTON: The chancellor has always been strange though he hasn't said much. And he was reprieved, but it cost him his whole fortune. I can't help feeling sorry for Master Olof. I've always liked him all the same, even though he has been difficult.

WIFE: Should they make a young boy like that pastor?

SEXTON: Well, he was pretty young; but that's probably what was wrong with him; but he'll most likely get over it in time.

WIFE: Nonsense—why, he's going to die today!

SEXTON: Yes, good Lord, I almost forgot, but it seems to me that's crazy.

WIFE: Do you know if he has repented?

SEXTON: I doubt it—he's still pretty stiff-necked, I guess.

WIFE: But he'll soften up when he sees his confirmands, whom he can't confirm.

SEXTON: I must say the king's pretty small when he turns that side. Having the pastor do penance in the church the very day his pupils are confirmed! It's almost as horrible as when he made Dean Göran drink a toast of friendship with the hangman or when he had the bishops ride through town with birchbark baskets on their heads.

WIFE: And his brother Lars is to prepare him for death.

SEXTON: See, here come the confirmands. They look sad; I don't blame 'em. I think I'll have to go in my room and cry . . .

(*The confirmands—girls and boys—march past* OLOF *with flowers in their hands. They are distressed and walk with their eyes cast down. People follow them. Curious ones among them point at* OLOF; *others reprove them.* VILHELM, *the pupil from Strängnäs, comes last in the procession, stops shyly before* OLOF, *falls to his knees, and puts his flowers at* OLOF's *feet.* OLOF *does not notice this because he has pulled his hood over his face. Some of the people murmur disapprovingly, others approvingly.* MÅRTEN *steps up to take away the flowers but is pushed back by the people. Soldiers make a path for* ARCHBISHOP LARS PETRI, *who appears in the ceremonial garb of his office. The people leave.* LARS, OLOF, *and* GERT *are alone. The organ becomes silent. The bells continue ringing.)*

LARS (*to* OLOF): Olof! The king has rejected the burghers' plea for mercy! Are you prepared to die?

OLOF: I can't think that far!

LARS: They have assigned me to prepare you.

OLOF: Better do it fast! The blood's still surging in my veins.

LARS: Have you repented?

OLOF: No!

LARS: Do you want to enter eternity with an unforgiving heart?

OLOF: Put aside your formulary if you want me to listen. I don't think I can die now; there's too much of the power of life left in me!

LARS: I think so, too, and it's for a new life in this world I'm preparing you.

OLOF: So I'm to live?

LARS: If you'll admit that what you've done was an error, and if you'll retract what you've said about the king.

OLOF: How can I? That would be death!

LARS: This is what I had to tell you. Decide for yourself.

OLOF: A man doesn't compromise about a conviction!

LARS: Even an error can become a conviction. I'll go, so you can think it over. (*Goes*)

GERT: What we had planted was not ready for harvest. A lot of snow must fall if the seed planted in autumn shall grow, yes, centuries will pass before anyone will see even a sprout. The conspirators have been caught, they say, and they offer thanks to God; they're mistaken; the conspirators are everywhere, in the rooms of the royal palace, in the churches, and on the squares, but they don't dare to do what we dared. But the day will come! Farewell, Olof! You ought to live longer, for you are young; I shall die with great satisfaction: The name of every new martyr will be a battle cry for a new host. Never believe that a lie has lighted a fire in a human soul; never doubt the emotions that have shaken you to the very core of your being when you have seen anyone suffer because of spiritual or physical oppression. Even if the whole world says you're wrong, believe your heart if you have the courage! The day you deny yourself, you're dead, and eternal damnation will be a favor to the one who has committed the sin against the Holy Ghost.

OLOF: You speak with certainty about my being set free!

GERT: The burghers have offered five hundred ducats to ransom you.[48] When it cost only two thousand to get Birgitta declared a saint, five hundred ought to be enough to declare you innocent. The king doesn't dare to take your life!

LARS SPARRE (*enters, accompanied by the hangman and soldiers*): Take Gert Bookprinter away!

GERT (*as he is taken away*): Farewell, Olof! Take care of my daughter, and never forget the great day of Pentecost!

SPARRE: Master Olof! You're a young man who has been led astray. The king forgives you because you are very young, but demands as surety a retraction in which you take back what you have done above and against his orders.

OLOF: So the king still needs me?

SPARRE: There are many who need you. But don't count on mercy before you have met the condition. Here is the king's order: your chains can be removed this very moment if you wish, but even this order can be torn to pieces.

OLOF: The one who's satisfied with five hundred ducats isn't likely to bother about a retraction—

SPARRE: That's a lie! The hangman is expecting you, too! But I beg you to listen to a few words from an old man. I, too, have been young, and have been driven by powerful passions; that's part of being young, but it's intended that the passions be conquered. I did what you've done; I went about blurting out truths, but I got no thanks, at best only ridicule; I wanted to build a little heaven on earth (*with emphasis*) on other bases than you, of course; but I soon brought my mind under control, and banished my false

dreams. I don't want to maintain that you're a man who wants
to become famous by attracting attention to yourself—I don't believe that—you mean well, but meaning well can do a lot of
harm. You're so hot-blooded you're blinded because you don't
control yourself; you preach freedom and plunge thousands into
the slavery of license. Go back, young man, and atone for the
wrong you've done; restore what you've torn down, and the people will bless you.

OLOF (*bewildered and shaken*): You speak the truth, I hear, but
who has taught you to speak it?

SPARRE: Experience! You lack that!

OLOF: Have I lived and fought for a lie? Will I have to declare my
whole youth and the best years of my manhood lost, pointless,
wasted? I'd rather die with my delusions!

SPARRE: You should have let your dreams go a little sooner! But
calm yourself. Life is still ahead of you; the past has been a school,
a hard one to be sure, but all the sounder. So far you have lived
for fancies and follies; you have neglected some things reality
demands of you. Outside this door stand your creditors with their
bills. Here are their papers. The clergy of the new church demand
that you live to complete what you have begun so beautifully.
The burghers of the city demand their secretary in their town
hall; the congregation demands its pastor, and the confirmands
their teacher. Those are the legal creditors. But there's yet another out there, the one to whom you owe most, but who doesn't
demand anything—your young wife. You have torn her from her
father and are casting her out into the storms of life; you have
robbed her of her childhood faith, you have made her mind anxious; your folly has made a crude mob drive her out of her home,
and she doesn't demand even love from you; she asks only that
she may suffer a lifetime at your side; you see, even we are concerned about others, though you call us selfish. Let me open this
door which will lead you out into the world again; humble your

spirit while it is still flexible, and thank God who still gives you time to serve humanity!

OLOF (*weeps*): I am lost!

SPARRE (*signals to the hangman, who removes* OLOF's *chains and prison garb; then the marshal opens the door to the sacristy, and deputies of the council, the clergy, and the burghers enter*): Olaus Petri, formerly pastor of the Great Church of Stockholm, do you hereby apologize for your offenses, do you retract what you have said against and above the king's orders, and will you keep your oath to the king of Sweden and serve him faithfully?

   (OLOF *remains silent.*)

   (LARS PETRI *enters with* KRISTINA; *they approach* OLOF. *The people make gestures of appeal.*)

OLOF (*coldly and firmly*): Yes!

SPARRE: In the name of the king, you are free!

   (OLOF *and* KRISTINA *embrace each other. The people take* OLOF *by the hand and congratulate him.*)

OLOF (*coldly*): Before I leave this room, let me be alone with my God! I must! Here I struck my first blow, and here . . .

LARS: Here you have won your greatest victory—today! (*All but* OLOF *leave.*)

   (OLOF *kneels.*)

VILHELM (*comes in very quietly. Becomes amazed to find* OLOF *alone and free*): Master Olof, I've come to say farewell.

OLOF (*rises*): Vilhelm, you didn't desert me! Let me weep with you over the memory of the happy moments of my youth.

VILHELM: Before you die, I want to thank you for all the good you've done for us. I was the one who gave you these flowers, but you haven't seen them . . . They've been crushed under foot, I see . . . I wanted to remind you of the time we played under the lindens in the monastery gardens of Strängnäs; I thought it would do you good to know we haven't thanked God you didn't come back as you said we would. We never forgot you, because you freed us from the cruel punishments, and you opened the heavy monastery doors and gave us freedom and the blue sky and a happy life again. Why you're going to die we don't know, but you could never do anything but what is right. If you're to die because you have supported a few oppressed people, as they say, it shouldn't pain you if it hurts us very, very much. You told us once how they burned Huss at the stake because he had dared to say the truth to the mighty, you told us how he stepped onto the pile and commended himself into the hands of God, prophesying about the swan who would come and sing new songs in praise of the new freedom. I've thought of you going to your death like that— with your face radiant and your eyes raised to the sky while the people shout: So dies a martyr!

(OLOF *crushed, leans on the pillory.*)

GERT's VOICE (*far off in the church*): Renegade!

(OLOF *collapses on the pillory, completely crushed.*)

CURTAIN

Notes on
'Master Olof'

THE CHARACTERS

SEE ALSO *The Last of the Knights, The Regent, Earl Birger of Bjälbo* (Seattle: University of Washington Press, 1956) for information about several of the characters.

Olaus Petri (or *Olavus Petri,* the Latinization of *Olof Petersson, ca.* 1493 or 1497–1552) was the son of the Örebro smith Peter Olofsson and his wife Kristina Larsdotter. Educated at the Carmelite cloister school in Örebro and the universities of Uppsala, Leipzig, and Wittenberg, he received his master's degree at Wittenberg in February, 1518. How well he knew Luther personally is not known, but it is certain that Luther's religious ideas became the decisive element in his career. Upon his return to Sweden in 1519, he became the secretary of Bishop Mattias of Strängnäs, who in 1520 ordained him as deacon and canon. He became a teacher at, and later the director of, the cathedral school. Accompanying the bishop to the coronation of Christian II, Master Olof probably saw the bishop executed in the bloodbath. Upon his father's death in 1521, he and his brother Lars fought successfully to prevent the monks in Örebro from taking possession of property their father had willed them. (The detailed account in the sources of this struggle probably gave Strindberg the basic material for the mother's deathbed scene.) In 1523, Master Olof began to preach against such papal practices as the sale of indulgences and continued to do so in spite of the protests of Bishop Brask and others.

From 1524 to 1539, Master Olof worked in varyingly close cooperation with the king for the reformation. From 1524 until 1531, he was secretary to the council of the city of Stockholm and preached the Lutheran doctrines in the Great Church there although he was not ordained until 1539 and did not become pastor of the church until 1543. In 1524, he was excommunicated by the Catholics on the grounds of heresy. In 1525, he married in defiance of the law of celibacy. In 1531, he became the king's chancellor. During the 1530's, Master Olof irritated the king increasingly by his insistence on speaking bluntly about the king's faults, on writing a history of Sweden according to scholarly standards rather than as Gustav would have liked, and on fighting for the relative independence of the Church of Sweden which Gustav wanted to control completely. In 1539–1540, he was brought to trial for treason and sentenced to death, but was reprieved when the burghers of Stockholm paid a heavy fine for him. From then until his death, Master Olof was never fully in the confidence of the king, who nevertheless continued to use his services when they were needed.

The historical Master Olof was an idealist and an intellectual, who not only believed in the Lutheran ideas he fought for but also was a strong man in his younger years, with little inclination to compromise with the king. It may well be that Strindberg is right in his interpretation of Master Olof as (1) an enthusiastic young reformer who did not understand fully the implications of the use Gustav Vasa was making of him, and (2) a disappointed but resigned servant of "the wonder man of God" in his later years. (See *Gustav Vasa*.)

Lars Andersson (*Laurentius Andreae, ca.* 1470–1552), who ranks next to Master Olof in the Lutheran reformation of the Swedish Church, studied at Skara, Uppsala, Rostock, and Leipzig (where he got his master's degree), visited Rome at least three times, and, until 1523, served the church at the cathedral of Strängnäs, the first center of Lutheranism in Sweden. In 1520, he became archdeacon of Strängnäs and was thus in a position to further the career of the brilliant Master Olof. In 1523, Lars Andersson became the king's secretary. As such, he became the most important politically of the Lutheran reformers for he not only gave Gustav Vasa the ideas that justified—in their minds at least— the king's moves against the Roman Church, but he also was the man behind the king's actions that gradually made the break with Rome inevitable. A man with sincere convictions as to the rightness of his cause but not servile to the king, Lars Andersson gradually lost favor with Gustav from 1530 on. The king apparently wanted a church entirely in his control; Lars Andersson wanted a relatively independent state church. In 1531, he lost his position as the king's secretary, and by 1539 he had lost the king's favor so completely that he was brought to trial for treason, condemned to death, and reprieved only through the sacrifice of almost his entire fortune. During the last twelve years of his life he lived in retirement at Strängnäs.

Lars Petri (or *Laurentius Petri* or *Lars Petersson*, 1499–1573), the younger brother of Master Olof, was practically unknown when in 1531 he was made the first Lutheran archbishop of Uppsala. A man who may be said to have been a practitioner of "high thinking and simple living," Archbishop Petri more than any other person was responsible for the development of the Church of Sweden into a high church with an episcopal organization very much like that of the Church of England. Wise, tactful, yet firm when necessary, he became one of the great archbishops of his country; far less impulsive and less needlessly outspoken than his brother, Lars Petri remained on good terms with three kings—Gustav I, Erik XIV, and John III. He was married to Elisabet, a daughter of Brita Vasa, the king's cousin. As a writer, he was surpassed by his brother in both prose and poetry.

Bishop Hans Brask (1464–1538), native of Linköping and its bishop from 1513 on, studied abroad and received his doctor's degree at some continental university. On his return to Sweden, he rose rapidly in the hierarchy of the church largely because he was both brilliant and aggressive. Loyal both to his native country and to the Church of Rome, he became one of the most powerful men in Sweden. He believed that the country's freedom and strength depended on the aristocracy and the church whose foremost spokesman and defender he was during the fateful 1520's, when Master Olof, Lars Andersson, and the other Lutheran reformers were making it possible for Gustav Vasa to strip the Roman Church of much of its possessions and well-nigh all of its power in Sweden. A practical and admirable man of wide experience, Bishop Brask fled from Sweden after the decisive *riksdag* or parliament at Västerås in 1527, when he found that his protests against the reformers' "heretical" acts had gained essentially nothing and that all his other actions to preserve the Roman Church had led to no practical results. In the remaining years of his life he was a source of comfort and assistance to many Swedish Catholics who had fled because of their faith or because of their opposition to the king. On occasion Gustav Vasa had cause to fear the practical implications of the absent prelate's activities in his voluntary exile.

Bishop Måns or *Magnus Sommar* (died *ca.* 1556), the last Roman Catholic bishop of Strängnäs, was far less difficult for Gustav Vasa to deal with than was Bishop Brask. Trained both in Sweden and abroad, Sommar had been elevated from cathedral dean to the bishop's throne in 1522 partly through the influence of the young regent. A gentle, conciliatory prelate and a loyal Swede, Bishop Sommar played a significant role at the *riksdag* at Västerås in 1527 when he urged economic and political concessions by the church and others in order to protect the welfare of the country under Gustav Vasa. In 1528, Bishop Måns, a faithful son of the Church of Rome but one who believed that the church should be reformed from within, was a means of preserving the apostolic succession for the Church of Sweden. Until 1536, he remained on good terms with the king but in that year Gustav forced him to resign as bishop and placed him in prison on the charge that he was involved in the conspiracy against Gustav's life. Released in 1537, the former bishop received Krokek's deserted monastery as a residence. Bishop Måns is remembered particularly for his support of Gustav Vasa, his loyalty to his Catholic faith, and his willingness to compromise on nonspiritual and nonreligious matters.

Kristina Petri (dates unknown) is remembered only as Master Olof's wife. Little is known about her origins beyond the facts that her mother's name was Malin and that her family was one of some means. Almost as little is known of Kristina as a wife and mother; Master Olof, who had little to say about the more intimate details of his own personal life in his autobiography, had still less to say about the woman he had married in 1525 against the canonical law. Two children were born to the Petris: Elisabet in 1526 and the apparently unfortunate Reginald in 1527.

Kristina Larsdotter (died 1545), the wife of Peter Olofsson, smith at Örebro, and the mother of Olof and Lars Petri, was, according to the popular sources, a devout Roman Catholic who had sacrificed so that her two brilliant sons could study both at home and abroad and who learned with dismay that both her sons had accepted the teachings of Luther and were doing all they could to establish them at home. Very little is known about the historical Kristina.

Lars Siggeson Sparre (died 1554), as Strindberg emphasized in three plays—*Master Olof, The Last of the Knights,* and *The Regent*—was one of Gustav Vasa's most faithful friends among the lords and one of his most loyal and effective supporters. One of the six Swedish hostages kidnaped by Christian the Tyrant in 1518, Lord Lars returned to Sweden in 1520 and, when the war for independence from the union broke out, gave complete allegiance and support to Gustav Vasa. By 1523, Gustav Vasa made him a national councillor and the national marshal, and, in the remaining years of his life, the king entrusted one mission and duty after the other to him. Among these were bringing Princess Katarina to Sweden in 1531 as Gustav's first queen, serving as his spokesman on important occasions, and commanding the royal forces against the Småland rebels in the 1540's.

Hans Windrank, according to SB (III, 238), was "a poverty-stricken sea captain, who the same day [the day before the king was to be assassinated] was told the secret. He was heavily in debt and hoped through what was going to happen to free himself from his oppressive situation. When the company separated, the sea captain was drunker than was good for the conspirators, and, when he came home, he met a woman in the neighborhood, to whom he could not prevent himself from revealing the bright prospects which had suddenly changed his life. One word led to another, and it was not long before the woman had learned the whole plan. She did not delay telling her husband about it, and he hurried to the palace. . . . Hans Windrank was brought to the palace immediately, and during the course of the night all the conspirators were seized except Anders Hansson, the master at the mint, who threw himself from the tower Three Crowns and, by committing suicide, avoided the king's punishment." What use Strindberg has made of these details is obvious.

For information about *King Gustav,* see the introduction and the notes to *Gustav Vasa.*

1. These speeches are excerpts from *The Comedy of Tobias* (*Tobie Comedia*), the oldest extant Swedish play on a Biblical subject. The rhymed play was generally thought to be Master Olof's beyond Strindberg's day; recent scholars have questioned his authorship.

2. Jeremiah 1:4-7, 18-19.

3. Jeremiah 1:17.

4. Bishop Brask of Linköping, the ablest defender of Roman Catholicism, ruled his diocese with the aims of safeguarding the church, avoiding political innovations, and preserving his own power. Bishop Måns of Strängnäs was a much more pliable man who was willing to compromise with the new king and with Lutheranism. As Strindberg indicates, the clergy of Strängnäs had Lutheran leanings.

5. Johannes Huss (1369–1415) and Johann Ziska (*ca.* 1370–1424) were early Bohemian Protestants. Huss, a professor at the University of Prague, was excommunicated and then burned at the stake because of his Protestantism. After his death, the Hussite wars (1419–1436) broke out—Ziska was the leading Hussite commander—against the pope and the emperor. Tens of thousands of Bohemian and German peasants died in these exceptionally brutal wars.

6. The Anabaptists were a religious sect that rejected infant baptism, insisted on adult baptism, and wanted to set up a utopian religious-political society.

7. Until 1526 Bishop Brask had his own printing press at Söderköping.

8. See Acts 2:1-4 for the significance of Pentecost and the descent of the Holy Spirit.

9. Baal, the name of various deities worshiped by ancient Semitic peoples, signifies *lord* or *master*. Hence, Strindberg's allusion to the two pillars of Baal and the two masters of much of the western world in Master Olof's early days—the emperor and the pope.

10. The Fichtel Mountains in Bavaria.

11. See note 6. Rink and Knipperdollink, two German merchants and Anabaptists, arrived in Stockholm in 1524 on a trip designed to combine business and religion. They succeeded in stirring up some Stockholmers to the point of destroying images and other church property. Young

King Gustav expelled them from the country. SB (III, 134) says: "Churches and cloisters were stormed, their ornaments torn down, their altars destroyed, their organs broken to pieces, and their saints' images exhibited with arms and noses cut off on streets and squares." King Gustav had gone to Malmö for a conference with the Danish king.

12. See the Book of Daniel 6. Daniel was thrown into the lions' den when he dared to disobey the king.

13. See note 4.

ACT II

14. Christian II the Tyrant (1481–1559) succeeded in gaining the Swedish throne in 1520 and is generally considered primarily to blame for the Stockholm bloodbath in that year. See Strindberg's *The Last of the Knights, The Regent, Earl Birger of Bjälbo* (Seattle: University of Washington Press, 1956) for detailed information about Christian, who lost the Swedish throne in 1521 because of Gustav Vasa and the war for independence from the hated Kalmar Union.

15. Käpplinge Island (now Blasieholm) was the scene in 1389 of the burning to death of several Swedish burghers by a group of German burghers of Stockholm. Until 1371, the German (Hanseatic) influence was so great commercially that half of the members of the city council of Stockholm had to be Germans.

16. Lübeck did assist Gustav Vasa very much in winning the war for independence. For a recent account of Lübeck's role, see Ingvar Andersson's *A History of Sweden* (London: Weidenfeld and Nicolson, 1955).

17. The southern province of Småland had for centuries been a cattle-raising province and had enjoyed appreciable prosperity through the sale of cattle and other products to nearby Blekinge, Skåne, and Halland, which were Danish in Gustav Vasa's time. When Gustav, in order to work toward economic independence, for all practical purposes closed the borders and fixed the prices on cattle, the *smålänningar* felt resentful because they had to drive their cattle north to Stockholm and sell them at prices set by the king. The people of Småland rose in rebellion in 1542 and 1543.

18. In 1520. See note 14.

19. King Gustav made strenuous, and to a degree successful, efforts

to develop Swedish shipping in order to release Sweden from commercial dependence on Lübeck and the other Hanseatic towns.

20. See note 11. Belial, the ancient Phoenician god, is used here as a personification of evil or an equivalent of Satan.

21. When Master Olof began to preach in the Great Church, he had a pulpit set up in the shape of a basket. It was from this pulpit that Master Olof preached the new Lutheran doctrines in Swedish. SB (III, 131) says: "Many times it happened that his sermon was interrupted by the throwing of stones or other disturbances."

22. The Great Church (*Storkyrkan*) was originally called St. Nicholas' Church.

23. For an explanation of the allusion to St. George and the dragon, see Strindberg's *The Last of the Knights, The Regent, Earl Birger of Bjälbo*, p. 95, note 51. The sculpture of St. George killing a dragon which had been about to swallow a princess was placed in the Great Church in 1489 as a memorial of the victory at Brunkeberg. Windrank's Latin was obviously very little.

24. See note 21.

25. From 1248 on, the law of celibacy had been in effect in Sweden. By Master Olof's time, the Swedish people had come to regard a priest's marriage as sinful. See note 30.

ACT III

26. See the note on Master Olof, above.

27. Francis I (1494–1547), Renaissance king of France (1515–1547), appreciated the arts, including literature. Long before the first Swedish university was founded at Uppsala in 1477, young Swedes went to Paris to study. Travel on the continent and studies at a continental university were common for centuries for young Swedes from wealthy families.

28. See Numbers 22-24. Balaam was the diviner sent by a heathen king to curse the Israelites; on his way, he was confronted by an angel with a sword in his hand and was rebuked by his ass.

29. With Sweden on the verge of bankruptcy, King Gustav found it necessary to look upon the church as a source of badly needed income. Proceeding slowly and carefully, Gustav had "borrowed" from the church in 1522 (before he ascended the throne), 1523, 1524, and then

more and more frequently until, for all practical purposes, he eventually confiscated the extensive holdings of the church. Gustav's seizure of parish bells and other metal equipment from the churches in 1529 to get means to pay installments on the debt to Lübeck was particularly resented. See Strindberg's *Gustav Vasa*.

30. Master Olof's marriage on February 12, 1525, horrified the Catholics because they considered him a priest. Although he had been consecrated a deacon, Master Olof did not consider himself a priest. See SB (III, 139).

31. See note 5 above.

32. The Swedish translation of the New Testament (1526) was apparently the result of a committee or joint project rather than the work of one individual. Lars Andersson, the king's chancellor, and Master Olof are generally credited with an active part in the project, so highly essential to the Lutherans, who believed that everyone should have direct access to the Holy Scriptures. The Swedish translation of the Old Testament appeared in 1541.

33. In December, 1524, Master Olof accompanied the king and several members of the council to Uppsala, where Dr. Peder Galle, professor of theology, was the leading defender of the Catholic faith and the rights of the church. In the ensuing violent debate about religious questions, Dr. Galle used the writings of the church fathers as well as the Bible in supporting the Catholic cause while Master Olof was willing to accept only the Bible as a basis for argument. The debate was continued mainly in writing.

34. See notes 6 and 11.

35. In 1527, at the *Riksdag* (Parliament) of Västerås, King Gustav threatened to abdicate since the four estates were not ready to accept his proposals for making the country financially sound by providing new sources of national income. The threat of abdication and the support of the burghers and the farmers forced the lords and the clergy to accept the king's proposals: the transfer of surplus income of the bishops, cathedral chapters, and cloisters to the crown; and the transfer of castles held by bishops to the crown.

36. See note 35. Bishop Brask had been the most influential clerical opponent of King Gustav's proposals at Västerås.

37. See note 33.

38. See also note 35. Strindberg states the major decisions reached at Västerås. About 1454, Charles VIII (Karl VIII) confiscated many holdings of the church that had come into its possession illegally. Church property and most holdings of the nobility were not taxed, of course. The heirs were to receive all holdings given to the church after 1454.

39. King Gustav usually moved very slowly and cautiously in matters of religious doctrine and practice. The enthusiastic young reformer, who wanted to move swiftly and decisively, had preached in the Great Church from 1524 on, although he was not officially appointed pastor until 1543. See Conrad Bergendoff's *Olavus Petri and the Ecclesiastical Transformation in Sweden* (New York: Macmillan, 1928) for a fairly detailed account of Master Olof as a reformer.

ACT IV

40. The plague or pest in various forms recurred several times throughout Master Olof's time, although never with such violent results as in the Middle Ages.

ACT V

41. The conspiracy against Gustav involved many people. SB (III, 238) says that the conspiracy started in 1534 and that various plans for liquidating the king were made: "One of the conspirators agreed to try to poison the king's food; one—Anders Hansson, who worked in the mint and was often alone with the king in the silver room in Stockholm Palace—was to try to kill him with a dart; a third, the German Hans Bökmann got the assignment of carrying out the most important plan." He was to place under the king's chair in the Great Church powder which was to be set afire on Palm Sunday. Fortunately for King Gustav, several of the conspirators engaged in a drinking bout on Saturday evening, and one of them, the sea captain Hans Windrank, revealed the plan to a neighbor, who informed the palace authorities. Several of the conspirators were either hanged or imprisoned; Anders Hansson committed suicide. Olaus Petri and Lars Andersson had learned about the conspiracy through confession; neither had been a participant.

42. St. Clara's convent was founded in the thirteenth century during the reign of King Magnus Barnlock (Ladulås), who favored the Order of St. Clara or Second Order of St. Francis as well as its closely related Order of St. Francis (Gray Friars) by his protection and substantial gifts. St. Clara (1194–1253) had been canonized in 1255; her "Poor Clares" were dedicated to extreme poverty and to charitable activities, the most emphasized being the education of children.

43. For the Biblical account of Sennacherib (705–681 B.C.), the king of Assyria, see II Kings 18 and 19.

44. Salt was the most important condiment of the time and one of the commodities about which King Gustav was concerned. Strindberg says in *Svenska folket i helg och söken* (*The Swedish People on Holiday and Every Day,* Vol. I, "1500-talet," chapter i): In the large chapel [of the Great Church] to the south the king stores 468 lasts of salt and in the one to the north not much less. . . . The king sells [the salt] at lower prices or gives it away to restless farmers and other dissatisfied people or [sells] it at high prices when the demon avarice affects his otherwise great and honest soul." While most of the needed salt was imported, some was produced as Strindberg indicates at various points on the Swedish seacoast.

45. Thomas Münzer or Müntzer (not, as Strindberg says, Münster) was a German Anabaptist who was the leader of Thuringian peasants in the Peasants' War. Defeated at Frankenhausen in 1525, he was captured and beheaded.

46. See the note on Dacke, p. 241. The rebellion of the *smålänningar* occurred in 1542 and 1543. The Dalesmen had risen in three major rebellions (1525, 1527, and 1531).

47. Both Olaus Petri and Lars Andersson first pleaded innocent on the grounds that they had learned about the conspiracy from the conspirators during confession. Nevertheless, both were condemned to death. Fryxell (III, 139) says: "The archbishop himself had to pronounce and sign his brother's death sentence." Olaus Petri was not reprieved as readily by the king as Lars Andersson was, for the young reformer had irritated the king on many occasions, by preaching openly against swearing and using the king as an example of the habit, by speaking bluntly

about various acts of the king of which he did not approve, and by not being servile toward the king.

48. The burghers of Stockholm paid King Gustav five hundred Hungarian guilder (*gyllen*), according to Fryxell (III, 139), to secure Master Olof's reprieve.

Introduction to 'Gustav Vasa'

I. STRINDBERG'S INTENTION

TWENTY-SEVEN tempestuous years after he had written *Master Olof* (1872), Strindberg wrote *Gustav Vasa* (1899), a drama that he considered the second unit of a Vasa trilogy. The fifty-year-old dramatist had then established himself as the greatest living Swedish writer and had won recognition as one of the most significant European writers of his time. He had lived through two marriages, the details of which he had recorded in many works. A few years before, in the middle 1890's, his condition had been such that many who knew him well had thought that his day as a great writer was over. In the years following his Inferno period he amazed his contemporaries, however, by creating some of the greatest plays and nondramatic works ever to flow from his pen.

Far from least among the amazingly rich literary output, quantitatively and qualitatively, from the last years of the nineteenth century until relatively shortly before his death in 1912, were the new historical plays. Always interested in history and encouraged by the increased interest of the Swedish theater and the Swedish public in *Master Olof*, Strindberg took up again the composition of historical dramas, several of which were to gain recognition as among his most important plays, rivaling, on the one hand, such so-called "naturalistic" classics as *The Father, Lady Julie, Creditors, The Bond,* and *The Dance of Death I* and *II,* and, on the other, such expressionistic plays as the Damascus trilogy, *A Dream Play, The Ghost Sonata,* and *The Great Highway.* These plays and a few that fit into none of the three categories—historical, "naturalistic," or expressionistic— notably *Easter* and *The Crown Bride,* were to gain him recognition as one of the greatest and most influential dramatists of all time. Part of that recognition, it should be emphasized, was the rather general acknowledgment that he was the most important writer of historical plays since Shakespeare.

The 1890's saw a renewal of interest in Swedish history and the Swedish present among both the writers and the general public. Gifted young writers were exploiting the Swedish background as it was reflected in the various provinces and regions of Sweden. Inevitably, the renewal included among its most significant areas of interest the western mountain province of Dalarna with its colorful inhabitants and its rich traditional culture. As important as any chapter in the history of Dalarna was the mine of innumerable legends and historical details centering in the adventures of Strindberg's favorite king, Gustav Vasa, there in the sixteenth century. The semipopular sources as well as the standard accounts were filled with highly usable details; moreover, the material from Dalarna had been part of the training of Swedes down through the centuries. The time was right for the creation of a great play about the man who freed Sweden from an unsatisfactory union and the folk hero who has perhaps remained most consistently the object of Swedish admiration and even hero worship above all others.

For his *Gustav Vasa* (1899), Strindberg had the initial difficulty of selecting from among the masses of raw material available both in scholarly histories and in more popular works. He says in *Open Letters to the Intimate Theater (Öppna brev till Intima teatern,* 1919 edition, p. 247):

> The destiny of Gustav Vasa begins like a legend or a miracle story, develops into an epic, and is impossible to survey completely. To get this gigantic saga into one drama is impossible, of course. There- fore the only answer was to find an episode. That was the one

centering in the rebellion led by Dacke. The king was then in his second marriage with children by two wives, and at the height of his power. But Providence wanted to test him and temper its man, to whom the building of the kingdom was entrusted, and for that reason it [Providence] struck him with all the misfortunes of Job. That time of despair gives one the best opportunity to depict the great human being Gustav Vasa with all his human weaknesses.

This brief quotation suggests several matters, all of them pertinent to an understanding of the play. By selecting what he calls one episode for dramatic treatment instead of trying to depict representative episodes from the king's long life (*ca.* 1494–1560) and long reign (1523-1560), Strindberg avoided the loose form of the chronicle play. It is clear, too, that Strindberg's principal aim was to present the king both as the leader who "built Sweden from its foundation to its rafters" and as a thoroughly human being as well; in other words, *Gustav Vasa* was intended to be exactly what it is—a historical drama of character. The quotation suggests, too, Strindberg's psychoanalytical approach, which had been effectively illustrated in his plays of the late 1880's, discussed in the preface to *Lady Julie* (1888), and was now to be modified by Strindberg's recently acknowledged faith in the Eternal One, who selects human beings for the performance of great deeds and disciplines them whenever they show signs of disobedience or arrogance.

II. The Historical Background

From 1521 on, Gustav Vasa had worked for one goal: the development of a strong and independent Sweden. Neglecting only the cultural aspect of his countrymen's lives, Gustav had proceeded to change his country in every other area in the manner of a benevolent dictator who rightfully had the conviction that he was the man who could do it. In 1543, when he had put in twenty turbulent but successful years as king, he was faced with what was perhaps the biggest threat to the accomplishment of his goal: the rebellion of the yeomanry of Småland under Nils Dacke. It is that period that Strindberg has chosen as the time for *Gustav Vasa*.

Behind the king at this time were many experiences: the war for independence which he had waged successfully between 1521 and 1523 but, unfortunately for his program and peace of mind later on, not singlehandedly. He had had to depend on the help of friends like the Dalesmen (such as Måns Nilsson and Anders Persson), and he had had to borrow heavily from Lübeck and to rely on its friendship, knowing full well that both the Lübeckers and his other friends would present their bills or ask for special consideration later.

Behind him were three rebellions in Dalarna (1525, 1527–1528, 1531–1533); unrest and the threat of rebellion on the part of the lords of Västergötland (1529); and a rebellion in Småland under Jon Andersson (1538). Besides these there had been innumerable difficulties with his officials and other fellow Swedes, few of whom had any insight into what he was attempting to do. Worst of all for him as a human being were perhaps the numerous occasions when he had felt forced to discipline harshly and efficiently some of the men who had been his close friends and supporters in earlier days. Pressing were still the claims for gratitude from Lübeck.

Behind him were the major steps toward freeing Sweden from the control of Rome through the reformation. Gradually and surely, but compromising when absolutely necessary, he had created a national Church of Sweden and in the process had acquired means to carry out his nonreligious program. On more than one occasion, he had given offense to the adherents of both the new faith and the old. By 1543, the religious question had for all practical purposes been answered in a manner satisfactory to him. Even the most independent of the reformers, Master Olof, had been brought under control.

Behind him, too, was one unhappy marriage, entered into with a foreign princess (Katarina of Saxe-Lauenberg) in order to provide an heir to the throne and strengthen his country internally and internationally. The heir had been provided, but Prince Erik was not the sort of heir for which the great builder had hoped. Highly comforting to the king was his second marriage to the wise and beautiful Lady Margareta Lejonhuvud, who had brought him not only domestic happiness but also both sons and daughters. But the family picture was marred by a stubborn mother-in-law, who insisted on remaining a Catholic and in illegally keeping Vreta convent open; and by the oldest son, who neither liked his stepmother nor saw any real need for living up to his father's expectations.

In 1543–1544, the time of *Gustav Vasa,* the king faced one of the hardest tests of his lifetime—dealing with the rebels of Småland. They had been hard hit by Gustav's price-fixing on cattle, his closing of the Småland-Danish border to profitable cattle trading, his restrictions on the right of the commons to hunt at will in the forests, the privileges he had granted the aristocracy, and his taxes. They were also resentful because he had closed the Småland convents and monasteries, changed the church services, and deprived them of the many comforts of the Roman Church to which perhaps most of them were still deeply attached. The rebellion had succeeded remarkably well; the emperor, other princes, and even Lübeck, as well as Swedish enemies of the king, had encouraged or otherwise supported the able yeoman rebel leader, Nils Dacke. In 1542, Gustav had to agree to a formal armistice with Dacke. When the rebels penetrated into Östergötland and the Dalesmen showed signs of activity, Gustav—according to Strindberg's major sources—prepared for flight. The arrival of some two thousand Dalesmen to support him and the encouragement of others led Gustav Vasa to make one more effort. The rebellion was effectively ended in bloodshed and even brutality. Never again did the commons make any serious attempt to rebel against the king.

III. The Play

Dominated as the action is from the raising of the first curtain
to the last by the central character whether he is present or not—he
does not make his appearance until the opening of the third act—
Gustav Vasa is above all a character study of one man of destiny
who was, Strindberg believed, placed in a specific set of situations to
do a specific job: to make Sweden a strong nation free from an un-
desirable union, foreign allies, foreign interference, and internal disturbances. The play is, in other words, a study of a great leader who
is a highly complex and dynamic human being. It is a study of the
practical but idealistic realist—a generation later than his appearance
in *Master Olof*—who has almost in his grasp the achievement of his
goal.

The key to Strindberg's interpretation of Gustav Vasa and to the
play, both in form and content, may lie in the statement: "Providence wanted to test him and to temper its man, to whom the
building of the kingdom was entrusted, and for that reason it
struck him with all the misfortunes of Job." An analysis of the play
scene by scene reveals that "the misfortunes of Job" is the hint that
above all others suggests Strindberg's technique. The Job-like misfortunes that strike the king one after the other are not presented
and then neatly disposed of; instead they overlap, disappearing only
to reappear somewhat later, never to be fully and absolutely disposed
of so far as the central character is concerned.

Against the background of Dalarna and with a leading Dalesman's colorful home as the setting, Strindberg presents what must
have been the most continuing of all Gustav Vasa's Job-like difficulties in his attempt to make Sweden a strong and united kingdom.
With appropriate attention to the local color of the setting and to
the telescoped time of the action, Strindberg conveys the atmosphere
of a segment of Gustav Vasa's people who have always been among
the most individualistic and independent-minded of all Swedes and
have also always retained their own rich culture based on the tra-

ditions and practices of centuries. Note the details about the room itself both in the description of the setting and throughout the whole act. Note particularly that the wall paintings record major episodes in the adventures of Gustav Vasa back in the crucial years when he had needed the Dalesmen's help and had received it.

The Dalesmen gathered in Måns Nilsson's home are at once Gustav's friends and a most sensitive source of his difficulties. Self-confident, self-reliant, not very much inclined to humility, addicted to boasting a bit on occasion, they and their ancestors before them have never been completely subjected either to lord or to king. They had helped Gustav expel the Danes from Sweden, but not in order to subject themselves to a native king. Ever ready to act on their own initiative and for the protection of their own interests, these proud yeomen have been accustomed to receiving visits from a king only when they have granted him permission and have promised him safe-conduct.

But Gustav Vasa has upset many of their traditional ideas. Instead of remaining ever grateful for their help and leaving them pretty much to their old ways and in semi-independence, he has dealt severely with them on several occasions (for example, liquidating Jon of Svärdsjö, taking their treasured parish bells to help pay the national debt, replacing the Roman Catholic form of religion with the—to them—less satisfactory Lutheran one). The great leader has a goal that they do not really understand and appreciate; many of his acts have seemed neither admirable nor friendly to the Dalesmen, who are aptly characterized by Master Olof and Herman Israel:

> OLOF: A stiff-necked people, faithful as gold and suspicious through and through!
> ISRAEL: A very good people!
> OLOF: But a little naïve. Did you see how I trapped them?

As Strindberg makes clear, their reactions to the measures Gustav Vasa has taken are a blend of genuine liking for him as a human being, admiration for his courage and self-reliance, and dread of him as the king who is behaving toward them in a most unexpected and disconcerting fashion. They know he is "the wonder man of God," who has freed Sweden from foreign political bondage; they sense that he is doing great deeds; they know that they can never be sure what he will do to achieve his ends. They, too, are men of action in their own fashion.

That Gustav is "a gadfly that buzzes just before it stings" has begun to be clear as he has now entered Dalarna without asking the Dalesmen for permission or promise of safe-conduct, without coming to visit any of his friends, but summoning some of them, one by one, for questioning, hearing, and punishment. To the sound of muffled drums and the muted ringing of church bells, the king places the Dalesmen in uncertainty and dread that heighten the tension throughout the act until the bloody coats of the executed are tossed in, and are relieved very little by the qualified mercy meted out to Anders Persson and Måns Nilsson. These two principal Dalesmen, who had done much for Gustav Vasa, do not understand what the king is working toward or why he acts as he does. In that fact lies the promise of Gustav's further difficulties with his Dalesmen. The Job-like trial is, in other words, not neatly solved and disposed of.

Two others of Gustav's Job-like trials are introduced in this act— the realization of the Lutheran reformation throughout the whole country in order to relieve himself of one kind of foreign interference and to provide himself with the financial means to carry through his program, and the settlement of the whole problem of Lübeck and its claims. The religious problem has, to be sure, become somewhat less of a problem since Gustav Vasa succeeded in putting Master Olof in his place and making him accept a subordinate role, as shown in Olof's words: "I don't permit myself to judge my king's acts, both because I'm not equal to the task and because I know that above him he has a Judge, who guides his destiny." But the religious problem has not been completely solved. Note that the Dalesmen still are loyal to the memory of the executed Jon of Svärdsjö, who died for his childhood faith. Lübeck, too, presents problems of gratitude and demands, as Strindberg effectively demonstrates.

The first act is superb. Compact and without superfluous details of any kind, it provides an intensely dramatic demonstration of one of King Gustav's greatest afflictions, introductions to two others, a group of important secondary characters, admirable creation of atmosphere, and, perhaps above all else, effective introduction to the central character. Though Gustav is not physically present on the stage, he is constantly present in the minds of those who are. As Jacob Israel later says, "Always this giant hand, which one never sees, only feels!"

In Act II, Strindberg naturally and unobtrusively suggests the other major Job-like trials that the king has to face. Two of them— the problem of the crown prince and the problem of Lübeck—he illustrates in great detail, and the latest and most explosive one, the revolt of the southern province, Småland, under the effective leadership of Nils Dacke, he introduces through exposition sandwiched into the dialogue. While doing all this, Strindberg effectively drives home the fact that not only are the people on the stage keenly and even fearfully aware of Gustav Vasa but he is aware of well-nigh everything important that is going on. It is emphasized throughout that none of the problems has been settled once and for all; instead, they overlap and grow and accumulate, disappearing only to recur again.

The old claims of Lübeck, based on friendly treatment of Gustav Vasa in the days when he was a refugee from a Danish prison and on the financial and other means of support during the war for independence from the union, have been settled only in part: the financial debt has been paid, but the debt of gratitude cannot easily be paid without the sacrifice of part of the king's goal—freedom from foreign interference and control. Like the Dalesmen, the Lü-

beckers have helped Gustav Vasa for primarily realistic and therefore selfish reasons:

ISRAEL: You've noticed something big is secretly in the making . . .
No doubt you know Lübeck is fighting for its rights in the North;
I say rights because we are the pioneers who have blazed trails up
here—commercial trails, in this case—and we have the right to
demand returns and profits from the work we have invested in
this country. We have taught these people to use their products
and to trade them with others profitably; and we have freed
Sweden! Now they want to toss us aside when they've made use
of us. Use us—and toss us aside! But there's a bigger and more
powerful interest than business that forces the North to ally itself
with the Hanseatic cities. The emperor and the pope are as one;
the free cities won their independence from the emperor first and
then from the pope, and now when this country—with *our* help
and that of its great king—has done the same, we have to be allies
against the common enemy whether we want to or not. We have
stood by each other until recently, but an evil spirit has seized
Vasa, and, whether it's pride or weariness that has deceived him,
he wants to follow a new course that will ruin all of us!

JACOB: Wait a bit!—All of us? Say *"us Lübeckers,"* for the Swedes
would gain by taking that course.

Thwarted in their desires, the Lübeckers, though they respect, admire, and even love the king, are not only plotting with the *smålänningar* but willing to make use of the two Dalesmen.

Even more disturbing to the king is the problem of the crown
prince. Brilliant but emotionally unbalanced, the prince is hardly
the kind of son that the man of action with a definite goal and a
keen sense of duty can get any help from or look forward to seeing
as his successor on the throne. Strindberg presents the crown prince
sympathetically in action and as a product of his heredity and environment. Note these exchanges:

JACOB: You shouldn't speak ill of your father; it sounds bad. Forgive me!

PRINCE: But when he behaves badly, shouldn't I have the right to say so? Besides, I hate him!

JACOB: Don't say that! Don't say that! Your royal father's so infinitely great that you can't grasp his greatness . . .

PRINCE: It only looks like that, I know. Can you imagine: last night he came up to me and put his arm about my shoulders—for the first time in my life—and as I'd always thought that I only came to his hips, I was amazed that I was as tall as he. But when I looked at him again from a distance, he grew and became a giant!

JACOB: He is! And he looks like one of Michelangelo's prophets . . . Isaiah, I think! And, in truth, God the infinite One is with him.

PRINCE: Do *you* believe in God?

JACOB: For shame! You ought to be ashamed of yourself!

PRINCE: Well-ll, what should a person believe in times like these, when the king and the clergy persecute believers and desecrate everything that has been considered holy? Yet pretend to be defenders of the faith!

JACOB: Let's talk about something else.

PRINCE: That's what the king always says when I insist on an answer; so I hate him still more! As he hates me! Did you know your father was the one who got my mother from Lauenburg for him?

JACOB: No, I didn't.

PRINCE: Yes, but that marriage went wrong; you see, they hated each other thoroughly—and—(*gets up, excited*)—one day I saw him lift his cane against her—(*shouts*)—against my mother; and he struck her! After that day I was never young again—and I'll never forgive him—never!

Young Jacob Israel says that he has hardly seen a more useless crown prince, and "the wonder man of God" with his heavy hand deals with him brusquely as if he judges Erik as Jacob does.

In both scenes of Act II, Strindberg continues to develop his characterization of his central character from the points of view of other characters. The chosen of God with his deliberate moves and actions suggested in the first act takes on an almost Odin-like stature among his contemporaries. Even the most experienced and shrewdest one among them, Herman Israel of Lübeck, willingly grants the greatness of the king. Crown Prince Erik unconsciously reveals that he, too, senses that his father is a superior human being, and young Jacob Israel has made the king the object of hero worship. Strindberg carefully suggests, however, that the wonder man of God, while he has a stature above those about him, is nevertheless a very human being with flaws and weaknesses.

The opening of the third act is startling in its effect. In his first appearance the blond bearded king, of medium height, who stands in deep thought by an open window in the sunlight strikes one as a very human being, not as an Odin or an implacable dictator. From the entrance of his beautiful and beloved Queen Margareta, Gustav Vasa as the tender but firm husband, the prejudiced but firm father, and the family man, takes on dimensions. The very genuine love between king and queen, the gentle rejection of the queen's interference, the difficulties caused by his compromise because of his mother-in-law, his preference for his son John, his thoughtful but somewhat brusque treatment of Erik are all illustrations of the Job-like difficulties caused by the members of his own family. Why and how he deals with these is amply illustrated:

> QUEEN: The country first!
> KING: First and last: the country!

and

> KING: Do you consider that you'll be king some day?
> ERIK: If I become king, all this old carelessness will be forgotten.
> KING: You're wrong about that, too. To this day I have to go about picking up old bits of carelessness of my own. However, if you don't want to obey me as my son, you'll obey me as a subordinate.
> ERIK: The crown prince isn't a subject.
> KING: That's why I said subordinate; everyone's subordinate to the king.
> ERIK: Am I to obey blindly?

KING: Yes, as long as you're blind, you'll obey blindly; when your eyes have been opened, you'll obey with your eyes open; but you are going to obey! Just wait until the time comes for you to give orders, and you'll see how much harder that is, and how great the responsibility.

ERIK (*scornfully*): Huh!

KING (*furious*): You fool! Go and wash off the filth, and see to it you get combed; above all, rinse out your mouth so you don't go about smelling up my rooms. Go! Or you may sleep off your binge for eight days in the tower, and, if that's not enough, I'll have your ears cut off so you can never wear a crown! Is that language *you* can understand?

ERIK: The act of succession . . .

KING: I'll draw up as many acts of succession as I want to! Now you know! Enough! Out!

The characterization of Gustav Vasa deepens when he faces Herman Israel, with whom he would like to remain on cordial terms without making any concessions that could make Sweden in any way dependent on Lübeck—now that the financial debt has been paid. What he says and does reveals him as not only a man of action dedicated to one great goal but as a practical realist, a man with a rough sort of charm, and a man with an active conscience. The nuances are many and highly credible. Having searched his conscience and secured all the evidence he needs, he settles the case of the Dalesmen:

Silence! It is I who am talking. You intend to speak of friendship. I am not a friend of my enemies, and I don't even know you, since I've renounced your acquaintance. If I were to let old affection influence my decision, I'd not be an impartial judge; and the man who has brought disfavor upon himself isn't helped by my favor.

But the king who has just sentenced the two Dalesmen to death sinks down and buries his face in his hands.

Act IV, aside from developing the characterization of Crown

Prince Erik and thereby clarifying further the king's problem with his eldest son, presents King Gustav in the humiliating position of having to try to get assistance from Lübeck although he has shortly before rejected an alliance with it; having to face the beggars who remind him of the effects of one of his acts; and being confronted with his godchild Barbro and her mother, the daughter and widow of Måns Nilsson, whom he had sent to death.

In scene 2, the king faces the greatest of his Job-like trials—the spreading and apparently successful rebellion of the southerners under Dacke—and is forced to the humiliation of having the truth about his offenses told him by Master Olof and being given the advice that the only cure is to humble himself, even to the extent of writing to Nils Dacke.

In the final act, King Gustav has been humbled. The southern rebels are approaching the gates of Stockholm, and two thousand Dalesmen whose intentions are unknown are encamped north of the city.

> This is the situation. Dacke answers that he doesn't want to see that rebel, perjurer, and violator of safe-conduct Eriksson. He calls me Eriksson! Dacke's forces have invaded Södermanland—so we have them at our gates! Further! Two thousand Dalesmen are encamped just north of the city, and we don't know what their intentions are, but we can guess! You're a *fine* prophet, Olof!

Convinced that he is no longer the chosen of God, he has prepared for his abdication and for his flight. His Job-like problems are still with him in one way or another as he receives the news that the Dalesmen have come to help him again—in what, as all Swedes know, was the last rebellion of his long reign. It is a chastened miracle man of God who thanks God for his punishment and will march with renewed faith in his mission against the *smålänningar* and the other rebels. Engelbrekt, the Dalesman, says appropriately, as he shakes the king's hand, "That's a hell of a fist! It's hard, but it's clean."

The Gustav Vasa presented by Strindberg is one of the most well-rounded characterizations in modern drama. When you have read the play, you should be very much aware of the king's brilliance; his astuteness; his individualistic and simple religious faith; his capacity for friendship, love, and other human relationships; his insight into people; his grasp of situations; his hot and violent temper; his occasional soft-heartedness; his ability to act swiftly and surely once he is sure in his own mind that he is doing the right thing. Several matters should be particularly noted, for example, his faith in his own exceedingly important mission in life:

> MASTER OLOF: If it were a private matter, yes; but since it concerns the whole country . . .
> KING: I take care of that! I take care of the whole country.

Note, too, that he believes he is one of the chosen:

> You know! How do you know? You believe! I don't believe anything any more, but this: God is angry with me, and I'm only expecting the axe. Fine! I have served and have been given notice. So I'll leave before I'm driven away. Do you know what day this is? No one has thought of it, and it came to me just now. It's midsummer day. My day, which no one celebrates! A generation ago I made my entrance into my capital: that was the greatest moment of my life! I thought the work of liberation was done, and I thanked God. But it wasn't done, and I hadn't arrived at my goal. The Dalesmen rebelled; I defeated them, and I thought I had arrived, but I hadn't. The Dalesmen rebelled twice more; I thanked God and thought I had arrived, but I hadn't. The lords of Västergötland rebelled; I defeated them, and I was happy, because I thought I must have arrived; but I hadn't! And now, Olof: we'll never arrive before we've come to the end. And I'm there now.

Note his feelings of guilt:

> This lies heavy upon me. Herman, old friend, believe me: I never make a decision or pronounce a sentence without having asked the Eternal One, the Almighty, for counsel. When I've fasted, prayed,

and considered, and I've received the answer from above, I strike
cheerfully even if it should cut me to the heart. But . . . you remember Jon of Svärdsjö, Jon, the friend of my youth, who helped me in
my first bout with Christian. He changed his mind, and he raised
the Dalesmen in rebellion against me. He had to go, so he was executed! (*Gets up*) Since then I've had no peace of mind. My own
family look at me as they never did before. My wife, my beloved
Margareta . . . turns away when I want to kiss her pure forehead,
and—can you imagine this? Yesterday, at the dinner table, she sat
watching my hand as if she saw blood on it! I don't regret what I
did, I mustn't, because I was right; by God, I was right! But just
the same—I don't have any peace of mind any more.

It is a humbled man appreciably bereft of his own pride and arrogance and self-adequacy who can finally say in his moment of greatest victory, when his great goal of a united nation and a united
people is about to be realized, "Oh God, Thou hast punished me,
and I thank Thee!"

Since *Erik XIV* was written as a companion play to *Gustav Vasa*
and Strindberg thought of these two and *Master Olof* as the Vasa
trilogy, what Strindberg has to say about Crown Prince Erik in this
second play should be emphasized. From his first appearance it is
evident that Erik is a highly unfortunate human being, an unhappy
and unbalanced person, victim of both hereditary and environmental factors. All the information about him taken together comprises
a sort of case report in dramatic form: his shifting from one mood
to another without warning, his insensitivity to the feelings of
others, his fluctuation between a state of self-justification and a state
of despising himself, the effect on his behavior of whatever company
he is in, his obsession with his own ego. His heredity has been both
good and bad. On the one hand, there is the lack of emotional balance traceable to his mother, and, on the other, there are the tendencies to suspect everyone and his motives and to break out into
uncontrolled anger—both reminiscent of his father. The environmental factors have been even less fortunate—his parents' unhappy

marriage, his father's remarriage, his resentment of his stepmother and his stepbrother John whom his father prefers, and his feeling that no one loves him and that he is always in the way. Strindberg amply illustrates Erik's tremendous need for the affection and understanding which he did not get or which he was rarely willing to receive. Note, too, how effectively Strindberg demonstrates the effects of Erik's falling in love with the beautiful and admirable commoner Karin Månsdotter. Freed from his obsession with his own ego at least for the time being, Erik behaves gently and considerately toward the members of his family whom he has resented. Nevertheless, as Göran Persson says, "It seems to be serious this time. But you'll come back all right!" Göran is right, from Strindberg's point of view; too much damage has been done to Erik's personality; nothing that happens to him can help him to become a balanced and well-adjusted human being.

The Olaus Petri of *Gustav Vasa* is not the fiery young idealist of *Master Olof,* attempting to create a Utopia on earth, but a weary, middle-aged royal servant who no longer believes he has the answers to the fundamental questions of life and who has settled for the role of a loyal and effective servant of the king. Note his reply to Reginald, his son, who represents the world-weariness of a lost generation:

REGINALD: What is life?

MASTER OLOF: I don't know. But I think it's either a punishment or a trial. When I was your age, I thought I knew everything and understood everything. Now I know nothing and understand nothing; so I limit myself to doing my duty and patiently enduring everything.

Note, too, his answer to the king's question:

KING: Who are you?

MASTER OLOF: A humble instrument of God made to serve what is great: the great miracle man of the Lord, to whom it was given to unite Swedish men and Swedish lands into one.

Master Olof is here presented as a brilliant royal servant, a protestant who no longer believes in the niceties of theological distinctions, a man whose marriage (begun idealistically) has become almost a Strindbergian dance of death, and a person who has resigned himself to accepting a life neither evil nor good but a disconcerting and bewildering blend of both.

Aside from the superb characterization of Gustav Vasa and the secondary characters, there are many matters that help make *Gustav Vasa* one of the greatest historical dramas in modern literature. There are, for example, such effectively suggestive details as the tolling of the bells, the beating of the muffled drums, the hammer, and the tipsy behavior of Engelbrekt; the use of intimate domestic scenes (the Vasas and the Petris at home); the use of parallel actions all subordinated to the king's but in appreciable measure related to the king and his problems (the Petris, the Israels, Agda and Jacob, Erik and Karin); the natural and easy introduction of the Job-like misfortunes; the atmosphere of Gustav's own time; the tremendously effective use of the fact that to everyone the king appears as an ever-present giant. Without superfluous scenes and details and with no seams of dramatic composition in evidence, *Gustav Vasa* is probably unsurpassed as a modern historical drama.

Gustav Vasa · A Play in Five Acts

Characters

KING GUSTAV I (*Gustav Vasa*)

CROWN PRINCE ERIK

PRINCE JOHN (*Johan*)

QUEEN MARGARETA LEJONHUVUD

LADY EBBA LEJONHUVUD, *the king's mother-in-law and a nun in Vreta convent*

MASTER OLOF (*Olaus Petri*)

KRISTINA PETRI, *his wife*

REGINALD, *their son*

HERMAN ISRAEL, *councillor of Lübeck*

JACOB ISRAEL, *his son*

MÅNS NILSSON *of Aspeboda,* ANDERS PERSSON *of Rankhyttan,* INGEL HANSSON, *and* NILS *of Söderby, all mine proprietors in Dalarna.*

GÖRAN PERSSON, *Prince Erik's secretary*

MASTER STIG, *priest at Copper Mountain (Falun)*

MÅNS NILSSON'S WIFE

BARBRO, *the Nilssons' daughter*

AGDA, *a servant at an inn*

KARIN MÅNSDOTTER, *a flower girl*

MARCUS *and* DAVID, *clerks at the Hanseatic office*

ENGELBREKT, *now a miner in Dalarna and one of the skiers who caught up with Gustav Vasa on the Norwegian-Swedish border*

MINOR CHARACTERS

Settings

ACT I: *The living room in Måns Nilsson's home at Copper Mountain, Dalarna*

ACT II: *The Hanseatic office; the Blue Dove*

ACT III: *The king's study*

ACT IV: *A square before the Hanseatic office; Olaus Petri's study*

ACT V: *The terrace of Stockholm Palace*

ACT I

The living room in MÅNS NILSSON's *home in Aspeboda near Copper Mountain (now Falun).*[1] *At the back a door; windows on either side, through which can be seen town houses, with their roofs covered with snow, and the flames from the blast furnaces. To the right, an open fireplace with a log fire. Chairs in front of the fire. On the same side between the fireplace and the back, a door.*

In the middle of the floor a long table with benches, and at one end a high seat with cushions and tapestries.

To the left, wall benches.

On the walls above the panel are large simple paintings representing GUSTAV VASA's *adventures in Dalarna; to the left of the door at the back a painting of* GUSTAV I *in Pastor Jon of Svärdsjö's house; to the right, a painting of* GUSTAV I *in* ANDERS PERSSON's *house at Rankhyttan (the threshing).*[2]

A bell in the town can be heard tolling [as the curtain rises].

MÅNS NILSSON *at the table writing. His* WIFE *is placing silver cans, goblets, etc. on the fireplace mantel.*

MÅNS NILSSON: The bell's tolling four, isn't it?

WIFE: Of course.

MÅNS: It sounds like a fire warning.

WIFE: Does that have a special sound?

MÅNS: Yes, it sounds like a plea for help and mercy.

155

WIFE: It has sounded like that since the king took our church bells, I think.

MÅNS: Silence! No talking behind his back! And the king will soon be here himself.

WIFE: Has the king invited himself, since you're preparing to receive him?

MÅNS: Invited himself, no; but he has announced his arrival at the Copper Mountain, so he can't very well pass by his friend Måns Nilsson of Aspeboda. I helped him when he really needed help—against both Master Knut and Chancellor Peder and, what's more, against that man who claimed he was a Sture.[3] Besides, he's our daughter's godfather.

WIFE: That was long ago! When the king's bailiff was here to take the bells two years ago, you were one of those who helped kill him.

MÅNS: That was two years ago, and he was after our heads that time, most likely. But then Christian the Tyrant broke in from Norway.[4] Our king needed help, and, when he asked us Dalesmen for it, we stood by him like one man and helped him. So we're quits.

WIFE: That's what you think, but the king never forgives anyone or anything unless it's to his advantage.

MÅNS: Yes-s. But as long as Christian is at large, he won't dare to break with us.

WIFE: Is Christian really still at large?

MÅNS: As far as I know. Besides, the king owes me so many thousand *dalers* . . . not to mention old friendship . . .

WIFE: God bless you, and preserve you from such a friend, who breaks both his word and his promises.

MÅNS: Don't tear open old wounds! And we should be ready to forgive.

WIFE: If you're ready to forgive but he isn't, there'll be no reconciliation. Watch out for yourself!

MÅNS: That bell really sounds bad!

WIFE: It does to me—it always reminds me of the great bell of St.

Mary that the bailiff stole. Do you remember when it was cast of the finest copper and the whole town brought milk and cream for the clay mold to make it firm—and, when it was to be poured, we threw in half our table silver to improve its tone? And it was christened at Candlemas. It rang for the first time for my father's funeral . . . then Herman Israel of Lübeck got it, and made coins out of it.[5]

MÅNS: All that's true, but it has to be forgotten or we'll never get peace.

(BARBRO *their daughter enters, with a basket of spruce twigs; she is dressed in black and white; behind her are small girls, all of them carrying similar baskets and dressed in the same way as* BARBRO; *they strew the floor with twigs, without saying anything.*)

WIFE (*to* MÅNS): Is there going to be a funeral?

MÅNS: No, we'd have used leaves if it were spring.

WIFE: But at least the children shouldn't be in mourning.

MÅNS: On the contrary! When the king asks the children, "Whom are you mourning?"—what will you answer, Barbro?

BARBRO: "We're mourning our beloved Pastor Jon of Svärdsjö."

WIFE: And if the king asks, "Why?" what will you answer?

BARBRO: "He was King Gösta's friend in his youth and saved his precious life for the fatherland."

MÅNS: What year was that?

BARBRO: "The year Christian the Tyrant beheaded the Swedish lords."

MÅNS: That's right, child. And there you see Master Jon's picture, when he holds the towel for the outlaw thresher who has just come from the barn! (*To his* WIFE) There's no need to tell the children that the king had his friend beheaded two years ago.[6]

WIFE: So you still have that much sense! But do you think the king will like to be reminded of an act that does him no honor?

MÅNS: Like it or not, he's going to hear it! That was an ugly deed!

Jon of Svärdsjö was a saint and a martyr, for he died for his faith, his childhood faith, that he wouldn't give up.

BARBRO (*by the high seat*): Is the king going to sit here, father?

MÅNS: Yes, child, the wonder man of God is to sit there, with his friend Måns Nilsson of Aspeboda. His life's a miracle story of how God led him from Danish captivity up to Dalarna, children; of how after many dangers he finally freed his country from bondage. You can see all of it on these pictures on our walls, all the way to the last one where the skier fetches him at Sälen on the Norwegian border.[7]

BARBRO (*studies the last picture*): Father, did the skier really have the same name as Engelbrekt, the great national leader of a hundred years ago?

MÅNS: Yes, he did, child. Then we called it the finger of God; now they call it superstition.

WIFE: Don't teach the children stuff like that!

MÅNS: Silence! I teach the children only what's good and right. And remember, girls, never to believe or say anything bad about the king, no matter what you hear, for an ungrateful person is the heaviest burden this earth bears. So you are to sing the ballad about King Gösta when he comes. Do you remember it?

BARBRO: Oh, yes!

MÅNS: Let me hear it.

BARBRO (*recites*): *King Gösta rides on his horse so tall*
On the field both back and forth:
I want to thank my Dalesmen all
For your true loyalty.

CHILDREN: *I want to thank my Dalesmen all*
For your true loyalty.

BARBRO: *By my side you have stood*
As faithful Swedish men.
I shall repay that good
If God does grant me life.

CHILDREN: *I shall repay that good*
If God does grant me life.

MÅNS: Fine, children. Go into your room again and be ready when
he comes.

BARBRO AND CHILDREN (*exit to right*): Yes, but if we're frightened by
the king?

MÅNS: He's not dangerous, and he likes children very much. Besides,
he's your godfather, Barbro.

WIFE: Do you know what you're doing?

MÅNS: I hope so, but I know what you mean.

WIFE: What?

MÅNS: I ought to take your advice. I used to, but things went wrong
every time.

WIFE: Try once more!

MÅNS: No!

WIFE: God's will be done, then. (*Pause*)

MÅNS: I've never lived through such a long afternoon. And our
friends don't come.

WIFE: I think I hear them out there.

MÅNS: My word, you're right this time. (*Noise can be heard in the
entry;* ANDERS PERSSON *of Rankhyttan,* NILS *of Söderby,* INGEL
HANSSON, *and* MASTER STIG, *a clergyman, enter.*)

THE FOUR MEN: Good afternoon.

MÅNS (*shaking hands with them*): God's peace, Anders Persson;
God's peace, Nils of Söderby; God's peace, Ingel Hansson; God's
peace, Master Stig. Come in and sit down. (*They sit down at the
long table.*)

ANDERS PERSSON: You're getting ready, I see.

MÅNS: I'm getting ready. Where's the king?

ANDERS: The last skier saw him near the mountain.

MÅNS: That close! Why do you suppose he's here?

ANDERS: Ask Nils of Söderby.

NILS: They say he intends to march into Norway against Christian!

INGEL HANSSON: Some people say he wants to thank us Dalesmen for the good help we gave him in the last campaign.

MASTER STIG: That's not like him.

ANDERS: To say "thank you"? No!

MÅNS: Is there any danger?

NILS: Not as long as Christian is at large!

INGEL: It's strange we should depend on Christian.

STIG: We knew what we had, but not what we were getting! Christian took the heads of the lords and let the people go; this one lets the lords go and puts the people in bondage—who is the tyrant?

MÅNS: Silence!

ANDERS: And we waged our war for liberty *against* our liberator. Did we know what we were doing that time?

INGEL: We were going to rid the kingdom of Danes! Do you remember that the first man in Dalarna who raised his hand for the king against the Danes was Rasmus Jute, a Dane,[8] who killed Nils Västgöte, a Swede? A strange beginning . . .

NILS: A strange beginning, like the end. (*To* MÅNS NILSSON'S WIFE) Watch your silver, Mother Nilsson!

(WIFE *looks questioningly at him.*)

NILS: The king's coming!

MÅNS: Silence for God's sake! Talk like that won't get us peace! Everything you say is right in a way, no doubt, but what has happened has been with the will of Providence . . .

STIG: . . . that let the children get their way so they could see their foolishness.

ANDERS: Måns Nilsson, are you sure the king's coming here?

MÅNS: That's a question!

ANDERS: Remember Jon of Svärdsjö!

MÅNS: That must be forgotten! Everything must be forgotten.

ANDERS: I suspect you and Nils of Söderby would like to forget that two years ago you two burned the royal estate in Hedemora and plundered Rävelstad! [9] He'll never forget it! (*The sound of distant muffled drums can be heard.*)

ALL (*jump up*): What's that?

MÅNS: Don't you know the gadfly buzzes just before it stings?

ANDERS: That's how it sounded on Tuna Heath on Ash Wednesday! [10]

INGEL: Don't talk about that bloodbath, or I'll go mad! (*Beside himself*) Don't talk about it!

NILS: He purrs and purrs like a cat. Don't believe him! (*The beating of drums approaches.*)

STIG: Wouldn't it be wise if you men, his personal friends, went to meet and welcome our stern king?

MÅNS: Really? Maybe he wouldn't come here afterward.

WIFE: Stay, Måns Nilsson! Don't go!

MÅNS: It smells of spruce here, and the drums are muffled as at a funeral. (*Three blows on the door*) Who's there? (*Goes up to the door; opens it*)

WIFE (*to the clergyman as she goes out to the right*): Pray for us!

(MASTER OLOF *and* HERMAN ISRAEL *enter.*)

MÅNS: Who do me the honor?

MASTER OLOF: The king's acting secretary; and the honorable representative of the city of Lübeck.

MÅNS: Come in, gentlemen; and tell us the news.

OLOF: The king's here and has pitched camp on the heath; he, himself, has put up at St. George's Guild Hall.

MÅNS: Why has the king come over Long Heath and Brunn Brook without safe-conduct and permission? [11]

OLOF: He didn't say.

MÅNS: Well, then, I'll go ask him.

OLOF: With your permission: Our gracious lord, the king, has asked us to greet the good miners at the Copper Mountain and ask each one to remain at home in his own house. When he wants to talk to anyone, he'll have him summoned.

MÅNS: What does that mean?

OLOF (*sits down*): I don't know. (*Pause*)

ANDERS: Is the Danish war over yet, master? [12]

OLOF: I don't know.

ANDERS: Do you know whom you're talking to?

OLOF: No.

ANDERS: I'm Anders Persson of Rankhyttan. Do you know that name?

OLOF: Yes. It's a fine name! (HERMAN ISRAEL *scans the silver pieces on the mantel of the fireplace and the wall paintings speculatively; he is wearing glasses with large black horn rims; then he sits down in the high seat.*)

MÅNS (*to* MASTER OLOF, *gesturing toward* ISRAEL): Is the Lübecker a royal person?

OLOF (*softly*): No, he isn't. But he manages the national debt, and we must never forget that our gracious king freed our country from the Danes only with Lübeck's help.

MÅNS: Only with Lübeck's help! Not with the Dalesmen's?

OLOF: Yes, that, too.

MÅNS: Does he speak Swedish?

OLOF: I don't think so, but I don't know him.

MÅNS: Really?

OLOF: He got here just when I did, and I haven't spoken with him.

MÅNS: Strange! I suppose it's the king who sent him?

OLOF: Most likely.

MÅNS: Maybe he's the one who buys bells?

OLOF: Maybe.

MÅNS: And the church silver?

OLOF: And the church silver!

MÅNS: What was his name?

OLOF: Herman Israel.

MÅNS: Israel! (*Whispers to* ANDERS PERSSON, *who whispers to the others. Someone knocks on the door.*)

    (OLOF *rises quickly; opens the door.*)

(*Messenger clad in armor enters; whispers to* MASTER OLOF *and then leaves.*)

OLOF: Our gracious lord, the king, requests that Ingel Hansson meet him in St. George's Guild Hall.

INGEL (*gets up*): Goodness, am I to go first?

NILS: The oldest goes first.

MÅNS (*to* INGEL HANSSON): Don't give in, Ingel, and tell him the truth; the king's a gracious lord who's willing to hear a word at the right time.

INGEL: It'll be all right, for Ingel Hansson has exchanged words with kings before this! (*Goes*)

OLOF (*to* NILS *of Söderby*): Well, Nils of Söderby, how is mining going these days?

NILS: Not bad, thank you. A little water in the mine after the fall flood; otherwise, we can't complain.

OLOF: Good times, then?

NILS: If you want to put it that way. Hm! Good times mean higher taxes, eh?

OLOF: I wouldn't know about taxes. (*Pause*)

OLOF (*to* ANDERS PERSSON): And farming! You're a farmer, too?

ANDERS: Oh, yes. And we have cattle in our pastures, too.

OLOF: A good land, old Dalarna, eh?

MÅNS (*nudging* ANDERS PERSSON *in his side*): Very much so! Everything drips with fat so that we can even eat the bark off our trees.

OLOF: Yes, they've told me that the Dalesmen eat bark now and then and that they chew resin. Is that, so to speak, usual or unusual?

NILS: In time of famine we have to eat what we can get.

OLOF (*to* MASTER STIG, *who has stayed somewhat in the background*): You know this, Master Stig: How was it during the recent famine when the king distributed grain? [13] Did it go to the right people?

STIG: It went to the right people even though there wasn't enough.

OLOF (*to* ANDERS PERSSON): Was there enough?

ANDERS: That depends. What do you mean by enough?

OLOF (*to* MÅNS NILSSON): Måns Nilsson, do you know what enough means?

MÅNS: Good heavens, everyone knows!

OLOF (*to* MASTER STIG): Now that we know what enough means, I ask you, Master Stig Larsson, if anyone starved to death during the recent famine?

STIG: Man does not live on bread alone . . .

OLOF: There you spoke a word of truth, master, but . . . (*Someone knocks on the door.*)

OLOF (*goes to the door, opens it, and receives the messenger who whispers to* OLOF *and goes*): The king requests a meeting with Nils of Söderby in St. George's Guild Hall.

NILS: Isn't Ingel Hansson coming back first?

OLOF: I don't know.

NILS: Oh, well, we're not afraid and . . .

OLOF: What should you be afraid of?

NILS: Nothing! Anders Persson! Måns Nilsson! There's still the Mora bell in the valley of Siljan! [14] It's a fine bell, and, when it tolls, it can be heard 'way into Norway, and fourteen thousand men will stand like one!

OLOF: I don't understand.

NILS (*shakes hands with* ANDERS PERSSON *and* MÅNS): But you two do! God bless you and keep you!

MÅNS: What are you trying to tell us?

ANDERS: What are you thinking of, Nils of Söderby?

NILS: My thoughts are racing so I can't keep up with them, but I can feel that Ingel Hansson is in agony! (*Goes*)

OLOF: Is there always a cloud of sulphur smoke over this town?

MÅNS: Usually with the east wind, master. (MÅNS *and* ANDERS *sit down together in the left corner;* MASTER STIG *is obviously uneasy.*)

OLOF: Which smokes more—the hard or the soft ore?

ANDERS: Why do you ask?

OLOF: That's a poor answer.

MÅNS: May I ask you instead, doctor, if King Christian is still at large?

OLOF (*stares fixedly at him*): Do you place your hope in the enemy? (*Pause*) What sort of man is Nils of Söderby?

MÅNS: His friends say he's the best of men, his enemies the worst.

OLOF: What bell was he talking about?

MÅNS: Well, it's the biggest one in Dalarna.

OLOF: Do you have many like that?

ANDERS: We still have a lot of the kind that calls people together. (MÅNS NILSSON *nudges him.*)

OLOF: I'm glad to hear that, and it will please the king even more. Do people attend church regularly, Master Stig?

STIG: I can't say they do.

OLOF: Are the priests bad, or do they preach anything but the word of God?

STIG: There aren't any bad priests *here,* and only the pure word of God is preached.

OLOF: Of all you've told me, that pleases me most. Only the pure word of God! (*Pause*) Nils of Söderby just hinted that, when the Mora bell rings, fourteen thousand men take the field. That was just foolish boasting, wasn't it?

MÅNS: Huh, if you ring it in the right way, sixteen thousand will show up! Right, Anders Persson?

ANDERS: Sixteen? No, eighteen!

OLOF: Good! Then we'll ring it in the right way the next time the Danes come, for only seven thousand showed up last time— against our country's enemies!

MÅNS (*to* ANDERS PERSSON): He's a dangerous man! Let's keep still!

STIG (*to* MASTER OLOF): Why doesn't Ingel Hansson come back?

OLOF: I don't know.

STIG: Why is the king here? They say he's going to invade Norway. Is that true?

OLOF: I don't know.

STIG: Then I'll go and find out! (*Goes to the door, opens it, but is met by the messenger and soldiers*)

OLOF (*goes up to the messenger, who whispers to him; then* OLOF *says*): Master Stig Larsson is commanded to appear before the king immediately!

STIG: Commanded? Who commands here?

OLOF: The king!

MÅNS (*jumps up*): Treachery!

OLOF: Exactly! Treachery and traitors! Go, at once, master, or you'll have to ride bareback!

STIG: Hell!

OLOF: To Hell! Out! (MÅNS NILSSON *and* ANDERS PERSSON *go toward the door.*)

MÅNS: Do you know who I am? That I'm a yeoman miner and the king's friend?

OLOF: Then sit down and take it easy! If you're the king's friend, there has been a mistake. Sit down, Anders Persson and Måns Nilsson. No harm will befall you or anyone else who is innocent. Let the master go, and don't get excited. Who says violence is involved? Your own bad conscience?

STIG: That's true! We haven't done any wrong, and no one has threatened us. Calm yourselves, good friends. I'll soon be back. (*Goes*)

MÅNS: That's true!

OLOF: When one throws a stick to a pack of dogs . . .

ANDERS (*to* MÅNS): We've been foolish. Take it easy. (*Aloud*) Look, master, one gets suspicious with the years, especially when one has seen promises and words broken time and again . . .

OLOF: I understand. In times like these, when one changes allegiance as a snake changes skins, people tend to be fickle. That is forgivable in young men, but it is unforgivable in old, experienced men.

MÅNS: As far as the king goes, he's in his best years . . .

OLOF: And consequently is forgivable . . .

MÅNS (*to* ANDERS): I think he's the devil himself!

ANDERS (*to* MASTER OLOF): How long are we going to sit here waiting? What are we waiting for?

OLOF: For the king's orders, naturally.

MÅNS: Are we prisoners?

OLOF: Far from it. But it wouldn't be wise to go out for a while yet.
   (MÅNS *and* ANDERS *are uneasy; they change seats frequently.*)

MÅNS: Something bad's happening! I can feel it!

ANDERS: It must be hot in here—I'm sweating! Wouldn't you have a
   glass of beer, master?

OLOF: No, thank you very much.

ANDERS: Or a glass of wine?

OLOF: Thank you, no, not I.

MÅNS: But it's genuine Rhenish?
   (OLOF *declines by shaking his head. Beating of drums outside*)

ANDERS (*beside himself*): For God's sake, won't there ever be an end
   to this?

OLOF (*rises*): Yes, it's over now! (*Goes to the door, opens it; the
   messenger throws on the table three bloody coats belonging to*
   INGEL HANSSON, NILS *of Söderby, and* MASTER STIG.) See!

MÅNS AND ANDERS: A bloodbath again!

MÅNS: And without investigation or trial!

OLOF: Two years ago we both investigated and sat in judgment, but
   to let mercy take precedence over justice and to find out if they
   were serious in their repentance the king let the traitors go. When
   he learned through spies that they were incorrigible and went on
   with their rebellious talk, he decided to execute the sentence. You
   see, that's how the matter looks when it's presented accurately.

MÅNS: But there *was* a rumor that all would be forgiven and forgotten . . .

OLOF: Forgotten, provided the offenses were not repeated, but, in
   as much as they were repeated, they were not forgotten, merely
   concealed. That is as clear as logic. (*To* HERMAN ISRAEL) Councillor Herman Israel, these two trustworthy men . . . you are trustworthy, aren't you?

MÅNS AND ANDERS: We hope so!

OLOF: Answer yes or no! Are you trustworthy?

MÅNS AND ANDERS: Yes!

OLOF (*to* ISRAEL): Councillor, these two trustworthy men have in your presence as witness given a true account of conditions in Dalarna. They have agreed in their testimony that mining is yielding good profits; that farming and cattle raising are flourishing; that famine is rare; and that in the recent famine the king distributed grain that got into the proper hands and was at least not insufficient. These trustworthy and honest yeomen miners have also testified that there still are bells in all the churches and that no bad priests preach human notions but that only the pure word of God is preached here. Moreover, you have perceived, councillor, that Dalarna can mobilize between sixteen and eighteen thousand competent men—the figures vary with the rise and fall of their manly courage! So, since you are in charge of the national debt and have been empowered to investigate the condition of the province, you have heard from the people's own lips that all the Dalesmen's complaints are unjustified, and that those who have spread talk to the contrary are liars and traitors!

MÅNS: I deny that!

ANDERS: I object!

OLOF: If you deny your own words, you're doubly liars!

MÅNS (*to* ANDERS PERSSON): He's strangling us! Better keep still!

ANDERS (*to* MASTER OLOF): No, I want to speak! I want to know what fate is in store for us!

OLOF: I'll tell you. Your fate is in your own hands; you're invited to come to Stockholm on safe-conduct; and you're to go alone. As old faithful friends of the king, to whom he acknowledges a debt of gratitude.

MÅNS: New treachery!

OLOF: No treachery! Here's the letter of safe-conduct signed by the king himself.

ANDERS: We know his letters!

MÅNS (*to* ANDERS): Agree; give in, until we get time to think it over.
Master Olof, may we go into the next room and talk it over,
the two of us?

OLOF: Go wherever you want to except to the king—now!

(MÅNS *and* ANDERS *go to the left and open the door to the next room.*)

MÅNS: We'll give you an answer in a little while.

OLOF: When and as you wish. (*The two exit to the left.*)

OLOF (*to* HERMAN ISRAEL): A stiff-necked people, faithful as gold and
suspicious through and through!

ISRAEL: A very good people!

OLOF: But a little naïve. Did you see how I trapped them?

ISRAEL: A nice piece of work. Where did you learn that?

OLOF: Through long association with many people I've discovered
that the original sin, the mother of all vices, is pride. When I want
to get the truth out of criminals, I fool them into boasting.

ISRAEL: Wise, very wise, and you're not an old man, either. But there
are modest people, too. How do you get the truth out of them?

OLOF: Modest people boast with their modesty, so it amounts to the
same thing.

ISRAEL (*stares at him*): Excuse me, your name is Master Olof, isn't
it? Surely you're not Olaus Petri?

OLOF: Yes.

ISRAEL (*amazed*): The one who carried out the reformation of the
church?

OLOF: Yes.

ISRAEL: And who was later involved in a case of high treason, suspected of knowledge of plots against the king's life?

OLOF: Confidences I received in confession under the vow of silence
and which I consequently didn't have the right to reveal.

ISRAEL (*continues to observe* MASTER OLOF *with curiosity*): Hm, hm!
(*Pause*) That was a rather mysterious affair, wasn't it?

OLOF: Oh, not so very mysterious. Gorius Holst and Hans Bökman
were found guilty; and the mystery wasn't so great but the people

in Hamburg were talking about the assassination of the king as an accomplished fact before the conspiracy was discovered in Stockholm! [15]

ISRAEL: That's what I call mysterious, especially since we didn't know anything about it in Lübeck.

OLOF: I admit that's mysterious, for the road to Hamburg goes through Lübeck.

(ISRAEL *remains silent.*)

OLOF: At the same time there was a rumor that Marcus Meyer and Jürgen Wollenweber weren't ignorant of the plot.

ISRAEL: I've never heard that. And I don't believe it. (*Pause, then points at the coats*) Are those things to stay there?

OLOF: For the time being, yes.

ISRAEL: Royal visits are rather bloody up here.

OLOF: I don't permit myself to judge my king's acts, both because I'm not equal to the task and because I know that above him he has a Judge, who guides his destiny.

ISRAEL: That's beautifully put—and thought. Have you always been so wise?

OLOF: No. One often becomes what one hasn't been. (*Pause*)

ISRAEL: I wonder if they're thinking of flight in there?

OLOF: That possibility was foreseen. Just as their conference had been taken into account. Do you know what they're talking about?

ISRAEL: No, indeed.

OLOF: Well, they still think Christian the Tyrant is at large and they intend to get help from him.

ISRAEL: What a stupid idea!

OLOF: All the more since Christian's a prisoner!

ISRAEL: It sounds crazy, but when I hear how the good Dalesmen are loyal to the king I'm not amazed that they can think only of the oath that binds them to their only legal *lord* . . .

OLOF: I'm amazed . . .

ISRAEL: Dear me! I'm only looking at it from *their* point of view.

OLOF: It's dangerous to look at anything from a traitor's point of view! (*Pause*)

BARBRO (*appears in the door to the right, accompanied by the children*): Is father here? (*Looks about; sees* HERMAN ISRAEL *in the high seat*) Heavens, it's the king! (*Kneels; the other children also kneel*)

ISRAEL: No, dear children, I'm not the king. I'm only a poor merchant from Lübeck.

OLOF: Lovely! Lovely! (*To the children*) This is the famous and mighty councillor Herman Israel, who along with Cord König and Nils Bröms [16] saved your king from Danish captivity and provided him with the means to carry on our war for freedom. You'll find his portrait up in the main hall of St. George's Guild, where Gustav Vasa is being presented to the councillors of Lübeck. Honor to him who honor deserves! Hail the friend of Sweden and of your king!

(BARBRO *and the children applaud.*)

ISRAEL (*rises, visibly moved*): My dear little friends . . . No, I can only thank you . . . I don't deserve your applause, for a merchant gives only to be paid, and I have been richly paid.

OLOF: Don't believe him, but remember there are services that can never be paid for, and fine acts that can never be blotted out, neither by ingratitude nor by forgetfulness! . . . So go back to your room. Father will be here soon.

(BARBRO *and the other children exit to the right.*)

HERMAN: Master Olof! I hadn't expected this of you!

OLOF: I understand. Don't force us to be ungrateful, however! It's a heavy burden to be ungrateful!

ISRAEL: Well, there'll be no problem about that! No danger of that!

MÅNS (*he and* ANDERS *enter from the left*): Well, after talking it over, we've decided on this: to go to Stockholm on the king's promise of safe-conduct so we can talk at leisure with him and the lords of the realm.

OLOF: Then my mission has been accomplished. So: Welcome to

the capital of the kingdom, Måns Nilsson and Anders Persson!
(OLOF *and* ISRAEL *leave.*)

MÅNS: Thank you, master. (*Waits until they have gone; then he
picks up the bloody coats on the table*) Here are our banners of
blood! King Christian will supply the poles, and then . . . to
Stockholm!

ANDERS: *Against* Stockholm!

OLOF (*re-enters*): I forgot to tell you one thing. Are you listening?

ANDERS (*angrily*): Yes!

OLOF: King Christian has been caught and has been imprisoned in
Sönderborg Castle on the island of Als.[17]

(MÅNS *and* ANDERS *are struck by the news; and say nothing.*)

OLOF: Do you understand? Sönderborg Castle on the island of Als!

CURTAIN

ACT II

SCENE I

In HERMAN ISRAEL's *headquarters. A large room; the walls are
lined with cupboards. A door at the back; doors to the right and
the left. Only a few small windows. A fireplace to the left. In the
middle of the room a large table with armchairs. Lübeck's coat of
arms in black, red, and silver above the door and the fireplace.*

*To the right, a desk with writing utensils and a scale. Shelves
with parcels of merchandise here and there.*

*A cupboard door is open; gold and silver church vessels can be
seen in the cupboard.*

MARCUS *is by the desk weighing items;* DAVID *records their
weights.*

MARCUS: A silver crucifix, gilded; twelve ounces.

DAVID (*writes*): Twelve ounces.

MARCUS: Item: a monstrance of gold . . . a big fellow! Weighs . . . let me see . . . I see . . . it's hollow . . . and has lead in the base . . . put down a question mark.

DAVID: A question mark it is.

MARCUS: A paten of silver . . . Who the hell can tell? (*Bites into the vessel*) Tastes like copper at least . . . Put: a rather good white metal.

DAVID: Rather good white metal! Do you think the farmers are cheating us?

MARCUS: Us? No one can cheat us!

DAVID: Don't say that. Nigels Bröms, the goldsmith, insists a lot of Dutch swindlers are traveling through the country selling faulty church vessels, obviously meant to be traded for genuine goods.

MARCUS: We'll have to make up that loss through the bells. According to old tradition they contain a lot of silver.

DAVID: The bells, yes. They should go to Lübeck, but they go to the royal foundries to be made into field guns and howitzers.

MARCUS: That's what they say. The Dalesmen should know about that, and they'd come dancing down over Long Heath.

DAVID: Oh, I guess they're through dancing after the latest fall slaughter.

MARCUS: No, they won't be through as long as the two worst rascals are at large . . .

DAVID: You mean Måns Nilsson of Aspeboda and Anders Persson of Rankhyttan, who are here in town doing some speculating while they're waiting for an audience with the king?

MARCUS: Yes, they're the ones.

DAVID: "Rascals" is pretty strong, and our boss Israel thinks a lot of them, apparently.

MARCUS: Listen, David; don't forget a Lübecker's first and last duty: silence! Think of all the talkative young bookkeepers who have disappeared through water gates and cellar openings! Just think about that!

DAVID: I'll try, though it seems time for the Hanseatic League itself to think about the great silence. (*Pause*)

MARCUS: Do you know where the boss is?

DAVID: Most likely with the king making an inventory of the treasures in Eskil's chamber.[18]

JACOB ISRAEL (*enters; he is* HERMAN ISRAEL'S *young son, richly clad, with a tennis racket in his hand; a bandage on his forehead*): Is father in?

MARCUS: No, Mr. Jacob; he's up at the king's, I think.

JACOB: Then I'll sit down for a while. Go on with your work. I won't disturb you. (*Sits down by the big table*)

PRINCE ERIK (*enters; is somewhat older than* JACOB): Why did you leave me, Jacob?

JACOB: I was tired of playing.

PRINCE ERIK: I don't think that was why; someone insulted you, someone who's no friend of mine.

JACOB: No, Your Highness, no one hurt my feelings; but I have a feeling I shouldn't be seen at court.

PRINCE ERIK: Jacob, my friend, why have you quit calling me—your old schoolmate—Erik? Why do you look at me so strangely? . . . Give me your hand. No? Alone, deserted since mother died, hated by my stepmother, my father and my half-brother, I beg for the friendship you once had for me and now have taken back!

JACOB: No, Erik, I'm not taking it back, but we mayn't be friends. That we were friends as youngsters because of the same kind of suffering, our fathers have overlooked and put up with, but, now that you're about to marry a foreign princess and become a duke, they have state reasons for separating us.

PRINCE: Your words sound affected as if you wanted to conceal your thoughts, but you can't conceal your feelings . . .

JACOB: Excuse me, Erik, but this conversation ought to be carried on somewhere else . . .

PRINCE: You mean because this is a business place. As if that could be humiliating for either of us. It doesn't matter to me, though I do find the seller less prejudiced than the buyer!

(JACOB *indicates with a gesture the presence of the bookkeepers.*)

PRINCE: Oh, let them listen! Marcus and I are old friends—we ran into each other at the Blue Dove last night.

JACOB: Shame! Why does Your Highness go to such places?

PRINCE: Where should I go? I haven't anyone to talk to at home; besides, I think people are just as good or bad no matter where I go. I do prefer so-called bad company, though. Do you know Jon Andersson? [19]

JACOB (*embarrassed*): No, I've never heard of him. Who is he?

(MARCUS *and* DAVID *go out silently to the left.*)

PRINCE: He's a *smålänning* who has some very sound ideas. Do you still need that bandage on your forehead?

JACOB: Do you think I'm wearing it as a decoration? Or as a memento of the mob?

PRINCE: Don't be bitter toward our good people just because one rascal happened to misbehave.

JACOB: I'm not, and I know very well what a foreigner can expect in an enemy country. If you come to Lübeck, you'll see how they throw stones at a Swede!

PRINCE: You're just like Göran Persson. Do you know him?

JACOB: No.

PRINCE: He looks at things in the same way.

JACOB: What do you mean?

PRINCE: He thinks that everyone's right and that everything that happens is right! There's something sound and enlightened in his philosophy of life; that's why my father hates him . . .

JACOB: You shouldn't speak ill of your father; it sounds bad. Forgive me!

PRINCE: But when he behaves badly, shouldn't I have the right to say so? Besides, I hate him!

JACOB: Don't say that! Don't say that! Your royal father's so infinitely great that you can't grasp his greatness . . .

PRINCE: It only looks like that, I know. Can you imagine: last night he came up to me and put his arm about my shoulders—for the first time in my life—and as I'd always thought that I came only to his hips, I was amazed that I was as tall as he. But when I looked at him again from a distance, he grew and became a giant!

JACOB: He is! And he looks like one of Michelangelo's prophets . . . Isaiah, I think! [20] And, in truth, God the infinite One is with him.

PRINCE: Do *you* believe in God?

JACOB: For shame! You ought to be ashamed of yourself!

PRINCE: Well-ll, what should a person believe in times like these, when the king and the clergy persecute believers and desecrate everything that has been considered holy? Yet pretend to be defenders of the faith!

JACOB: Let's talk about something else.

PRINCE: That's what the king always says when I insist on an answer; so I hate him still more! As he hates me! Did you know your father was the one who got my mother from Lauenburg for him? [21]

JACOB: No, I didn't.

PRINCE: Yes, but that marriage went wrong; you see, they hated each other thoroughly—and—(*gets up, excited*)—one day I saw him lift his cane against her—(*shouts*)—against my mother; and he struck her! After that day I was never young again—and I'll never forgive him—never!

JACOB (*gets up; puts his arms about* PRINCE ERIK): Erik, look at me! I have a stepmother, too. She torments me when I'm at home . . . but I mustn't talk of it . . . If it can comfort you that I have it worse, much worse than you, listen to me! But remember, too, that such things do come to an end. When we grow up, we're free . . .

PRINCE: And you don't hate her?

JACOB: That feeling doesn't belong with the one that fills my soul now.

PRINCE: You mean you're in love?

JACOB: We could call it that . . . And, when your time comes, you'll find your hate turn to love or disappear.

PRINCE: *That* I want to see! But maybe you're right. The lovelessness in which I was born and brought up has become a fire that is consuming me; my blood was poisoned at birth, and I don't think there's any antidote. Why are you deserting me?

JACOB: Because . . . because we may not be friends, can't be friends.

PRINCE: Do you think I'm too worthless?

JACOB: No! I can't say any more. Let's not see each other again. I'll always follow your destiny with sympathy, for you were born to misfortune.

PRINCE: Why should you say what I've so often thought? But you know, I'm born to be in the way, too; I'm in the way of father's wish to see John as king. I'm in the way of father's wish to forget the hated German woman; my German blood's in the way of the purely Swedish. I don't have it: while I'm a Vasa, I'm Saxony and Lauenburg and Brunswick as well. I'm so little Swedish that I rejoice when the free city of Lübeck imposes penal taxes on my country—and keeps it humiliated.

JACOB (*stares fixedly at him*): Do you really mean that, or are you just being polite?

PRINCE (*reaches for his sword; then calms himself*): You see how much I like you when I let you ask a question like that? Yes, my friend, my mother taught me to talk in German, and I said my evening prayers in German, the beautiful old "Heil Dir Maria Mutter Gottes" . . . yes, that was when . . . when . . . (*Weeps*) The deuce! I think I'm crying! Jacob, come to the Blue Dove tonight . . . There'll be Rhenish wine and gay girls! Göran will be there; you ought to know him.

JACOB (*coldly, calculatingly*): I . . . will . . . come!

PRINCE: Thanks, Jacob. (*Gets up*) This place really looks like a pawn shop.

JACOB (*sharply*): That's what I tried to tell you.

PRINCE: So we agree on that, at least! Tonight, then! Do you know Agda?

JACOB (*curtly*): No!

PRINCE (*haughtily gives him two fingers by way of farewell, which* JACOB *pretends not to notice*): Good-bye. Where did the little pawnbrokers go?

(JACOB *says nothing.*)

PRINCE (*arrogantly*): Good-bye, Baruch! [22] . . . Have you read the book of Baruch? (*Goes toward the back; taps the church vessels in passing*)

To the sound of gold when the game is played
And the wine sparkles and the drunken eyes glitter,
Every path leads to the girl of joy—
When darkness hides the short hours of night!

Good, isn't it?—I wrote it myself! (*Goes out through the door at the back*)

HERMAN ISRAEL (*enters from the right*): Are you alone?

JACOB: Yes, father.

ISRAEL: But I heard a voice.

JACOB: That was the crown prince.

ISRAEL: What did he want?

JACOB: I don't think that fellow has the slightest idea of what he wants.

ISRAEL: Is he a friend of yours?

JACOB: Yes, father, he says he's my friend, but I'm not his. When he thinks he honors me with his friendship, he flatters himself by believing he has mine.

ISRAEL: You're shockingly wise, son, for one so young.

JACOB: No. It's part of the art of living not to be the friend of one's enemy.

ISRAEL: Can he be used?

JACOB: Perhaps to run errands if one keeps him in healthy ignorance of what it's all about. Aside from that I've hardly seen a more useless crown prince.

ISRAEL: Do you hate him?

JACOB: No, I feel too sorry for him—he's more unfortunate perhaps than he deserves to be. That he'll come to a bad end can be taken for granted; he knows that himself—so well that he seems to want to hasten the catastrophe.

ISRAEL: Listen, son; I've known for a long time that I can't keep any secrets from you; so I had better be the one to tell you everything. Sit down and listen to me while I walk. I think only when I walk.

JACOB: Speak out, father. I'm always thinking.

ISRAEL: You've noticed something big is secretly in the making . . . no doubt you know Lübeck is fighting for its rights in the North; I say rights because we are the pioneers who have blazed trails up here—commercial trails, in this case—and we have the right to demand returns and profits from the work we have invested in this country. We have taught these people to use their products and to trade them with others profitably; and we have freed Sweden! Now they want to toss us aside when they've made use of us. Use us—and toss us aside! But there's a bigger and more powerful interest than business that forces the North to ally itself with the Hanseatic cities. The emperor and the pope are as one; the free cities won their independence from the emperor first and then from the pope, and now when this country—with *our* help and that of its great king—has done the same, we have to be allies against the common enemy whether we want to or not. We have stood by each other until recently, but an evil spirit has seized Vasa, and, whether it's pride or weariness that has deceived him, he wants to follow a new course that will ruin all of us.

JACOB: Wait a bit—all of us? Say *"us Lübeckers,"* for the Swedes would gain by taking that course.[23]

ISRAEL: Are you on their side?

JACOB: No, I'm not, but I can see where their advantage lies. And, father, avoid conflict with Vasa, for the hand of the Lord is guiding him—don't you understand that?

ISRAEL: To think I was so foolish as to confide in a mere youngster!

JACOB: It certainly can't hurt to have your plans examined critically in time from someone else's point of view, and you know you can depend on me. So go ahead.

ISRAEL: No, I can't say any more.

JACOB: The pen won't write since the point's broken! If you won't be angry, *I* will tell you more!

MARCUS (*enters*): The man you were expecting has come, sir.

JACOB: He's Jon Andersson, I suspect.

ISRAEL (*gestures to* MARCUS *to go*): Let him wait. (*To* JACOB *after* MARCUS *has gone*) Do you know him, too?

JACOB: No, I've never seen him, but I can figure out who he is.

ISRAEL (*amazed*): You—can—figure?

JACOB: I add one thing to another!—Now that the Dalesmen have been crushed, one has to start with the people of Småland.

ISRAEL: The people of Småland?

JACOB: Yes. Jon Andersson is from Småland, I understand; but his name certainly isn't Jon Andersson, it's—(*softly*)—Nils Dacke! [24]

ISRAEL: Are you spying?

JACOB: No, I listen, watch, and add!

ISRAEL: You missed the mark this time!

JACOB: There! You've told me there are two people, and that Dacke's the invisible one who'll appear when the war breaks out.

ISRAEL: You frighten me!

JACOB: No, father, I don't dare to do any wrong. When I do, I suffer.

ISRAEL: Do you think I'd do wrong?

JACOB: Yes, for you're exactly like Prince Erik—you don't believe in anything. [25]

ISRAEL: I'm to hear this from my own child?

JACOB: You may hear it from others, later on.

MARCUS (*enters*): Two Dalesmen request an audience.

ISRAEL: Let them wait.

(MARCUS *goes.*)

JACOB: This will cost them their heads!

ISRAEL: Who do you think they are?

JACOB: Anders Persson of Rankhyttan and Måns Nilsson of Aspeboda, who've tried in vain to get an audience with the king. Now
in foolish anger they turn to you to get revenge.

ISRAEL: You know that, too?

JACOB: Without meaning any disrespect, father—how can you at
your age believe that there are any secrets?

ISRAEL: Time has passed me by; I don't know where I am.

JACOB: That's right. And I think you've miscalculated the consequences of what you're doing.

ISRAEL: Time will tell. Go now, for even if you know what I'm doing you mustn't be involved in it.

JACOB: I'll obey, but you must listen to me.

ISRAEL: No, you're going to listen to me! Go to Marcus and tell him
I'm expecting the visitors in the great hall; stay here with David,
and have everything of value packed in boxes, ready to be sent
south.

JACOB: Father!

ISRAEL: Silence!

JACOB: Just one word: don't rely on me if you do anything wrong.

ISRAEL: Take my word for this. In this house I have the power over
life and death. Every traitor will be judged and executed, whether
he's my son or not. My country first, then my family! But first
and last, my duty! (*Puts his hand on his sword*) Now: go!

CURTAIN

Scene 2

*A room at the Blue Dove Tavern. High paneled walls with jugs
and flagons on the panels. Benches fixed to the walls and supplied
with cushions and tapestries. At the back a corner tower with
flowers and bird cages on it. Bracket lamps holding candles on
silver plates on the walls; candelabras on the table. Fruit bowls,
wine flagons, beakers, and glasses; dice and cards, a lute.*

It is night. PRINCE ERIK *and* GÖRAN PERSSON *are sitting at the table, pale and exhausted, but are not drinking any more.*

PRINCE ERIK: You want to go home to sleep, Göran; I prefer to
dream when I'm awake. Going to bed is like going to death—for
me; to be shrouded in linen sheets and to stretch out in an oblong
bed as if in a coffin; and then there's the nuisance of having to
wash one's own corpse and to say the burial prayer, too.

GÖRAN: So you're afraid of death, Prince Erik?

PRINCE: Yes, as children are afraid of going to bed, and I'll probably
cry as they do. If I only knew what death is.

GÖRAN: Some people say it's a sleep, others that it's an awakening,
but no one really knows anything about it.

PRINCE: How can a person know anything about the next life when
he doesn't know anything about this one?

GÖRAN: Yes, what is this life?

PRINCE: It seems to me it's a madhouse. Just think of my very wise,
healthy, sensible father! Doesn't he behave like a madman? He
frees the country from the foreigners and then he beheads the
liberators; he frees the country from the foreigners and then
brings in foreigners and places them, Peutinger and Norman,[26]
above all the lords of the realm and the members of the government. He's crazy! He was going to free the church from human

contrivances. And then he imposes new ones on pain of death! This hero of liberty is the greatest tyrant that lives; this tyrant is the greatest liberator that lives! Can you imagine? He wanted to forbid my coming here tonight, and, when I went anyway, he threw his Hungarian hammer at me as the god Thor throws his at the trolls. He barely missed killing me—just as they say—maybe you haven't heard—he killed my mother!

GÖRAN (*becomes attentive*): No, good heavens, I've never heard that!

PRINCE: Yes! And I can understand that; there's something great about it! To feel that one is above human prejudice, to kill the person who's in one's way, and to go forward by trampling the rest underfoot. You know, sometimes when he comes, in his large felt hat and blue cloak, carrying his boar's spear like a walking stick, I think it's the god Odin himself. When he's furious in the attic, people say they feel it all the way to the cellar just as when it thunders. But I'm not afraid of him, that's why he hates me, but he respects me at the same time!

(GÖRAN *smiles skeptically*.)

PRINCE: You smile! (*Laughs*) Because you don't respect anything! Not even yourself!

GÖRAN: That least of all!

PRINCE: Are you really such a beast?

GÖRAN: Since everyone says I am, I must be!

PRINCE (*resuming his former thought*): And . . . this thought pursues me . . . I think he resembles the god Odin, I said. The Odin who returns and lays waste the temples of the Christians as once they plundered his . . . You should have seen them weighing and counting the church treasures at Herman Israel's yesterday; it was terrible . . . And, you know, he's lucky in everything; if he's sailing, the wind's good; if he's hunting, the game appears; if he's fishing, he gets fish; if he gambles, he wins. They say he was born with a caul—

GÖRAN: He's an extremely unusual man.

PRINCE: You don't know young Jacob, Herman Israel's son—he

promised to come here tonight. He's a little old for his age, but has pretty sound ideas about this and that, and I admire him for various qualities, most likely because I don't have them.

GÖRAN: Oh.

PRINCE: Besides, he's probably as terrible a rascal as his father.

GÖRAN: Then I'll be happy to meet him.

PRINCE: Because he's a rascal? (*Laughs*)

GÖRAN: In spite of that!

AGDA (*enters from the left*): Did you call me, Your Highness?

PRINCE: No, but you're always welcome. Sit down here.

AGDA: That's too great an honor for me.

PRINCE: Yes, it is.

AGDA: So I'll go before I lose—that honor.

PRINCE: Mosquito! Do you bite?

AGDA: No, Your Highness misunderstood. I have enough sense and am too insignificant to dare to offend great lords like you, Your Highness.

PRINCE: Good! Very good! Let's talk some more.

AGDA: If Your Highness commands, I'll have to talk, but . . .

PRINCE: Give me your love. I've begged for it for a long time.

AGDA: I can't give what I don't have.

PRINCE: Ah, ha!

AGDA: I've no love for Your Highness, so I can't give you any.

PRINCE: *Diantre!* Let me enjoy your favor, then!

AGDA: One doesn't give that away; one sells it.

PRINCE: Listen to her. It's as if Jacob the wise himself were philosophizing! (*To* GÖRAN) Have you ever heard the like?

GÖRAN: Ah, all wenches learn that from their lovers.

PRINCE: Don't say that. This girl has won my heart.

GÖRAN: But somebody else has won hers.

PRINCE: How do you know?

GÖRAN: Why, you can hear it, even if it doesn't show.

PRINCE: Do you believe in love?

GÖRAN: I believe it exists, but not that it lasts.

PRINCE: How can one win a woman's love?

GÖRAN: All you need is to be the *right one,* nothing else. But if you aren't, you never can.

PRINCE: That's strange.

GÖRAN: It's one of the great riddles.

PRINCE: Who do you think my rival is?

GÖRAN: A clerk, a jailer, or a rich horse trader.

PRINCE: And I who am not afraid to court the virgin queen, the proud ruler of England! [27]

GÖRAN: That's how it is, anyway.

PRINCE: But maybe Agda's bashful . . . and doesn't dare to believe I'm serious . . .

GÖRAN: I, on the contrary, don't believe you are!

(*Noise outside the door at the back*)

PRINCE JOHN (*enters*): Pardon me, Erik, for forcing my way in here at this late hour, but our gracious father sent me out of affectionate regard for your . . .

PRINCE ERIK: Johnny! Make it short and snappy, or sit down and have a drink! It all amounts to this: the old man wants me to get home to bed. My answer: the crown prince determines his own bedtime.

JOHN: I don't want to deliver that answer, especially since your disobedience in this case can have disagreeable consequences.

ERIK: Won't you sit down and have a drink, duke?

JOHN: Thanks, crown prince, but I don't want to cause my father sorrow.

ERIK: Heavens, how serious that sounds!

JOHN: Yes, it is very serious. Father has great new troubles as there are rumors of unrest in the southern provinces, especially Småland, and, as it's possible the king will have to leave his capital, he counts on the assistance of the crown prince in the administration of the government.

ERIK: Half of that's a lie, of course; and there are so many to attend

to the government, anyway. Go in peace, brother; I'll come when
I come.

JOHN: I've done my duty, and I regret only that I have so little of
your ear; I haven't any bit of your heart. (*Goes*)

ERIK (*to* GÖRAN): Can you make head or tail of that boy?

GÖRAN: No.

PRINCE ERIK: Does he believe in his chancery-style sermons himself?

GÖRAN: That's the worst of it: he does! Ordinary rascals like you and
me, who don't believe in anything, couldn't get words like that
across our lips, and so we don't fool anybody.

PRINCE: You're a beast, Göran!

GÖRAN: Yes!

PRINCE: Isn't there a trace of good in you?

GÖRAN: Not a trace! Besides: what is good? (*Pause*) My mother always said I'd end on the gallows. Do you think one's destiny is
predetermined?

PRINCE: Yes, that's what Master Dionysius [28] says—he's a Calvinist,
and he proves by means of the Bible that election by grace does
not depend on oneself.

GÖRAN: Let it be the gallows, then! That's the grace they've elected
for me!

PRINCE: Just think—Jacob says I'm born to misfortune. Father says
so, too, when he's angry. Where do you think I'll end?

GÖRAN: Wasn't it St. Augustine who first said that the one who's
intended for a penny will never be a *daler*?

PRINCE: Yes, he was the one. But we haven't been drinking so much
we need argue about theology. They've been arguing about that
for a generation so that all the prophets are at loggerheads, and
Luther himself has refuted St. Augustine, but Calvin has refuted
Luther, and Zwingli Calvin, and John of Leyden has refuted the
whole lot so now we know exactly how it is. [29]

GÖRAN: Yes, it's all humbug, and, if it hadn't been for that humbug,
I'd never have been born.

PRINCE: What do you mean?

GÖRAN: You must know my father was a monk, and, when the monasteries were closed, he went off and got married. So I was born of perjury and fornication since my father broke his vow and had illicit intercourse with an impure sheep.

PRINCE: You are a beast, Göran.

GÖRAN: Have I ever denied it?

PRINCE: But there are limits . . .

GÖRAN: Where?

PRINCE: Here and there. The innate sense of what's proper usually suggests—the approximate limits.

GÖRAN: Are you dreaming, dreamer?

PRINCE: Beware! There are limits even in friendship . . .

GÖRAN: No, for mine's limitless!

(JACOB ISRAEL *is brought in by* AGDA, *whose hand he squeezes.*)

PRINCE (*rises*): There's Jacob, at last! You've certainly kept me waiting—I was longing for you just now!

JACOB: Excuse me, Your Highness, but I had depressing thoughts, which I didn't want to bring to a merry company.

PRINCE: We're devilishly merry, Göran and I—this is Göran Persson, my secretary and friend; an extremely enlightened and clever man, and complete beast, besides. You can tell from his ugly looks and false eyes.

GÖRAN: At your service, sir.

PRINCE: Sit down, Jacob, and philosophize with us. I offered you beautiful women, of course, but we have only one here, and she's spoken for.

JACOB (*shocked*): What do you mean—spoken for?

PRINCE: That she has given her heart away, so there's no point in your trying to get at her heart . . .

JACOB: Are you talking about Agda?

PRINCE: Do you know the virtuous Agda? Who declares she doesn't give away her favors but sells them?

AGDA: God in Heaven, I never, never meant that!

JACOB: She can't have meant that!

PRINCE: That's what she said.

JACOB: That must be a lie!

PRINCE (*with his hand on his sword*): Mind your manners!

GÖRAN: This is a tavern brawl in the best form! The words in question were spoken approximately like that, but understood in an unintended sense.

PRINCE (*to* GÖRAN): Rascal, are you against me?

GÖRAN: My friends . . . listen . . .

PRINCE: *For* a slut, *against* your lord?

JACOB: She's not a slut!

AGDA: Thank you, Jacob! Tell them the truth . . .

PRINCE: So, there is something . . . See! (*To* GÖRAN) And you come to the defense of innocence! (*Thrusts with his sword toward* GÖRAN, *who leaps aside*)

GÖRAN: You always try to cut me down when someone else behaves foolishly. Stop, damn it!

PRINCE (*to* JACOB): And there's my rival! (*Laughs*) A fellow like that! *Ventre Saint-Gris!* (*Beside himself, collapses in a chair in a sort of epileptic fit*)

JACOB (*holds* AGDA's *hand*): Your Highness! You honored me once with your friendship, to which I could respond with pity alone; I didn't want to be a hypocrite and asked that you let me go . . .

PRINCE (*rushes up*): Go, go, damn it . . .

JACOB: Yes, I'm going, but you're going to know what there is between me and Agda. It's something you'll never understand, for you understand only hate, and so can never win anyone's love . . .

PRINCE: *Diantre!* I who can have the virgin queen, the proud maid of England, at my feet whenever I want to . . . (*laughs*)

JACOB: King David had five hundred proud maidens, but he sought happiness with his humble servant's only wife . . .[30]

PRINCE: Am I going to hear more of that?

JACOB: A lot more!

PRINCE (*rushes at Jacob*): Die, then!

    (*Guards enter at the back.*)

COMMANDER (*an old, white-bearded man*): Prince Erik! Your sword, if you please!

PRINCE: What's that?

COMMANDER (*hands him a parchment*): From the king! You're under arrest, Prince Erik!

PRINCE: Go to hell, old Stenbock! [31]

COMMANDER: That was not a fitting princely answer to a king's command!

PRINCE: Blab away!

COMMANDER (*goes up to* PRINCE ERIK *and seizes his sword; the guards surround him and lead the prince out*): Out with him! To the tower! That's order number one. And then number two. Secretary Persson! (*To the guards*) Put handcuffs on him! And take him to the green vault! Tomorrow at cock's crow: ten double lashes!

(*Guards put handcuffs on* GÖRAN PERSSON.)

GÖRAN: Am *I* to get the whipping because *he* didn't want to go to bed?

PRINCE: Do you dare to lay hands on your crown prince? God's death!

COMMANDER: God still lives—and the king! March! (*To* AGDA) And the tavern's to be closed. Remember that. No questions and no answers. (*Follows the guards, who have taken* PRINCE ERIK *and* GÖRAN PERSSON *out*)

JACOB: Always this giant hand, which one never sees, only feels. Just now it was thrust forth from the clouds to take hold of our insignificant destiny, Agda. The national liberator has descended in the darkness of the night and freed you, dear little bird. Will you fly away with me?

AGDA: Yes, far away, and with you.

JACOB: But where?

AGDA: The world is wide.

JACOB: Come, then!

CURTAIN

ACT III

The KING's *study. Large windows consisting of painted panes at the back; some of the windows are open. No door at the back. Outside can be seen trees green with the foliage of spring; above the trees, the masts of ships with flags flying and the spires of towers. Benches attached to the walls and covered with many-colored pillows under the windows. To the right a large open fireplace richly decorated and with the national coat of arms above it; on the same side a door leading to the waiting room. To the left a throne chair with a canopy; in front of the chair a long oak table; on it a green cloth, a folio Bible, writing utensils, candlesticks, a steel hammer, etc. On the same side farther away a door opening into other rooms.*

On the floor, fur rugs and carpets.

On the walls paintings of scenes from the Old Testament; the most striking depicts "God visiting Abraham in the grove of Mamre." The Abraham closely resembles the KING.

An Arabian pottery decanter with a silver beaker on a cupboard table.

By the door to the right hangs a large, long, blue cape and a very large black slouch hat; next to them stands a short wild-boar spear.

The KING *is standing in deep thought by an open window in the middle of the sunlight; he is dressed in a black Spanish costume lined in yellow, which shows in the slits and seams; his cape has a sable border. His hair is blond, and his giant beard, which extends down over his chest, is somewhat lighter.*

QUEEN MARGARETA *enters from the left; she is dressed in yellow trimmed with black.*

KING (*kissing her forehead*): Good morning, my rose.

QUEEN: A glorious morning!

KING: The first spring day after a long, long winter.

QUEEN: Are you gracious today, my king?

KING: The king's grace doesn't depend on the weather and the wind.
—But go ahead.—Is it about Erik?

QUEEN: Yes.

KING: Fine. He'll have my favor when he has sobered up in the
tower. And Göran Persson, too?

QUEEN: Yes.

KING: He, on the contrary, won't have my favor until he reforms.

QUEEN: But . . .

KING: That fellow's corrupt through and through; he'll ruin Erik
completely. I can't do anything about the causes of his wickedness,
whatever they are, but I have to prevent the effects. Do you have
still more protégés of the same kind?

QUEEN: I won't say anything more.

KING: Then we'll talk about something else.—How's my mother-in-
law?

QUEEN: You already know.

KING: And John?—Where is John?

QUEEN: He's about.

KING: I wish he were nearer, nearer to me, so near that he could succeed me when the time comes.[32]

QUEEN: It isn't right to think like that, still less to say it since Providence has chosen Prince Erik.

KING: Yes, I don't know if vanity fooled me into looking for a foreign princess that time or if wisdom made me stay away from
the homes of the Swedish lords, I can't say.—Who ever knows
what he's doing?

QUEEN: True.

KING: But becoming brother-in-law of the Danish king[33] through
that marriage benefited the country. We got peace as a result, so
no one can complain.

QUEEN: The country first!

KING: First and last . . . the country! So we'll arrange for Erik's marriage.

QUEEN: Do you really think he has any chance of marrying the English queen?

KING: I don't know; we'll have to find out—but without risking our national honor. It's not impossible—we've had an English princess on our throne before.

QUEEN: Who?

KING: You don't know? That Queen Philippa was the daughter of Henry IV? [34]

QUEEN: I didn't know.

KING: Then you don't know either that you're descended from the Folkungs or that you're a descendant of Valdemar the Victorious, too?

QUEEN: Oh, no! I thought the bloody saga of the Folkungs was over!

KING: Let's hope so! At any rate your ancestress, Princess Jutta,[35] was the daughter of Erik Plowpenny and had a son with her brother-in-law King Valdemar, the son of Earl Birger . . .

QUEEN: Why do you tell me such horrible stories?

KING: I thought it might amuse you to know you have royal blood while I have yeomen's blood! You're too modest, Margareta, and I want to see you raised so high that Erik, that fool, will respect you.

QUEEN: To have been born in sin must make a person modest.

KING: Well, that's that. Was there anything else?

　　(QUEEN *hesitant*)

KING: You mean Anders Persson and Måns Nilsson? You may not talk about them.

　　(QUEEN *falls to her knees.*)

KING: No, get up! Well, then, I'll go! (*Exits to the left*)

　　(PRINCE ERIK *enters from the right; besotted, uncombed, pale.*
　　QUEEN *rises, frightened.*)

ERIK: Did I frighten you?

QUEEN: No!

ERIK: Well, I can leave. I was just looking for a glass of water. (*Goes to the water decanter, fills a beaker and empties it; then another, etc.*)

QUEEN: Are you ill?

ERIK: No, just a little parched.

QUEEN: What's that?

ERIK: Dry, a bit dry, then. The more wine one drinks, the drier one's throat gets; the wetter, the drier. That's crazy—like everything else!

QUEEN: Why do you hate me?

ERIK (*cynically*): Surely I mayn't love you! (*Keeps on drinking*) One may not love his stepmother, but one should love her. That's crazy, too!

QUEEN: Why do you say stepmother?

ERIK: That *is* the word, isn't it? Right? Right! So it isn't crazy!

QUEEN: You have a tongue like a serpent . . .

ERIK: And a mind, too!

QUEEN: But no heart!

ERIK: What would I do with it? Throw it to the women to befoul? . . . Besides, my heart's lying in a coffin down in a cathedral vault with my mother. I was only four years old when it happened, but it happened all the same, and they say she had a hole in her head from Thor's hammer, but I didn't see that. At the funeral when I asked to see my mother for the last time, they had already fastened the lid. And there lies my only heart—I never got any other . . . Besides, what do you have to do with my vitals? As little as with my feelings. But watch out for my mind! I understand your thoughts before you've had time to put them painfully into words; I understand you'd like to see the crown on that red devil's still redder hair, whom you call son, and whom you want to force me to call brother. He insists he has a far greater ancestry than I and that he's the descendant of Danish kings! If that's so, he has fine ancestors: Erik Plowpenny was beheaded; Abel, who murdered his own brother, was beaten to death; Christopher was poisoned; Erik Glipping was butchered like a pig—I don't have fine ancestors like them! But, if he should take after them, I'd better keep an eye on my dear brother!

QUEEN: You all talk only about blood and poison today. I don't know how the sun could rise this beautiful morning.

ERIK: That sun's false; don't have any faith in it. Blood will flow before evening. Erik and Abel were the two fine ancestors. Not Cain and Abel! And it was Abel who killed Cain—I mean Erik— that time! Good omens in that ancestry—Erik was killed! Poor Erik!

(QUEEN *sighs deeply.*)

ERIK: But you shouldn't believe in superstitions, for I came into this vale of tears with my fist filled with blood!

QUEEN: Now you do frighten me!

ERIK (*laughs*): Göran wouldn't believe that. That I could frighten anyone, I mean.

QUEEN: Whose blood is to be shed today?

ERIK: I wouldn't know, but they say the Dalesmen are to lose their heads today.

QUEEN: Can't that be prevented?

ERIK: If it has been decided, it can't be prevented but will come like the thunder after lightning! Besides, what's wrong with that? Heads fall here like ripe apples.

(KING *has entered, reading a document.* QUEEN *goes up to him imploringly.*)

KING (*eagerly*): Margareta, if you have confidence in me, stop trying to judge in this matter of state. I have investigated it for two years, and I haven't quite made up my mind yet. How then can you understand it? Won't you join the children? I want to say a word to Erik.

(QUEEN *goes.*)

KING: If you could see yourself, Erik, you'd despise yourself.

ERIK: I do.

KING: That's merely boasting, for, if you despised yourself as you are, you'd change.

ERIK: I can't make myself over.

KING: Have you tried?

ERIK: I have tried.

KING: Then it's your bad companions that ruin your good intentions.

ERIK: Göran isn't worse than others, but he has the merit of seeing that he isn't any better.

KING: Do you consider that you'll be king some day?

ERIK: If I become king, all this old carelessness will be forgotten.

KING: You're wrong about that, too. To this day I have to go about picking up old bits of carelessness of my own. However, if you don't want to obey me as my son, you'll obey me as a subordinate.

ERIK: The crown prince isn't a subject.

KING: That's why I said subordinate; everyone's subordinate to the king.

ERIK: Am I to obey blindly?

KING: Yes, as long as you're blind, you'll obey blindly; when your eyes have been opened, you'll obey with your eyes open; but you are going to obey! Just wait until the time comes for you to give orders, and you'll see how much harder that is, and how great the responsibility.

ERIK (*scornfully*): Huh!

KING (*furious*): You fool! Go and wash off the filth, and see to it you get combed; above all, rinse out your mouth so you don't go about smelling up my rooms. Go! Or you may sleep off your binge for eight days in the tower, and, if that's not enough, I'll have your ears cut off so you can never wear a crown! Is that language *you* can understand?

ERIK: The act of succession [36] . . .

KING: I'll draw up as many acts of succession as I want to! Now you know! Enough! Out!

(ERIK *exits.*)

COURTIER (*enters from the right*): Herman Israel, councillor of Lü-beck.

KING: Let him come.

(ISRAEL *enters*.)

KING (*comes up to* ISRAEL, *takes his hand, then puts his arm about his shoulder and they walk upstage*): Good day, Herman, old friend, and welcome. Sit down, sit down. (*The* KING *sits down on the throne chair;* HERMAN ISRAEL *sits down directly opposite him*.) You come from Dalarna?

ISRAEL: Directly from Dalarna.

KING: I was there, too, as you know, and straightened up a little after the Dalecarlian thief and the feud about the bells, and you stayed on. Well, you kept your eyes on Master Olaus Petri! What sort of man is he nowadays? Can I rely on him?

ISRAEL: Completely! He's not only the most loyal but also the ablest negotiator I've ever seen.

KING: Really, Herman. I'm glad to hear that. Really, Herman. Well, you know about the old trouble between him and me and how it was settled! [37] Yes, yes. It was settled. Yes, it was. That's that! Shall we talk about our affairs?

ISRAEL: Yes. But let's keep our common sense both in word and deed.

KING (*fingers his hammer*): Gladly—you keep it.

ISRAEL (*gestures toward the hammer*): For the sake of old friend-ship, couldn't we put that away?

KING (*laughs shortly*): Gladly, if you're afraid of it, Herman. Be-gin. But make it brief!

ISRAEL: Then I'll begin at the end. The national debt to Lübeck has been paid, and we're about to part.

KING: That sounds as if it were written. Oh, well, then we'll part as friends.

ISRAEL: Rather as allies . . .

KING: Are you at that again, Israel? Well, I want no more depend-ence.

ISRAEL: Listen, Your Grace, or king, or whatever I should say . . .

KING: Say Gösta as you used to when I called you father.

ISRAEL: Well then, my son, many things divide us, many things, but one thing unites us: our mutual and justified opposition to the emperor . . .

KING: Right! And for that reason we can rely on each other without written treaties.

ISRAEL: You forget one thing, my son; I'm a merchant . . .

KING: And I the customer. Haven't you been paid? [38]

ISRAEL: Paid? Yes . . . There are things that aren't paid for with money . . .

KING: It's my duty to speak of the debt of gratitude that I owe you and your free city since the day I came, very young, and deserted —as I thought—by God and—as I knew—by my fellow human beings. Let that gratitude become the friendly feelings I cherish and demonstrate for you. This debt can't be paid with money, still less with treaties. What do you want a treaty for? To bind me and my country during an uncertain future? . . . Don't make me ungrateful, Herman; by my salvation, I have so much that lies heavy upon me anyway. So very much!

ISRAEL: What, my son?

KING: This lies heavy upon me. Herman, old friend, believe me: I never make a decision or pronounce a sentence without having asked the Eternal One, the Almighty, for counsel. When I've fasted, prayed, and considered, and I've received the answer from above, I strike cheerfully even if it should cut me to the heart. But . . . you remember Jon of Svärdsjö,[39] Jon, the friend of my youth, who helped me in my first bout with Christian. He changed his mind, and he raised the Dalesmen in rebellion against me. He had to go, so he was executed! (*Gets up*) Since then I've had no peace of mind. My own family look at me as they never did before. My wife, my beloved Margareta . . . turns away when I want to kiss her pure forehead, and—can you imagine this? Yesterday, at the dinner table, she sat watching my hand as if she saw blood on it! I don't regret what I did, I mustn't, because I was right, by God, I was right! But just the same—I don't have any peace of mind any more.

ISRAEL (*discreetly*): That does honor to your heart, my son, and I must admit I hadn't thought you were that sensitive . . .

KING: No matter. And no boasting! But now I'm back to the same problem. Tell me, Herman, what do you think of Anders Persson and Måns Nilsson?

ISRAEL (*uneasy*): Will my opinion make any difference in your judgment, or have you already made up your mind?

KING: I'm still uncertain—as you ought to understand.

ISRAEL: Then I beg that you'll allow me to say nothing.

KING: Are you my friend?

ISRAEL: To a certain extent, yes. But you can't rely on me, because I'm not independent, and I can't give away what isn't mine.

KING: For shame! How wise you are!

ISRAEL: Go and be likewise!

KING: I'll try. First, give me the receipt for full payment of my country's debt.

ISRAEL: I don't carry it with me; besides, it has to be signed by our council in executive session.

KING (*strikes the table with his hammer*): Herman!

ISRAEL: Couldn't we put that thing away?

KING: I understand you want to lead me where I don't want to go, but you must have some purpose I don't understand. Speak out, old man, or you'll make me furious! You want to fool me into signing something! What is it?

ISRAEL: A treaty of trade and friendship, nothing more. Nothing more.

KING: I'll never sign it, for I know Lübeck's friendship, and its trade. Talk about something else.

ISRAEL: I've nothing else to talk about. Why don't you believe me?

KING: Because you're lying!

ISRAEL: Since you unfortunately enough believe I'm lying, you'll never learn the truth.

KING: Unfortunately! Yes, I'm as unfortunate as a human being can be, for I don't have one friend!

ISRAEL: Gösta, it hurts me to hear you talk like that, and ... it pains me to see human greatness and high station bring you so little true happiness. I'll not speak of gratitude, for that's entirely too vague a concept for us human beings, but I have loved you as a son from the moment your destiny was delivered into my hands by the God of Hosts. I have followed your brilliant career as if it were my own; I have rejoiced over your victories and have grieved over your griefs ... My duty to my own people has often forbidden me to extend a helping hand to you; your own harshness has often come between us; but now when I see you so thoroughly crushed and you have dealt with me with a trust I'd like to call childlike, I'll forget for a moment that I'm your enemy—for as a Lübecker I am your enemy, but as Herman Israel I am your friend—I'll forget I'm a merchant, and—(*pause*)—may I never regret this!—(*pause*)—and—and—do you know Jon Andersson?

KING: No.

ISRAEL: But I do; and I know Anders Persson and Måns Nilsson as well! Yesterday, I received them as visitors, and—tomorrow the southern provinces will rise in rebellion!

KING: So *that* was it! So! Who is Jon Andersson?

ISRAEL: Hard to tell; but behind his face appears another's which seems to be the devil's. Have you heard the name Dacke?

KING: Yes, but as in a dream. Dacke—Dacke! It sounds like a rook's cry! Who is he?

ISRAEL: No one knows. He's invisible; everyone knows him; but no one has seen him. But his name has been seen on a letter, signed by—the emperor.[40]

KING: The emperor!

ISRAEL: The emperor of the Holy Roman Empire!

KING: Fables!

ISRAEL: You don't believe me? Look into it!

KING: I believe you and I thank you. You say Anders Persson and Måns Nilsson have plotted with the rebels—here in my own city? [41]

ISRAEL: Yes, if I can believe my own ears.

KING: My God! My God! Then I'm through with them! Two years of struggle with myself and my conscience, and I'm through with them at last! At last!

COURTIER (*brings in* JACOB ISRAEL): Jacob Israel of Lübeck.

KING: Who dares disturb me?

JACOB (*comes forward; kneels, without observing his father is present*): Great king! A humble youth dares disturb you because it concerns your life!

KING: Speak! Go on! Who are you?

JACOB: Jacob Israel, Your Majesty.

KING (*to* HERMAN ISRAEL): He's your Jacob, isn't he?
      (JACOB *amazed, when he sees his father.*)

ISRAEL: He's my son.

KING (*to* JACOB): What do you want? Quickly, or go!
      (JACOB *silent*)

KING: Who's threatening my life? Jon Andersson or Dacke? I know about that already. Because of your good intention and your youth, but most of all for your father's sake, I forgive you.

ISRAEL: But I don't have the right to forgive him so quickly. You came here to accuse your father. Yes or no?

JACOB: Yes!

ISRAEL: Get out of here, and take my curse with you!

JACOB (*kneeling before his father*): Father, forgive me!

ISRAEL: No, not father any more! Shameless, foolish youngster who believed you understood politics and laws of honor better than the one who gave you life! You hadn't anticipated the possibility I might change my mind.

KING: Oh, Herman, forgive him.

ISRAEL: I have forgiven him, but our sacred laws have not. Jacob, take this ring and go to—you know whom—but say good-bye to me first.

JACOB (*rushes into his father's arms*): Take away the curse, father!
(ISRAEL *wets his finger, makes a sign on* JACOB's *forehead, and mumbles something. Then he kisses him on both cheeks and leads him out to the right.*)

KING (*as* HERMAN ISRAEL *comes back*): What are you up to?

ISRAEL (*deeply moved*): That is a family secret. Now we can proceed.

KING: Or stop! You've given me proof of your irrevocable friendship and I thank you for the last time. Give me your hand.

ISRAEL: But not by way of promises, which I can't keep.

KING: All right, not any promises, then. Farewell and God's peace.

ISRAEL (*moved*): Thank you.

KING: What? You're weeping.

ISRAEL: Perhaps, for I'm just as unhappy as you. I have lost my son.

KING: He'll come back.

ISRAEL (*goes*): Never! Farewell.

KING (*accompanies him to the door*): Farewell, old friend.
(KING's MOTHER-IN-LAW *enters from the left. She is dressed in the garb of the Cistercian nuns.*)

KING (*friendly*): Good morning, mother-in-law.

MOTHER-IN-LAW: Are you busy?

KING: Very busy.

MOTHER-IN-LAW: But not so busy that you can't listen to the just complaints of one of your subjects.

KING: How humble you are. But let me decide if your complaint is justified. There are, God knows, so many unjustified ones.

MOTHER-IN-LAW: If I deign to complain, you can be sure I have reasons for it.

KING: But they must be good reasons; so often we get bad ones. Is it about Anders Persson and Måns Nilsson?

MOTHER-IN-LAW: No, it's about me.

KING: Then you ought to be well informed, at any rate.

MOTHER-IN-LAW: Are there law and justice in this country?

KING: Both law and justice, but also injustice.

MOTHER-IN-LAW: Do you know that your queen's mother—*I*—have been insulted by the mob?

KING: No, I didn't know, but, as I've told you before, I've always expected it.

MOTHER-IN-LAW: You consider it just, then . . .

KING: Then? No, I consider it wrong of you to wear that costume *publicly* since it's forbidden; and it's only out of respect for you and your sex—hm!—that I haven't had it torn off your back long before this!

(MOTHER-IN-LAW *laughs disdainfully.*)

KING: And that I haven't had Vreta cloister,[42] where you've been permitted to stay, torn down was wrong of me, for, according to the law, I should have.

(MOTHER-IN-LAW *laughs disdainfully.*)

KING: Since you used my first concession to let Vreta cloister remain standing, and put me into the difficult situation of looking like a lawbreaker to the people, you should be considerate enough not to appear in that dress on the streets. And, since I've let you come to the capital at your *own* risk, you'll have to take that risk. To show you that there is justice, I'll have the ones who insulted you sought out, for they haven't the right to insult you, not even if you had been the humblest woman in the land. Now that's settled. (*Goes to the door to the right and talks with the courtier who can be seen*) Call four of the guards. Place two by that door —(*points to the left*)—and two by that one. (*Points to the right*)

MOTHER-IN-LAW: I'm to be treated like a thief and murderer by my own kinsman.

KING: You haven't been, but you may be . . . that depends on how you behave.

MOTHER-IN-LAW (*with a threatening look*): This is freedom!

KING: It is freedom—for me—to be free of unreasonable people!

(*Two guards enter.*)

KING (*points to the left door*): Just inside that door. And don't let anyone in; literally, no one. (*As the guards tarry*) And, if anyone comes, no matter who it is, and wants to force his way in, strike 'im down; strike 'im down. (*To his mother-in-law*) I can't force you to leave, but I want to prepare you for this: two executions will take place in this room in a little while.

MOTHER-IN-LAW: Here?

KING: Here! Do you want to watch?

MOTHER-IN-LAW (*going to the left*): I'll go, but you're going to listen to a word first, for your own good . . .

KING: Then I can understand, since it's for *my* good. Go ahead— vomit!

MOTHER-IN-LAW: That Herman Israel, who you think is your friend, is slandering you!

KING: When I *do* anything bad, he has the right to *speak* badly about me! Right?

MOTHER-IN-LAW (*goes, angry*): There's no point in trying to reason with you.

KING: No! Now you know—at last! (*Goes to the door to the right*) Let Master Olaus Petri come in.

(MASTER OLOF *enters.*)

KING: Good day, Olof. I've read your report on the investigation of conditions at Copper Mountain, and I'm pleased with you. Have they arrested Anders Persson and Måns Nilsson?

MASTER OLOF: They were arrested last night.

KING (*goes to the door to the right*): Have Anders Persson and Måns Nilsson brought in immediately. (*To* OLOF) Have you evidence that the prisoners have plotted with Jon Andersson?

MASTER OLOF: Proof and witnesses.

KING: Fine! Tell me something . . . What is your opinion of Herman Israel as a person and especially in his relationship to me?

MASTER OLOF: He seems to me to be a good and faithful friend of

Your Majesty; as a private person he's honorable in every way, noble in his thinking and just in his actions.

KING: I'm glad to hear that just now when I was about to lose my faith in friends. You believe I can rely on him?

MASTER OLOF: Completely.

KING: Have you heard about the unrest in the southern provinces? [43]

MASTER OLOF: Unfortunately, yes.

KING: Rather serious, they say.

MASTER OLOF: So serious that only quick and vigorous intervention can save the country.

KING: Have you heard the emperor's name mentioned in connection with the unrest?

MASTER OLOF: Yes, I have.

KING: Give me a bit of advice, though I don't promise to take it. If you were in my place, what would you do with Anders Persson and Måns Nilsson?

MASTER OLOF: Have them beheaded before the sun has set!

KING: You are severe, Olof.

MASTER OLOF: Why not?

KING: Would you sleep nights, do you think, after such—severity?

MASTER OLOF: Then I'd be able to sleep calmly for the first time . . .

KING: Fine! Have you anything to ask?

MASTER OLOF: Yes, I have; but it's a delicate matter.

KING: Go on.

MASTER OLOF: It's about the queen's mother . . .

KING: The people are complaining?

MASTER OLOF: Yes, the people think that the king, who has harshly imposed a new faith, shouldn't let the law be broken because of private family considerations . . .

KING: It isn't the people but you who say that . . .

MASTER OLOF: Assume that I were free to speak a truth to my king . . .

KING: You're no court fool, I trust, so you have to go about dropping truths! (*Pause*) I'll admit my gracious mother-in-law's lack

of consideration puts me in a false position as far as the followers
of the new faith go. But this isn't the bedroom, and I'll settle
that question behind the curtains. Anything else?

MASTER OLOF: Nothing else; but this question . . .

KING (*violently*): I'll solve it myself!

MASTER OLOF: Can Your Majesty solve it?

KING: It seems to me you ask too many questions!

MASTER OLOF: If it were a private matter, yes; but since it concerns
the whole country . . .

KING: I take care of that! I take care of the whole country; and, if
you insist on knowing, that question was just settled right here.
So your advice comes a little too late, and Vreta cloister will be
closed before you have time to do anything. Don't you understand
I've the right to get angry about your unnecessary and uncalled-
for questions?

MASTER OLOF: I admit it.

KING: I have to put up with you because of my sins, and I'll have to
take your faults with your great merits . . . But this is the end!
Go back to your pulpit and thunder there. Here *I* do the thun-
dering!

(MASTER OLOF *goes out to the right.*)

KING (*in front of the closed door to the right; speaks, softly, with
folded hands*): Oh, eternal God, who directs the destinies of peoples and princes, enlighten my understanding, and strengthen
my will so that I may not pass judgment unjustly! (*He makes
the sign of the cross and mumbles a short prayer; then he opens
the door.*) Bring in the prisoners! (*The door remains open, and
the* KING *goes over to the throne chair and sits down on it.*)

(ANDERS PERSSON *and* MÅNS NILSSON *are brought in; at first they
look about uneasily and then try to approach the* KING's *table.*)

KING: Stop there! (*Pause*) Anders Persson and Måns Nilsson! There
was a time when I called you friends; you know why very well;
that was long ago. My debt of gratitude to you Providence was
gracious enough to let me repay when I pardoned you in terms

of both your life and your property, although you had forfeited both.[44]

Two years have gone since you renounced your allegiance to me and began to wage war against me because of that matter of the bells. As victor, I had the right to behead you, but I let you go, and so my debt to you was paid. Your ingratitude canceled my gratitude, and with that the bill was settled.

Now there's to be a new settlement, but now you're on the list of arrears. To discover your way of thinking I invited you to my capital, and you ought to have suspected I'd keep my eyes on you. But I've had my ears open, too; so I learned you had started plotting again. Do you know Jon Andersson?

ANDERS PERSSON AND MÅNS NILSSON: No!

KING (*rises and goes, furious, toward them*): Do you know Dacke?

ANDERS PERSSON AND MÅNS NILSSON (*kneel*): Mercy!

KING: No! No more mercy! You got it once, but you'll not get it twice!

(ANDERS PERSSON *and* MÅNS NILSSON *try to speak.*)

KING: Silence! It is I who am talking. You intend to speak of friendship. I am not a friend of my enemies, and I don't even know you, since I've renounced your acquaintance. If I were to let old affection influence my decision, I'd not be an impartial judge; and the man who has brought disfavor upon himself isn't helped by my favor. Now enough has been said. (*In the door to the right*) Guards, take the criminals away!

ANDERS PERSSON: And the sentence?

KING: Life, honor, and property!

(MÅNS NILSSON *makes a gesture as if he wanted to shake the* KING's *hand.*)

KING: My hand? No! You can shake hands with the hangman, and you may kiss the hangman's block!

ANDERS PERSSON: One word!

KING: No, not one!

(ANDERS PERSSON *and* MÅNS NILSSON *are taken out.*)

(KING *has turned his back to them and gone up to the throne chair, on which he sinks down and buries his face in his hands.*)

CURTAIN

ACT IV

SCENE I

A square at the foot of Brunkeberg.[45] *In the center a fountain. To the right the house that serves as headquarters of the Hanseatic League—a red brick building with Gothic windows provided with large iron gratings outside and shutters inside. Bolted and barred entrance. Above the entrance the coat of arms and flags of Lübeck.*

To the left a tavern with the sign "The Golden Apple"; benches and tables under verdant trees in front; an arbor with a table and a bench in the foreground.

At the back can be seen Brunkeberg ridge, on which can be seen a great many gallows and wheels (instruments of torture). Outside the Hanseatic House is a bench.

AGDA *and* KARIN *are standing by the well.* AGDA *has a water pitcher, and* KARIN *has a basket filled with flowers and wreaths.*

AGDA: This large red house was St. Clara's cloister a few years ago, but it's the Hanseatic office now.

KARIN: Would they buy flowers in there?

AGDA: I don't think so, but I used to bring flowers when there was an image of the Virgin Mary in the corner. I wish she were still there.

KARIN: What are they up to in there? I've heard a lot of strange stories about them, and they never let anyone in . . .

AGDA: Have you heard that, too? They sell and buy like Lübeckers, I suppose.

KARIN: Of course, but they say that people disappear in there and that they're heathens who sacrifice—

AGDA: Have you heard that, too? It can't be true. Can it?

KARIN: I wouldn't know, of course. But why does that upset you?

(AGDA *does not answer.*)

KARIN: They say you have a friend in there. Do you?

AGDA: Yes—since you already know. But I wonder if he's still there. If I only knew!

KARIN: I'll ring the bell and ask.

AGDA: No, no! You don't know those people.

KARIN: Do you think they'll eat me alive? (*Goes to the entrance and rings; a bell can be heard.*) Listen! It's the old vespers bell! I recognize it. Ding, dong! Ding, dong!

AGDA: Stop! Someone might come!

KARIN: That's the idea, isn't it? But no one's coming. Dear! It's a terrible house! And I certainly won't disturb it.—Agda, you know Prince Erik, don't you?

AGDA: Yes. It's his fault the Blue Dove was closed. I'm working at the Golden Apple over there, now.

KARIN: Was he polite to you?

AGDA: No, he was very impolite. Very vulgar!

KARIN: Then he was drunk; he's usually unhappy, they say.

AGDA: Do you know him?

KARIN: No, I've only seen him, and I'll never forget his sad eyes or his long face—he looks like a doll I once had. I called it my blind Paleface—they're mean to him at home, too, I think.

AGDA: Maybe, but he doesn't have to be a pig just because he's unhappy.

KARIN: Why do you say that? He drinks wine like all young lords . . . and . . . sh-h . . . someone's coming . . .

AGDA: Good-bye, Karin, I have to hurry . . . (*Goes into the tavern to the left*)

KARIN (*exits to the right*): I'll be back.

(PRINCE ERIK *and* GÖRAN PERSSON *enter from the back*.)

ERIK: This is my new tavern . . . come over here into the arbor, quickly.

GÖRAN: And Agda's here, too.

ERIK: So? (*Raps on the table*)

(AGDA *comes out.*)

ERIK (*to* AGDA): Bring Rhenish wine. And then disappear. (*To* GÖRAN) Göran, do you know we're at such a crucial point I'll have to be ready to take a hand? The king has lost his mind and is doing things that can't be defended. Last night he had the Dalesmen executed, and today there's a report his troops have been defeated by the Småland farmers, who've crossed Holaved Forest! [46] So the Dalesmen will revolt, and everything will be lost.

GÖRAN: How does that concern us? Let the whole world perish, and I'll laugh!

ERIK: But the height of his madness is this: when the treasury is empty, he goes in his unbelievable naïveté to the Lübeckers to borrow money from them—from his enemies.

GÖRAN: From whom should one take money if not from his enemies?

ERIK: If I'm not crazy, you'd make me! Be serious for a moment!

GÖRAN (*declaims*): *By the sound of gold when the game is played*
And the wine sparkles, and the drunken eyes glitter,
Every path leads to the girl of joy
When darkness hides the short hours of night.

(AGDA *has come out with wine.*)

ERIK (*laughs foolishly at* GÖRAN PERSSON's *declamation*): That's good! But I made it up myself.—Well, Agda or Magda, where's your pawnbroker today?

(AGDA *silent*)

ERIK: Do you know those Lübeckers in there used to butcher boys to send them to the unspeakable Turks?

AGDA: Is that true?

ERIK: There's probably something to it.

GÖRAN: Let the girl go before she starts crying. I don't like tears.

ERIK: You've never cried, Göran, have you?

GÖRAN: Yes, once, when I was born, and once from fury.

ERIK: You're a beast, Göran!

(AGDA *goes into the tavern.*)

GÖRAN: However! You want to figure out the course of events and on that false reckoning arrive at a conclusion. Haven't you noticed how all our expectations are thwarted? The gods are playing! Sometimes we act wisely, and everything goes to hell; sometimes we do what's really crazy, and everything goes just right. The whole thing's a damned mess!

ERIK: That's what I think, too, but I rather think there's some sort of sense to it.

GÖRAN: I can't discover it. It's just like gambling.

ERIK: Let's gamble, then.

GÖRAN: That's it! Let's gamble! That's it! Now they're going to play for crown or halter to see if Dacke will get the crown and the king the halter! Well, who's that coming?

(KARIN *enters from the right.*)

ERIK (*stares at her*): Who—is—she?

GÖRAN: A flower girl.

ERIK: No—she—is—something else! Don't you see?

GÖRAN: What am I supposed to see?

ERIK: What I see, but you can't, of course.

(KARIN *comes up to them, kneels before* ERIK, *hands him a wreath.*)

ERIK (*rises, takes the wreath, and puts it on* KARIN's *head. To* GÖRAN): See! Now there's a wreath on her crown!

GÖRAN: Crown?

ERIK: Didn't you see it? (*To* KARIN) Rise, my child! You mustn't kneel before me, but I before you! I won't ask you what your name is, for I know who you are, though I've never seen you or heard of you before. What may I do for you? Speak!

KARIN (*simply*): Will Your Grace buy my flowers?

ERIK: Put your flowers there. (*Slips off a ring and gives it to her*) Here you are.

KARIN: No, Your Grace. I can't wear that ring. It's too fine for me, and I couldn't sell it, because then I'd be arrested as a thief.

ERIK: You're just as wise as you're beautiful. (*Gives her money*)

KARIN: Thank you, Your Grace; but that's too much.

ERIK: When you haven't mentioned the price, I'll set it.

(KARIN *exits. Pause*)

ERIK: Didn't you see?

GÖRAN: No, I didn't see anything at all.

ERIK: Didn't you hear? Didn't you hear that voice?

GÖRAN: An ordinary servant girl's voice—a little impertinent.

ERIK: Silence, Göran! I love her!

GÖRAN: Well, she isn't the first one.

ERIK: Yes, the first one. The only one!

GÖRAN: Well, seduce her then.

ERIK (*draws his sword*): Watch out, or, by God!

GÖRAN: Are you up to that again?

ERIK: I don't know what has happened, but from this hour, I despise you; I can't be in the same city as you; your eyes make me unclean, and your whole being smells! So I'll leave you, and I never want to see you again. I'll leave you as if an angel had come to fetch me from the dwellings of the devil; I despise the past as I despise you and myself! (*Goes out the same way* KARIN *did*)

GÖRAN: It seems to be serious this time. But you'll come back all right! (*Raps on the table*)

(AGDA *enters.*)

GÖRAN: Do you know Karin, the flower girl?

AGDA: Yes, I do.

GÖRAN: What sort of girl is she?

AGDA: She's very kind and good. I've never heard anything bad about her.

GÖRAN: Do you think she's at all beautiful?

AGDA: No, but she's rather pretty, and she looks like goodness itself.

GÖRAN: So that's what he saw!

AGDA: Listen, Mr. Secretary, you're really not so bad as people say, are you?

GÖRAN: Child, I'm never angry with anyone, but the whole world has been angry with me ever since I was born.

AGDA: Why don't you always talk like that?

GÖRAN: However: the prince is in love; he's bewitched!

AGDA: Poor fellow!—Tell me, Mr. Secretary, is the prince bright?

GÖRAN: What strange questions you ask! Let me ask you one—hm! —Do you think a woman could ever—hm!—love me?

AGDA: No!

(GÖRAN *hurt*)

AGDA: Yes, if you became a good man.

GÖRAN: How in hell can one become good?

AGDA: Shame!

GÖRAN: When I never see any good, how can I believe in it?

AGDA: Tell me, Mr. Secretary, did the prince mean what he said about the Lübeckers and what they were up to in there?

GÖRAN: No, child, that was only a cruel joke. But whatever they do in there no Swede can do anything about. That much you ought to know if you're anxious about your Jacob.

AGDA: Would you do me a great favor? It won't cost you anything.

GÖRAN: With all my heart, my girl.

AGDA: Find Jacob for me. He was to meet me, but he didn't show up. We've rung the bell, but no one opens the door.

GÖRAN: I don't want to make you sad, Agda, but unfortunately I have reasons for believing the Lübeckers have left because of the new rebellion.

AGDA: And he won't come back?

GÖRAN: I'm not anxious to prophesy, because my prophecies always turn out wrong, but I don't think he'll be back very soon.

AGDA (*falls down*): Lord Jesus!

GÖRAN (*rises and lifts her up*): What's wrong, Agda? Tell me.

(*Softly*) Are you going to have a baby?

AGDA: He promised to marry me!

GÖRAN (*with genuine emotion*): Poor woman!

(AGDA *looks at him.*)

GÖRAN: Always misery . . . when it's a matter of love.

AGDA: You don't despise me?

GÖRAN: I pity you . . . as I pity all of us.

AGDA: You see; there is good!

GÖRAN: Where?

AGDA: In you!

GÖRAN: Bosh! Is there anything else I can do for you?

AGDA: Yes, if you'd write to Lübeck, sir, and ask Jacob . . .

GÖRAN: I don't like love affairs like this, of course, but I'll write in any case, provided, of course, I find out for sure that he's gone.

AGDA (*wants to kiss his hand, but he draws it quickly away from her*): Thank you!

GÖRAN: What are you doing, girl? I'm no bishop, I hope! But hush now. Fine company's coming; so I'm going.

(*The stage has become darker.*)

AGDA: Don't forget me, Mr. Secretary!

GÖRAN: You don't believe me. Well, I'm not much to believe in.

(*Exits to the left*)

(*The* KING *dressed in his blue cape, big slouch hat, and with his wild-boar spear as a staff.* PRINCE JOHN, *simply dressed as if he didn't want to be recognized*)

KING (*looks about*): Do you think they've recognized us?

PRINCE JOHN: No, father, I don't think so.

KING: Ring the doorbell, then.

JOHN (*rings at the Hanseatic entrance*): The bell isn't ringing.

KING: Knock, then!

JOHN (*knocks*): There's no answer!

KING (*sits down on the bench*): I have to see Herman Israel tonight; I have to.

JOHN: You're uneasy, father.

KING: Yes, I'm certainly not calm. (*Pause*)

JOHN: Are you worried about financial matters?

KING: Don't talk about it. Knock once more.

JOHN (*knocks*): No one's there.

(*Several* BEGGARS *enter, kneel before the* KING, *and stretch out their hands.*)

KING: Are you mocking me?

BEGGAR I: Stern knight, we're perishing.

KING: I'm perishing, too. Why are you begging?

BEGGAR II: Well—I'll tell you. The king abolished the tithe for the poor and told us: Beg!

KING: What was he going to use the money for?

BEGGAR I: To support Prince Erik's mis-mistresses . . .

KING: To pay the national debt, rascals! (*To* JOHN) Give them money so they can go.

JOHN (*distributes money*): There, you can divide this, but go. Right away!

(BEGGARS *exit.*)

KING: Who sent them? Someone did. Knock again!

(JOHN *knocks.*)

KING: Humiliation beyond compare! There you see, son, that no one is ever in so high a position that he doesn't have to step down occasionally. But I never dreamt that it would come to this. (*Removes his hat and wipes the perspiration from his forehead*)

JOHN: May I say something?

KING: No, you mayn't, for I know what you want to say.

(*The widow of* MÅNS NILSSON *is led in by her daughter* BARBRO. *Both are dressed in mourning.* BARBRO *has a document in her hand.*)

BARBRO (*to her* MOTHER): There's the councillor himself!

MOTHER: Is that Herman Israel sitting there? Sorrow has weakened my eyes.

BARBRO: It must be.

(MOTHER *and* BARBRO *approach the* KING.)

BARBRO (*to the* KING): Are you the councillor?

KING: What do you want of him?

BARBRO: Lord councillor, we are the late Måns Nilsson's widow and daughter and have come to ask you to recommend our appeal to the king.

KING: What can the councillor do about that?

BARBRO: They say you're the king's only friend; that's why we'd like to have you try to get the property that was unjustly taken from us restored to us.

KING: Unjustly? As a traitor Måns Nilsson was sentenced to lose his life *and* his property. And that was just.

BARBRO: But the innocent widow's dowry should not have been taken.

KING: What is your name?

BARBRO: I was christened Barbro, and the king himself was my godfather. He was up in Dalarna then.

KING (*rises, and then sits down again*): Barbro! Have you ever seen the king?

BARBRO: Not since I was too small to recognize him again. But when he was at the Copper Mountain last time, father expected him to come to our house. We children were going to greet him with a song.

KING: What song was that?

BARBRO: It was a song about King Gösta and the Dalesmen, and it ended like this:

By my side you have stood
As faithful Swedish men.
I shall repay that good
If God does grant me life.

KING: Say something bad about the king!

BARBRO: No! Father said we mustn't, even if we heard others say it!

KING: Did father say that?

BARBRO: Yes.

KING: Go in peace. I'll talk with the king, and you'll get justice, for he wants what is just and does what is just.

BARBRO (*kneels; takes the* KING's *hand and kisses it*): If the king were as kind as you, sir, there would be no suffering.

KING (*puts his hand on* BARBRO's *head*): He is, my child, and he won't deny his goddaughter anything. Go in peace.

(BARBRO *and her* MOTHER *go.*)

KING (*to* JOHN): Who sent them? Who? Here I, the highest of judges, sit on the bench of the accused.

JOHN: May I say one word?

KING: No! I can tell myself everything you have in mind. I can say to myself that the hand of the Lord is resting heavily on me, but why I don't understand. If God speaks through my conscience and my prayers, *He* has persuaded me to act as I have acted. Why my obedience punishes me now, I don't grasp; but I bend before the higher wisdom, which surpasses my understanding. (*Pause*) That was my goddaughter! And her father was my friend, whose head I had to take. Cruel life, that has to be lived in spite of everything. (*Pause*) Knock again!

MARCUS (*dressed for traveling; enters from the right*): Your Majesty! (*Kneeling*)

KING: Still more?

MARCUS: A message from Herman Israel.

KING: Finally. Speak.

MARCUS: Herman Israel had the anchor raised at Älvsnabben [47] this afternoon and has sailed home to Lübeck.

KING (*rises*): Then I'm lost—God help me!

JOHN: And us all! (*They exit.*)

(MARCUS *goes up to the tavern and raps on the table.*)

AGDA (*comes out*): Is it you, Marcus?

MARCUS: Yes, Agda, it's I.

AGDA: Where is Jacob?

MARCUS: He has gone on a journey, a very long journey.

AGDA: Where?

MARCUS: I can't say, but he asked me to greet you and give you this ring.

AGDA: As a memory or as an engagement gift?

MARCUS: Read the inscription.

AGDA (*reads*): I can spell a little. "For ever and ever," it says. What does that mean?

MARCUS: Most likely: Farewell for ever!

AGDA (*cries out*): No! It means he's dead!

(MARCUS *says nothing.*)

AGDA: Who killed him?

MARCUS: The law and his crime. He rebelled against his father and betrayed his country!

AGDA: To save *my* country! What will become of me?

MARCUS (*shrugs his shoulders*): Ta! That's how it is in this world. Nothing but treachery and uncertainty.

AGDA: He was like all the others.

MARCUS: Yes! They're pretty much alike, all human beings. And if they're no worse, they're no better, either. Good-bye.

CURTAIN

SCENE 2

MASTER OLOF's *study. A door to the right, and one to the left.* MASTER OLOF *is sitting writing.*

KRISTINA (*is standing beside him, holding a letter in her hand*): Am I disturbing you?

MASTER OLOF (*calmly, coldly*): Since I'm writing, yes.

KRISTINA: Are you sure you're writing?

MASTER OLOF: Quite sure.

KRISTINA: But your pen hasn't moved for a long time . . .

MASTER OLOF: I was thinking.

KRISTINA: There was a time . . .

MASTER OLOF: Yes, there was a time . . .

KRISTINA: May Reginald [48] come in to say good-bye?

MASTER OLOF: Is it that late already?

KRISTINA: The driver's waiting, and everything's packed.

MASTER OLOF: Let him come, then.

KRISTINA: Are you sure he's going to Wittenberg to study?

MASTER OLOF: You know I've seen too much to be sure of anything.
—If you do have any reason for doubting that his plan for the
trip can be carried out, speak up.

KRISTINA: Even if I did have any doubts, I wouldn't want to bother
you with them.

MASTER OLOF: As charming as ever! Would you ask Reginald to
come in?

KRISTINA: I always obey your orders.

MASTER OLOF: As I never give orders but ask . . .

KRISTINA: If you'd give orders to that son of yours, for once, he'd
probably be a little politer and more obedient to his mother!

MASTER OLOF: Reginald's no doubt difficult, but you're wrong if you
want to bring him up only for your special pleasure.

KRISTINA: Do you side with the children, against the parents?

MASTER OLOF: I believe I always have when it's been a question of
the children's justified demands.

KRISTINA: Justified? Are children justified in demanding anything?

MASTER OLOF: Certainly! Have you forgotten how we . . .

KRISTINA: Yes, I've forgotten all that old nonsense; I've forgotten
how you promised to love me; and all that talk about the pope's
beard, and the theft of silver and the swindle about the bells, and
the *pure* confession, and roasted geese and cackling swans, and
martyrs with *goutte militaire,* and the imitation of Christ with
wine and women, and how they tore each other's eyes out and
the hair off each other, so that there are now twenty-five faiths

instead of one holy universal church. I have forgotten the whole
thing!

MASTER OLOF: You probably did the right thing. Would you call
Reginald?

KRISTINA: Yes. I'll call him. That will be a very real and a very great
pleasure. (*Exits at the left*)

MASTER OLOF (*alone; talking to himself*): She's lucky—to have forgotten the whole thing! I remember it, all too well!

(KRISTINA *enters with* REGINALD.)

REGINALD: Mother has to leave—I can't talk when she's here.

MASTER OLOF: We won't talk very much.

KRISTINA: I won't say a word; I'll only listen, and above all look at
you. (*Sits down*)

REGINALD: No, you mayn't look at us!

MASTER OLOF: Take it easy, my boy. And be polite to your mother.
When you're going away, you never know if you'll come home
again.

REGINALD: So much the better!

MASTER OLOF (*pained*): What's that?

REGINALD: I'm tired of everything! I wish I were dead!

MASTER OLOF: That's how young people talk nowadays.

REGINALD: Why? Because we don't know what we should believe.

MASTER OLOF: Really? Don't you know the articles of faith? Believe
them!

REGINALD: Believe them! Don't you know that it's God who gives
you faith?

MASTER OLOF: Are you a Calvinist?

REGINALD: I don't know what I am! When I talk with Prince John,
he says I'm a Catholic, and when I happen to be with Prince Erik,
he says I'm a Calvinist.[49]

MASTER OLOF: Do you want to go to Wittenberg and acquire your
faith from Martin Luther?

REGINALD: Why, I know his doctrines, but I don't believe in them.

MASTER OLOF: Really?

REGINALD: No, for him faith is everything and deeds nothing. I've been a believer, but my deeds didn't get one whit better, and finally I felt just like a hypocrite.

MASTER OLOF: Is Prince John a Catholic?

REGINALD: He must be since he insists on good deeds, which must be the main thing, anyhow.

MASTER OLOF: And you say Prince Erik's a Calvinist?

REGINALD: In so far as he believes in election by grace. And Göran Persson's a satanist, I think; and young Sture's definitely an Anabaptist . . .

MASTER OLOF: All this is news to me. I thought the time of disunity was over . . .

REGINALD: Disunity, yes! That's what John always says; we had a universal church, and then . . .

MASTER OLOF: Shut up and go to Wittenberg!

REGINALD: Since you want me to, father, but I don't want to study theology any more.

MASTER OLOF: Why not?

REGINALD: I think it's the devil's device to make people each other's enemies!

KRISTINA: Good, Reginald! Good!

MASTER OLOF: I live to hear this in my own house! *Pulchre, bene, recte!* Reginald, who do you think is to blame for this disunity from which you and your generation suffer?

REGINALD: That's obvious!

MASTER OLOF: I see! You mean my generation! But we were children of our time, too, and were robbed of our childhood faith by our prophets. Who's to blame?

REGINALD: No one.

MASTER OLOF: What sort of future do you want?

REGINALD: My future? I see it like a gray mist through which the sun can never shine; and, if a ray of light should ever penetrate it, it would prove to be a will-of-the-wisp that leads people astray.

MASTER OLOF: I thought so, too, once; and at your age I saw my

whole terrible future as in a vision; I foresaw the cup of agony
and the pillory; yet I had to go on, had to enter the mist and
carry *the* will-of-the-wisp which was to lead the wanderers astray.
I even predicted this hour when my son would come to me and
say: Here I am as you have made me. That's why you noticed
I wasn't amazed.

REGINALD: What shall I do? Give me one bit of advice.

MASTER OLOF: You wouldn't take it any more than I did.

REGINALD: Tell me, then: What is life?

MASTER OLOF: I don't know. But I think it's either a punishment or
a trial. When I was your age, I thought I knew everything and
understood everything. Now I know nothing and understand
nothing; so I limit myself to doing my duty and patiently enduring everything.

REGINALD: But I want to know.

MASTER OLOF: You want to know what we're not permitted to
know. Go ahead, try to find out! And go under! However, are
you going or aren't you?

REGINALD: I'm going to Wittenberg to tear down Luther!

MASTER OLOF (*not ironically*): That's the idea! Youth, how glorious
you are, with your regret like Alexander's [50] that there isn't anything more to tear down!

KRISTINA: Aren't you a Lutheran?

MASTER OLOF: I'm a Protestant!

KRISTINA: If you're done, I'd like to say in one word what Luther
is, just one!

MASTER OLOF: Say it, by all means, before you burst!

KRISTINA: Luther is dead! [51]

MASTER OLOF: Dead?

KRISTINA: Yes, that's what my brother-in-law writes from Magde-
burg—in this letter.

MASTER OLOF (*gets up*): Dead! (*To* REGINALD) Poor Alexander, what
will you tear down now?

REGINALD: The universe first, and then myself!

MASTER OLOF (*shoves him gently toward the left door*): Go, then, but begin with yourself. The universe will always remain.

KRISTINA (*has risen, follows* REGINALD): Will there be peace on earth now?

MASTER OLOF: There never will be. Let me have the letter. (*She gives it to him.*)

(KRISTINA *and* REGINALD *exit to the left.*)

(*While* MASTER OLOF *reads the letter, someone knocks very hard on the door to the right.*)

MASTER OLOF: Come in.

(*The knocking is repeated.* MASTER OLOF *goes and opens the door.* KING *enters, wearing his hat and cape, which he promptly removes.*)

MASTER OLOF: The king!

KING (*beside himself*): Yes, it's the king himself! But how long will I be king? Do you know who Dacke is? A hired man who has killed a bailiff, a parish thief, an incendiary, who writes to me and demands an answer! I'm to take my pen and correspond with a bumpkin! Do you know he has crossed Kolmården Forest and has one leg in Västergötland and the other in Östergötland? But who's behind him? The emperor, the Palatinate Count Fredrik, who offers him ennoblement and a coat of arms; the runaway Bishop Magnus Haraldsson; Duke Albrekt of Mecklenburg.[52] But the emperor! Who wants to restore the children of Christian the Tyrant! And what hurts me most: the Lübeckers and Herman Israel! My friend Herman! I'm still asking myself: Is it possible? And who has done this to me? Who? *You* don't say anything!

MASTER OLOF: What shall I say, and what may I say?

KING: Don't be harsh now, Olof, and revengeful. I'm only an unfortunate man who has swallowed humiliations like water, and I come to you as to a pastor. I'm in despair, for I think God has forsaken me forever. What a damnable idea to have the Dalesmen killed now, just now, when I need them. Do you think that

that displeased God? If I sinned as David, you were my Nathan! [53]

MASTER OLOF: I have lost the call to prophesy, and I'm not the man to punish you.

KING: Olof! Comfort me, then!

MASTER OLOF: I can't, because only the penitent receive comfort.

KING: If you mean I have offended, gone too far, speak up! But say it as a servant of the Lord and not as an arrogant schoolmaster. Have I gone too far?

MASTER OLOF: The question shouldn't be put like that, but the question is if the others have any justification.

KING: Put it that way.

MASTER OLOF: Well, then. Dacke represents justified discontent. As Christian II's brother-in-law the emperor is the advocate for Christian's children, who have the right of succession to the Swedish throne, because rebellion does not annul the law. Bishop Magnus Haraldsson is the spokesman for the unjustly exiled bishops.

KING: Unjustly!

MASTER OLOF (raises his voice): Yes! Because the law of Sweden does not exile anyone because of his faith!

KING: Watch out!

MASTER OLOF: Now it's too late. The discontent of the people is justified because the decision of the parliament of Västerås gave the king permission to take only the property of bishops and cloisters, but, when the king took the property of parish churches and private individuals, he committed a crime! [54]

KING: You are a brave man!

MASTER OLOF: I used to be braver! So far as Herman Israel goes, he was here not long ago and offered you a treaty of friendship, but, when the king refused it, he was stupid!

KING: Watch it!

MASTER OLOF: Not yet! The church's gold and silver were to go toward the payment of the debt to Lübeck, and much of it did, but much of it went into Eskil's chambers under the palace, and from there it flowed out to pay, among other things, for Prince Erik's foolish courtships, which . . .

KING: What the hell!

MASTER OLOF: Yes, Queen Elizabeth of England is only making fun of him.

KING: You know that?

MASTER OLOF: Yes, I do! In the same way, the bells were to go toward the payment of the debt to Lübeck, but some of them went to the foundry to be made into cannons, and that wasn't right.

KING: Really!

MASTER OLOF: Add to that: after the order for the closing of the cloisters, Vreta cloister was allowed to remain open, because it pleased the king's mother-in-law to be a Catholic. That was cowardly and bad and has stirred up much bad blood . . .

KING: Vreta will be closed.

MASTER OLOF: Yes, but it should have been closed! And it isn't! If I were to summarize all that's blameworthy in the great king, I'd lack respect.

KING: What's that? That's the worst I've ever heard!

MASTER OLOF: Respect is the consideration the stronger man, even if he is a man chosen by Providence, must have for the feelings of weaker men, when these have sprung from a childlike and therefore pious spirit.

KING: So that's what it is.

MASTER OLOF: Now I have spoken.

KING: Yes, you have spoken!

MASTER OLOF: And if the king had been willing to *listen* once, he would have learned more. But it's the bad habit of princes that they listen only to themselves.

KING: I've never heard the like! I'm amazed, mostly because I haven't killed you.

MASTER OLOF: Why don't you?

(*The* KING *gets up and approaches* MASTER OLOF, *who remains standing calmly, his glance fixed on the* KING. *The* KING *then walks backward and sits down. They observe each other for a couple of seconds silently; then the* KING *speaks.*)

KING: Who are you?

MASTER OLOF: A humble instrument of God made to serve what is great: the great miracle man of the Lord, to whom it was given to unite Swedish men and Swedish lands into one.

KING: That was given to Engelbrekt,[55] too, but he was rewarded with the poleaxe. Is that to be my lot, too?

MASTER OLOF: I don't think so, but that depends on you, my king.

KING: What shall I do?

MASTER OLOF: Exactly what you advised me to do when I was very young and zealous.

KING: And you have to return that advice now?

MASTER OLOF: Why not? I have learned from life, but you have forgotten.

KING: What shall I do?

MASTER OLOF: Answer Dacke's letter!

KING: Never! Should I humble myself for a tramp?

MASTER OLOF: God sometimes makes use of tramps to humble us. Think of it as the ordeal by fire.

KING (*gets up; paces the floor*): I feel that there's truth in what you say, but it doesn't quite penetrate into my mind. Say one word more.

MASTER OLOF: Dacke is right as long as you act wrongly, and God will be with him until you do what is right.

KING: I can't humble myself.

MASTER OLOF: Then someone else will humble you!

KING (*paces back and forth*): You mean the Dalesmen? Have you heard that they've rebelled after the late executions?

MASTER OLOF: So they say.

KING: I am lost!

MASTER OLOF: Write to Dacke!

KING (*weakly*): No.

MASTER OLOF: The emperor writes to him!

KING: That's true. The emperor writes. Why shouldn't I? But it's absolutely unreasonable. Who is this mysterious man who's never seen?

MASTER OLOF: Perhaps a miracle man of God—in his way!

KING: I want to see him. I'll write that he's to come here on safe-conduct so that I may talk with him. Let it be done! Give me paper and pen. Or—you write; I'll dictate.

(MASTER OLOF *sits down at the table.*)

KING: Let's start. What shall I call him?

MASTER OLOF: We'll write simply: "To Nils Dacke."

KING: Is his name Nils? Nicholas? The one who comes the sixth of December with birch sticks for the children? [56] (*Pause*) Write! No, I'll go home and write myself. Have you heard that Luther is dead?

MASTER OLOF: Yes, Your Majesty.

KING: He was a splendid man—may he rest in peace!—he was very good as he was, but it got to be a little too much of Luther!

MASTER OLOF: Too many articles of faith and too little religion!

KING: Yes, he was a stubborn fathead and went too far. He should have had a gadfly like you to take him down a peg or two now and then!

MASTER OLOF: May the time of disunity be over now!

KING: Disunity! Yes! Good-bye, Olof! (*When* OLOF *makes a facial gesture as if he wanted to speak*) I *will* write!

CURTAIN

ACT V

*The terrace of the royal palace. Clipped hedges. Statues; a foun-
tain. Chairs, sofas, tables.*

*At the back a balustrade of Tuscan columns with flowers in
jars of faïence. Below tops of trees. Above and beyond them the
tops of masts with blue-and-yellow flags, etc. Farthest away the
spires of church towers.*

The KING'S MOTHER-IN-LAW *in Cistercian garb.*

QUEEN (*enters*): Mother, for the last time, I beg you not to wear that
dress.

MOTHER-IN-LAW: It's my festival dress, and I'm just as proud of it
as you are of your scarlet mantle.

QUEEN: Don't be proud; the day of misfortune is upon us—we have
to stand united.

MOTHER-IN-LAW: Yes, let's do that, and keep peace.

QUEEN: That's what you say, but you don't want to change even
your dress for the sake of peace in our country.

MOTHER-IN-LAW: I don't change faith as you change a coat, and this
dress represents a promise to God. The people threaten my life—
let them take it. I'm wearing my shroud.

QUEEN: We may have to flee today, if the news is as bad as yesterday's.

MOTHER-IN-LAW: I won't flee!

QUEEN: But the king has already had everything packed, and the
yacht is ready to sail by the southern heights.

MOTHER-IN-LAW: I haven't anything to pack, for I own nothing.—
"Be faithful unto death, and the crown of life shall be yours!"

That's what I taught you once, but you sold your birthright for a crown, which you won't have much longer.

QUEEN: That's right; punish me; that comforts me—a little.

(PRINCE ERIK *has entered; he looks neat and docile.*)

MOTHER-IN-LAW: Do you know what has happened to Erik these last few days? He looks gentle, and his face isn't so hard.

QUEEN: I don't know, but he has changed his ways, they say, and can't stand Göran's company. There's a rumor he has fallen in love . . .

MOTHER-IN-LAW: Oh, no!

QUEEN (*to* PRINCE ERIK): What news do you bring?

ERIK (*gently and respectfully*): No news, mother.

QUEEN (*to her* MOTHER): He called me mother. (*To* PRINCE ERIK) How are you, Erik? Is life difficult?

ERIK: More difficult than the day before yesterday.

QUEEN: Why, what happened yesterday?

ERIK: What happens to a person only once in his lifetime. Do you understand?

QUEEN (*to her* MOTHER): How childlike he has become! (*To* PRINCE ERIK) Have you heard anything from your friend Jacob?

ERIK: Yes, he was really my friend; that's why they cut off his head.

QUEEN: That's unjust! They certainly won't behead Göran . . .

ERIK: He isn't my friend any more! (*Furiously*) But I don't want to be questioned any more, least of all about my secrets—the secrets of my heart, I mean!

QUEEN (*to her* MOTHER): Why, he's really lovable in his childishness. He'd be happy to tell his secret!

(PRINCE JOHN *enters.*)

ERIK (*approaches him*): John, soon we brothers probably won't have much to quarrel about; and . . . it seems to me we ought to be friends.

JOHN: Gladly, Erik. Nothing has ever been dearer to me.

ERIK: Give me your hand.

(JOHN *gives him his hand.*)

ERIK: I don't want to be the enemy of anyone in the whole world any more. (*Goes out; agitated*)

MOTHER-IN-LAW (*to* PRINCE JOHN): What has happened to Erik?

JOHN: He has a sweetheart, they say.

QUEEN: Wasn't I right?

MOTHER-IN-LAW (*to* PRINCE JOHN): You're coming with me to mass down in the chapel, aren't you, John?

(JOHN *hesitates*.)

QUEEN (*sharply*): John!

JOHN: Mother!

MOTHER-IN-LAW: Doesn't he have freedom of conscience?

QUEEN: Leave his conscience in freedom, and he'll have freedom!

MOTHER-IN-LAW: I'll go! John knows where! (*Goes*)

QUEEN: John!

JOHN: What?

QUEEN: Don't give up your childhood faith!

JOHN: My childhood faith, which I learned from my nurse, and not from you, was the faith of my father when he was young! Why didn't you teach me yours?

QUEEN: Punish me! You're right! Everything comes back! I was young, life was a game for me; the king wanted me beside him at festivals and entertainments, and your cradle stood alone, unguarded. That was in the heady days of victory and good fortune. And now! John, go where you can worship, and pray for your mother.

JOHN: If it would trouble you, mother, I won't.

QUEEN: Pray for all of us. (*Softly*) For I don't know the new prayers and I may not utter the old ones.—Hush! The king is coming!

(JOHN *goes through the same exit as the* MOTHER-IN-LAW.)

(MASTER OLOF *and the* KING—*with a letter in his hand—enter*.)

KING (*to the* QUEEN): Have everything ready for our departure.— We are lost!

QUEEN: God's will be done!

KING: It seems to be done. Go, my dear, and set your house in order.

(QUEEN *goes.*)

KING (*to* MASTER OLOF): This is the situation. Dacke answers that he doesn't want to see that rebel, perjurer, and violator of safe-conduct Eriksson. He calls me Eriksson! Dacke's forces have invaded Södermanland—so we have them at our gates! Further! Two thousand Dalesmen are encamped just north of the city, and we don't know what their intentions are, but we can guess! You're a *fine* prophet, Olof!

MASTER OLOF: We haven't seen the outcome yet.

KING: Where did you get your confidence?

MASTER OLOF: I can't put it into words, but I know this will end well.

KING: You know! How do you know? You believe! I don't believe anything any more, but this: God is angry with me, and I'm only expecting the axe. Fine! I have served and have been given notice. So I'll leave before I'm driven away. Do you know what day this is? No one has thought of it, and it came to me just now. It's midsummer day. My day, which no one celebrates! [57] A generation ago I made my entrance into my capital: that was the greatest moment of my life! I thought the work of liberation was done, and I thanked God. But it wasn't done, and I hadn't arrived at my goal. The Dalesmen rebelled; I defeated them, and I thought I had arrived, but I hadn't. The Dalesmen rebelled twice more; I thanked God and thought I had arrived, but I hadn't. The lords of Västergötland rebelled; I defeated them, and I was happy, because I thought I must have arrived; but I hadn't! And now, Olof: we'll never arrive before we've come to the end. And I'm there now.

MASTER OLOF: No, you still have far to go.

KING: Where do you get your fancies? Has a bird been singing, or have you been dreaming?

MASTER OLOF: Neither!

KING (*listens intently*): Do you hear that? They're blowing their birchbark horns! Am I to be crowned with the birch crown . . .

like Peder the Chancellor [58] and Master Knut? Or am I to go to the scaffold like ... like ...

MASTER OLOF: No!

KING: What did you call it? Respect! Wouldn't respect have been fine at Larv's Heath and on Tuna Field! [59] No, I was right, right, right! God help me! Amen!

(MASTER OLOF *remains silent.*)

KING (*listens*): They have drums, too! Everything comes back to one.—Do you think I'll get out of this, Olof?

MASTER OLOF: Yes—and—a last bit of advice. Don't leave.

KING: I can't avoid leaving, I suspect. Do you think I want to let them take my head? Think of it: I can hear them tramping as they march through the city gates. And they're the Dalesmen, my Dalesmen! Life is cruel! Hear it? One two—one two—do you think I'll get out of this?

MASTER OLOF: Yes.

KING: Just think of it: tomorrow at sunrise I'll know my fate. If only I were there! No, now I hear something else. (*A Latin litany is being recited offstage by a woman and a man.*) What is it?

MASTER OLOF (*walks toward the balustrade*): It's the queen's mother reciting the Catholic litany.

KING: There's a man's voice, too.

MASTER OLOF: Prince John!

KING: John! Even this I must take! Won't I have taken enough soon? So everything I have built is to be torn down.

MASTER OLOF: Everything you've torn down shall be rebuilt.

KING: John a Catholic! Erik a Calvinist! Do you remember when we rejoiced with von Hutten: [60] "The spirits are awake, and it is a joy to be alive!" A joy to be alive! (*Laughs bitterly*)—and the spirits awoke with their feet on the pillows! Were you the one who said the gods are playing with us? Silence! I was wrong—they're marching over North Bridge. Can't you hear their heavy steps on the planks of the bridge? Let's flee! (*Puts a parchment on the table*) I'll put my act of abdication here!

MASTER OLOF (*takes the parchment*): I'll take care of this. I'll keep it—as a memento! And now we'll hoist the flag of truce! (*Takes a white cloth from a table and hangs it on a branch of a tree*)

PRINCE ERIK (*enters*): Father!

KING: Croak, you raven!

ERIK: All hope's gone! The yacht has torn loose from the anchor and gone aground!

KING (*rapidly, wildly*): And lightning has struck in the nursery, the grasshoppers have eaten up the crops, and the water's rising . . .

ERIK: The Dalesmen are negotiating with the palace guards and are drunk!

KING (*sits down*): So: come, death!

ERIK (*listens*): I can hear wooden shoes on the garden stairs! (*At the balustrade*)

KING (*counting on his fingers*): Anders Persson, Måns Nilsson, Jon of Svärdsjö!

ERIK (*draws his sword*): Now he's here! (*Follows someone below the balustrade with his eyes*)

KING (*as before*): Ingel Hansson, Master Stig, Nils of Söderby! God is just!

ENGELBREKT (*comes in; merrily drunk, but steady in his movements; looks about somewhat embarrassed but with happy amazement and a broad smile. To* ERIK): Are you the king? (*Puts his hat on the ground and scuffs off his wooden shoes*)

KING (*rises; shoves* ERIK *aside*): No, I am.

ENGELBREKT: Yes-ss-ss! You are!

KING: Who are you?

ENGELBREKT (*slowly*): You don't recognize me!

KING: No!

ENGELBREKT (*draws a dagger with a silver handle from his stocking*): Do you know this, then? (*Smiles broadly*)

KING: I don't understand! What's your name?

ENGELBREKT: Well—(*pause*)—my name's really Engelbrekt!

KING: Eng-el-brekt?

ENGELBREKT: Well, yes, it sounds big, but I don't belong to *that* family! [61]—You see, a long time ago the king—you weren't king then, of course—no, I'm so drunk, so drunk! Well, I was the one who went on skis after you on the Norwegian border, and then you gave me this dagger and said: "If you should ever need me, just come!" Well, I've come, and here I am! It's a shame I'm so drunk!

KING: What do you want now?

ENGELBREKT: What I want? Just like the others, I want to go against Dacke, of course.

KING: *Against* Dack-e?

ENGELBREKT: Where the hell should we otherwise go?

KING (*lifts his hands*): Oh God, Eternal One, Thou hast punished me!

ENGELBREKT: Do we agree? For the others are waiting down there. And want to celebrate a bit in honor of the day.

KING: If we agree? Ask me for something!

ENGELBREKT (*ponders*): May I shake your hand?
    (KING *extends his hand.*)

ENGELBREKT (*looks at the extended hand*): That's a hell of a fist! It's hard, but it's clean. You're a deuce of a fellow, and I was a little afraid when I came!

KING: Are the others just as drunk as you?

ENGELBREKT: Just about! But they can blow all the same! (*Goes to the balustrade, waves, and calls as Dalesmen do when they call the cattle*) Po-alla! Po-Alla! Po! Oj-ola! Oj-ola! Oj!
    (*Below the horns sound and the drums beat out a fanfare.*)
    (KING *goes up to the balustrade; beckons with his hand.*)
    (MOTHER-IN-LAW *enters, wearing her court dress.*)
    (QUEEN *enters; goes up to the* KING, *who takes her in his arms.*)
    (PRINCE JOHN *enters; goes to the balustrade.*)

KING (*lifts his hands*): O God, Thou hast punished me, and I thank Thee!

CURTAIN

Notes on
'Gustav Vasa'

THE CHARACTERS

FOR INFORMATION about the following characters, see the pages indicated: Master Olof (Olaus Petri), p. 123; Kristina Petri, p. 126; Reginald, p. 243; Herman Israel, p. 238; Prince Erik, p. 246; Prince John, p. 331; Göran Persson, p. 329; and Karin Månsdotter, p. 330. See also the genealogical table.

For information about *Gustav Vasa* (*ca.* 1494–1560), see also *The Last of the Knights, The Regent, Earl Birger of Bjälbo* (Seattle: University of Washington Press, 1956) and the notes on *Master Olof.* Professor Andrew A. Stomberg's account of the king's appearance and personality (*A History of Sweden* [New York: Macmillan, 1931], pp. 283–284) deserves to be quoted:

> Gustavus Vasa is described in his mature years as a stately individual of medium size, with keen, penetrating blue eyes, ruddy complexion, flaxen hair, and a long, flowing beard. By nature he was jovial and delighted in the companionship of congenial souls, loved music, in which he was himself quite proficient, and wholesome frolic. People who were associated with him marvelled at his extraordinary memory; he knew the roads over which he had not travelled for thirty years and persons with whom he had once come in contact were decades later recognized by him and called by their right names when he chanced to meet them again. In his acts he was generally actuated by the highest motives of public interest, and keenly felt an overpowering sense of responsibility to God and to the Swedish nation. A quick temper which often got beyond control, a tendency to suspect everyone of evil designs, intolerance and harshness against those who dared to oppose him, and a thriftiness which

often tended upon penury were the main weaknesses in his otherwise sturdy personality. In his private life he set a noble example of rectitude; in the whole list of calumnies that his enemies and traducers cited against him, there was never even a hint of licentiousness or scandal; he was a good husband and a kind, perhaps too indulgent, father.

Queen Margareta (*ca.* 1514–1551), the second queen of Gustav Vasa, was the daughter of the Lord Erik Lejonhuvud who was executed in the Stockholm bloodbath in 1520 (see *The Last of the Knights*). In her girlhood, she and young Svante Sture fell in love and apparently became secretly engaged. When King Gustav asked for her hand, her family saw to it that she became his wife in October, 1536. The happiest of Gustav's three marriages, this union with Margareta gave him love and understanding as well as several children, eight of whom survived both parents—Princes John, Magnus, and Charles (Karl or Carl) and Princesses Katarina, Cecilia, Anna, Sofia, and Elisabeth. Queen Margareta was a beautiful, charming woman who not only won the king's heart and served as his good and competent companion, but also won the hearts of her subjects through her thoughtfulness, kindness, and tact. According to the sources, she was frequently the means of protecting Swedes from the king's anger and resultant punishment. It should be noted that she apparently tried to be a good mother to her stepson, Crown Prince Erik, but did not succeed in her efforts. It should also be emphasized, perhaps, that Queen Margareta's mother, *Lady Ebba Vasa Lejonhuvud,* was one of many Swedes who refused to give up their Catholic faith when Sweden became Lutheran; it was largely because of her that Gustav Vasa allowed Vreta cloister to remain open after he had ordered convents and monasteries closed.

Måns Nilsson of Aspeboda, a mine proprietor in Dalarna, was the wealthy benefactor of Gustav Vasa not only in 1520, when he began the war for independence, but also in 1527–1528 when he actively supported Gustav and again in 1529 when he prevented the Dalesmen from rebelling. In 1531, he became a leader in the revolt because of the confiscation of the church bells, was taken prisoner in 1532, and was executed as a traitor in 1534.

Anders Persson of Rankhyttan, like Måns Nilsson a mine proprietor in Dalarna, had been a schoolmate of Gustav Vasa at Uppsala, was the young leader's faithful supporter in the war for independence, and remained loyal to the king until 1531 when the confiscation of the bells led to open resistance. Anders Persson's imprisonment, stay in Stockholm, and execution in 1534 were apparently parallel to Måns Nilsson's.

Nils of Söderby was the leader of the Dalesmen's armed resistance to the king's attempts at taking the parish bells. He had been in command of the rebels when they had plundered the king's estate at Hedemora and the estate at Rävelstad. He was executed at King Gustav's command in 1533 along with four other yeomen in the presence of the assembled Dalesmen. Like many another rebel, Nils was "crowned" with a birchbark crown at the place of execution. Among the supporters of the rebel leaders were the parish priests or clergymen, including *Master Stig.* According to Afzelius' *Svenska folkets sagohäfder* (*The Legends and History of the Swedish People*) ([Stockholm: Norstedt, 1881], I, 180): "After the investigation was over, the priests received mercy, although they had been the most active in the rebellion and had incited the simpler people against the king."

Ingel Hansson was a native of Dalarna who had been appointed bailiff largely to satisfy the Dalesmen's demand that no outsiders be appointed to official positions in the province. Involved in the rebellion about the bells, Ingel Hansson was, according to SB (III, 222), arrested, taken to Stockholm, and executed at the same time as Måns Nilsson and Anders Persson.

ACT I

1. Mining in Dalarna prospered in the fifteenth and sixteenth centuries so that, by Gustav Vasa's time, the mine-owners and proprietors in Dalarna and the neighboring provinces were among the most well-to-do and influential commoners in the country. The proprietors not only carried on mining but usually owned forest and farming lands as well. The proprietors were among the most influential and active in the war for independence. The Copper Mountain (Kopparberget at what is now Falun) had been mined since the Middle Ages.

2. Gustav Vasa had landed at Kalmar in May, 1520, but, when neither the Swedish forces there nor the commoners of Småland were willing to help him, he turned north to his family estate of Rävsnäs, where

he learned of the bloodbath in which his father and a brother-in-law had lost their lives. Disguised as a laborer—a price had been set on his head —Gustav fled to Dalarna, where his experiences became the source of numerous widely known stories. Among the most prominent Dalesmen who played important parts in these stories were Anders Persson of Rankhyttan, the priest Jon of Svärdsjö, and Måns Nilsson of Aspeboda. By Christmas, 1520, Gustav appealed to the Dalesmen to rise in rebellion, and, when they did not respond favorably, he set out on skis for Norway in an attempt to escape abroad. Shortly after his departure, the Dalesmen, having received confirmation of Christian II's outrageous behavior from other fugitives, sent two of their best skiers after Gustav. They caught up with him at Sälen. On January 1, 1521, he was elected commander of the Swedish rebels at Mora.

3. In 1525, King Gustav, without securing the approval of the pope, had voided the election of the former Sture chancellor Peder Sunnanväder as bishop of Västerås and had deposed Master Knut, the cathedral dean there. Fleeing to nearby Dalarna, these men urged the Dalesmen to rebel. Both prelates were captured and executed later on. The false Sture was the leader of the Dalesmen's rebellion in 1527 who passed himself off as a son of the beloved Sten Sture (see *The Last of the Knights*). The impostor finally fled to Germany and was there, at Gustav's request, beheaded. (Ibsen's *Lady Inger of Östråt* in part concerns the same impostor.)

4. In 1531, Christian II made his last attempt to invade Sweden, but King Gustav and his forces defeated him and forced him to withdraw into Norway. A year later Christian was put into a Danish prison for his lifetime. See note 17.

5. In 1529, Gustav seized the largest bell in every parish church and convent in the country in order to secure the means with which to pay installments of and interest on the debt to Lübeck. Herman Israel, as the representative of Lübeck in Sweden, received the payments. See note 38.

6. See note 2. The priest, Jon of Svärdsjö, who not only had helped Gustav Vasa when he was a fugitive in Dalarna but had been his companion at Uppsala, was executed as a rebel supporter of the false Sture in the presence of the king at Tuna on Ash Wednesday, 1528.

7. The skiers Engelbrekt and Lars of Mora were the messengers

sent to catch up with Gustav Vasa and bring him back to lead the commons against the Danes.

8. Rasmus Jute, a Danish-born resident of Dalarna and an early admirer of young Gustav Vasa, killed Nils Västgöte, a Swede by birth and a sub-bailiff in Danish employ, when he (Rasmus) discovered that Nils intended to seize Gustav and turn him over to the Danes. Thus, a Dane was the first person to come to the armed support of Gustav.

9. The Dalesmen, under the leadership of Nils of Söderby and with the implicit support of Måns Nilsson, plundered the king's estates, according to Fryxell (III, 113).

10. On Ash Wednesday, 1528, King Gustav summoned the yeomen of Dalarna to Tuna Church; when they had assembled, he surrounded them with soldiers and cannons, had one of the members of the council deliver his charges against them for their support of the false Sture and other misdeeds, and then, when they had pointed out the leaders, had several of the latter including Jon of Svärdsjö tried and executed.

11. The Dalesmen insisted on their right to keep Swedish rulers from entering Dalarna without specific permission.

12. This Danish war was the last war with Christian II (1531–1532). See note 17.

13. One of the worst crop failures and resultant famines occurred in 1526. Gustav helped the victims by having grain distributed, as Strindberg says. There are innumerable stories of the eating of bark bread in times of famine. Linné in his eighteenth-century *Dalaresa* (*Linné's Journey to Dalarna* [Stockholm: Hugo Gebers Förlag, 1953], pp. 14 and 176) speaks of the Dalesmen's habit of chewing resin.

14. Lake Siljan, one of the most attractive lakes in all Sweden, has been called "the eye of Dalarna" and the territory about it "the heart of Sweden."

15. See *Master Olof* in this volume, notes 41, 47. Holst and Bökerman (Bökmann) were two of the Germans who conspired to kill King Gustav in the late 1530's; Meyer and Wollenweber (or Wüllenwever) were councillors of Lübeck who tried to improve the position of their city commercially and politically by encouraging dissatisfied people in both Sweden and Denmark to rebel.

16. Both Nils Bröms, burgomaster, and Cord König, councillor of

Lübeck, not only protected Gustav Vasa when he fled from prison in Denmark but also helped him return to Sweden in 1520.

17. In 1532, when Christian the Tyrant came to Copenhagen on safe-conduct, his uncle—Fredrik I—imprisoned him. A. A. Afzelius in *Svenska folkets sagohäfder* (I, 176) says: "He was placed in a hard prison at Sönderborg Castle. In the appalling room, in which the miserable wretch sat, the door was bricked shut, so that the poor food that he grudgingly got had to be shoved in through an opening in the wall. A little deformed dwarf was the only person who was allowed to approach his dark prison. In that way the former ruler of three kingdoms remained for seventeen years. He seems to have had plenty of time in which to shed tears of bitter regret over all the suffering that he had caused innocent people."

ACT II

18. Eskil's chambers, according to SB (III, 295), consisted of four vaulted basement rooms in the palace. By the time of his death, the thrifty and economy-minded king had filled these rooms with silver and other precious articles.

19. Gustav Vasa's efforts to strengthen Sweden economically and otherwise led to dissatisfaction in many parts of the country. When the Småland farmers assisted the farmers of neighboring Skåne (then Danish) in their rebellion against the aristocracy even though King Gustav sent military forces to assist the Danish lords, the king disciplined the *smålänningar* severely. A great many of the latter fled to the woods where they formed outlaw or partisan groups that harassed the Swedish forces and officers. In the late 1530's, Jon Andersson, a Småland yeoman, led the groups in the opposition to King Gustav and his men. Jon Andersson was succeeded as leader by the much abler Nils Dacke. See note 24.

20. Michelangelo Buonarroti (1475–1564), the Italian sculptor, painter, poet, and architect. Isaiah was the Hebrew prophet of the eighth century B.C. who attacked corruption in the national life of the Hebrews.

21. In January, 1531, Herman Israel began negotiations with Duke Magnus of Lauenburg for the marriage of his daughter Princess Katarina to King Gustav. On September 8, the Swedish ships sent to fetch

the royal bride arrived in Stockholm; on September 22 or 24, the wedding was held in the royal palace. Fryxell (III, 116) says: "This marriage began with much joy. But the continuation was quite different. Whimsical, strange Katarina could never win her consort's love. Nor was she able to appreciate his greatness. Mutual coldness and dissatisfaction became the constant rule, and in this unhappy marriage was born— to the misfortune of Sweden—the unhappy Erik XIV." Strindberg probably got the questionable ideas about the king's mistreatment of Katarina from Fryxell (III, 134), who says, among other things: "The great man's misbehavior was converted in his little enemies' eyes into horrible crimes. They spread abroad that he had spoken harshly to Katarina, and at times struck her. They said a page at court, who had listened at a door, had heard the words [of blame and complaint] she spoke to the Danish king and had told them to Gustav. The latter in his violent rage had then beaten and struck her so hard with a hammer that she died as a result."

22. Baruch was the secretary of the prophet Jeremiah (see Jeremiah 36). He may have been the author of the apocryphal book of Baruch.

23. Lübeck, one of the most powerful of the Hanseatic cities, had helped Gustav Vasa win Sweden's independence primarily, no doubt, to protect and, if possible, increase Lübeck's power, commercially and politically. As king of Sweden, Gustav's efforts were directed toward Sweden's political and commercial growth.

24. See note 19. Nils Dacke was the chieftain of the Småland rebellion (1542–1543), perhaps the most dangerous of all the rebellions against Gustav Vasa.

25. See *Erik XIV* in this volume.

26. George Norman (Normann, died 1553) was a German nobleman whom Gustav I had brought to Sweden as Prince Erik's tutor. Conrad von Pyhy (or Peutinger, died *ca.* 1554) was a German adventurer who, along with Norman, became one of Gustav's favorite officials. The two Germans were apparently responsible for having Master Olof and Lars Andersson brought to trial.

27. See note 2, following *Erik XIV*, for a brief account of Erik's courtship of Elizabeth.

28. Dionysius Burreus, a French Calvinist, was Erik's tutor, favorite, and, later, adviser.

29. See *Master Olof*.

30. For the story of David, Uriah, and Bathsheba, see II Samuel 11.

31. Apparently Lord Gustaf Stenbock, King Gustav's friend and the father of his third queen.

ACT III

32. Most of the sources agree that John was King Gustav's favorite son.

33. Princess Dorotea of Saxe-Lauenburg, the sister of Queen Katarina of Sweden, was already married to Crown Prince Christian (later Christian III), the son of King Fredrik I of Denmark.

34. The wise and courageous queen of Erik XIII (union king; king of Sweden, 1396–1439) was Philippa, daughter of Henry IV of England. She is buried at Vadstena cloister. For information about the Folkungs, see Strindberg's *Earl Birger of Bjälbo*. Valdemar the Victorious (1170–1241) was one of Denmark's greatest kings.

35. See Strindberg's *Earl Birger of Bjälbo*. Queen Margareta was a descendant of Princess Jutta's illegitimate son.

36. In 1544, the *riksdag* of Västerås made Sweden a hereditary monarchy, the throne to be inherited according to primogeniture. The country had been an elective monarchy.

37. See *Master Olof* in this volume.

38. Andrew A. Stomberg says in *A History of Sweden*: "These trade privileges . . . were, however, not the only reimbursement that the merchant cities exacted from bankrupt Sweden; a few months after Gustavus's election, their representatives appeared in Stockholm and presented a bill for their aid in the siege of the city. This amounted to 116,472 marks, which already a year later, in spite of some payments by Sweden, had grown to 120,817. . . . The extreme poverty of Sweden at the time is revealed by the fact that Gustavus was driven almost to distraction in attempting to raise this small amount. The debt to Lübeck was to harass Gustavus during the early part of his reign and was to have a most important bearing upon the king's policies and acts."

39. See note 10.

40. The sources agree that Emperor Charles V not only corresponded with Dacke but promised him support.

41. Fryxell (III, 124), for example, says: "The real leaders in the rebellion were taken to Stockholm. A more careful investigation then revealed that Måns Nilsson and his friends had actually been in secret contact with Christian and Gustav Trolle. They were sentenced to loss of life and property. The help they had earlier given Gustav in the hour of need, the loyalty to him they had for such a long time evinced could not move him to mercy; their confiscated property was returned to their widows and their children."

42. Lady Ebba Lejonhuvud, the widow of the Erik Lejonhuvud who was the first Swedish lord to be executed in the Stockholm bloodbath, and the mother of Queen Margareta, never became a Lutheran.

43. See notes 19, 24, and 40.

44. See notes 1-3, 5-14, 19, 24, and 41.

ACT IV

45. Brunkeberg, a height on Norrmalm, has been leveled.

46. Holaved is the forested area between Lakes Vättern and Sommen.

47. Älvsnabben was a harbor in the Stockholm archipelago.

48. Strindberg's major sources say very little about Reginald, Master Olof's only son. A recent biography, Robert Murray's *Olavus Petri* (2nd ed.; Stockholm: Svenska Kyrkans diakonistyrelse, pp. 148-150), says that Reginald was born on November 30, 1527, was sent in 1542 to study at Rostock and Wittenberg, was dismissed from Wittenberg by Melanchthon because of misbehavior at a student celebration, returned to Sweden in 1545, but left for studies in Leipzig the same year. In 1547, he visited his parents and went to Poland; he returned to Sweden with his master's degree in 1549, went to Germany again in 1550, and was in part subsidized at Wittenberg by King Gustav. He may have become a teacher in Stockholm for a time, but, Murray says, nothing about his later life is known with certainty.

49. Strindberg says Zwinglian in this speech but Calvinist below. For all practical purposes, the two terms are interchangeable.

50. Alexander the Great (356–323 B.C.), the king of Macedonia, is said to have regretted he had no other worlds to conquer.

51. Luther died on February 18, 1546.

52. See notes 19, 24, and 40. Kolmården is a forested hilly area in

northern Östergötland and southern Södermanland. The point is that Dacke's rebels were approaching Stockholm. Bishop Magnus Haraldsson of Skara had, after the *riksdag* of Västerås (1527), become involved in the plotting of the lords of Västergötland, which did not result in actual rebellion because of the loyalty of the farmers to the king. In 1529, the bishop found it wise to flee from Sweden. The sources suggest that he and the foreign princes mentioned in this speech did support Dacke.

53. See II Samuel 12. Nathan was the Hebrew prophet who reproved David for causing the death of Uriah, whose wife had become David's mistress. See note 30.

54. Apparently Gustav did go beyond the provisions made by the *riksdag* of Västerås (1527), as Strindberg suggests.

55. For information about the fifteenth-century hero Engelbrekt, see *The Last of the Knights, The Regent,* and *Earl Birger of Bjälbo.* Engelbrekt succeeded in freeing the Swedes from the union but was assassinated by a fellow Swede in 1436. See also Strindberg's play, *Engelbrekt.*

56. December 6 is the day of St. Nicholas, patron saint of children, schools, and seafarers. St. Nicholas comes with presents for the good children but with punishment for the bad ones.

ACT V

57. King Gustav made his triumphal entry into Stockholm at midsummer, 1523. See Strindberg's *The Regent.*

58. See note 3.

59. Larv's Heath (*Larfs hed*) was the meeting place of the Västergötland rebels in 1529, and Tuna the place in Dalarna where Gustav disciplined the Dalesmen in 1528.

60. Ulrich von Hutten (1488–1523) was the aristocratic supporter of Luther.

61. See note 7.

Introduction to 'Erik XIV'

I. STRINDBERG'S INTENTION

SHORTLY AFTER completing *Gustav Vasa* in 1899, Strindberg wrote *Erik XIV* as the last of the plays in the Vasa trilogy and, above all, as a companion play to *Gustav Vasa*. In writing a play about Erik, Strindberg was doing what many of his countrymen before him had done—centering his attention on one of the most interesting though not most admirable rulers Sweden has ever had. But Strindberg's approach to Erik differed greatly from that of his predecessors' in drama, prose fiction, and poetry; in contrast to the almost invariably romantic approach of earlier writers, Strindberg's was realistic but highly sympathetic in a very personal way. As an examination of either his own autobiographical works up to 1899 or of any of the biographies will reveal, Strindberg's own experiences had led him to feel a kinship to the Renaissance king not only in formative environmental factors but in actual experiences as well.

In the volume that has been quoted frequently in the introductions to the plays in this series, namely, *Open Letters to the Intimate Theater* (*Öppna brev till Intima teatern,* Stockholm, 1919 edition, p. 248), Strindberg says, "My *Erik XIV* is a characterization of a characterless human being." Anyone who has read his preface to *Lady Julie* (1888) will find this statement reminiscent of what Strindberg says about dramatic characterization there. What he says about vacillation and disintegration, the incredibility of the human automaton fixed in a static role, and the fact that human beings are "hard to catch, classify, and keep track of," is as applicable to King Erik and Göran Persson as to either Lady Julie or Jean. *Erik XIV* is essentially a realistic drama planned with great care and skill in keeping with its central character and his story. What that story was, according to the sources, is briefly told below.

II. The Historical Background

Erik XIV (1533–1577) was an exceptionally handsome, well-built man, and an excellent rider, swimmer, and dancer. Reared as a Renaissance prince, he learned several foreign languages and received broad training in history, logic, mathematics, military science, the arts, and astrology. A lover of music, he is said to have written songs, composed music, and demonstrated skill as a painter. The keenness of his mind and his imagination were counterbalanced by his fantastic interest and faith in astrology and his strong tendency to be extremely suspicious, irritable, and violent tempered. Erik was the product of an unhappy marriage and certainly not his father's favorite child, and his misfortunes probably stemmed from hereditary factors as well as the factors in his childhood and youth that Strindberg emphasizes in *Gustav Vasa*: the unhappy family situation and the unhappy influence of some of his companions. His drinking to excess as a youth and his indulgence in other forms of escape may very well have been the result of his feeling that he was not wanted and was in the way.

The Renaissance prince who ascended the throne as Erik XIV in 1560 might have become a highly successful ruler if it had not been for such qualities in his character as abnormal suspicion and anxiety, a lack of emotional security, dependence on his leading favorite, and tendencies to impulsive actions as well as certain facts in his family and national background.

Leading among Erik's favorites and advisers was Göran Persson, the son of a Catholic priest who had married after the reformation had begun. One of the ablest and most learned men of his time, Göran Persson has been labeled both "Erik's evil genius" and the friend of the common people in their struggle with the powerful lords. An advocate of a strong central government, he undoubtedly played a major role in Erik's reign. The relationship between King Erik and Göran Persson was exceptionally close.

Erik's reign began with promise. Within a relatively short time, he set up a badly needed supreme court (*konungens högsta nämnd*) and summoned a meeting of the estates in 1561 at Arboga, where he corrected one of the relatively few serious political blunders his great father had committed. In his last will and testament, Gustav had given his younger sons hereditary duchies with almost complete power over them: John, his favorite, was given southwestern Finland; Magnus, Dalsland and part of Östergötland; and Charles (Karl or Carl), Närke, Värmland, and most of Södermanland. By the so-called Articles of Arboga, Erik was able to reduce his brothers from virtually independent princes to subjects and to restrict their rights within their particular duchies. The duchies were not taken away from his brothers, however, and the actions of two of them— particularly John—were the source of many of Erik's principal troubles.

When Erik became king, the crown was in very good financial condition and the royal family itself was wealthy. Erik's vanity, ambition, and love of color and display helped waste the wealth that his father had so carefully accumulated. Strindberg's sources emphasize particularly Erik's coronation—the most brilliant and costly that had ever taken place in Sweden; his extravagance in living (he liked good food and drink, art and music, splendid clothes and display); and, above all, his extended and futile courtships of Elizabeth of England, Mary of Scotland, Renata of Lorraine, and Kristina of Hesse. In keeping with these matters was his creation of new ranks within the aristocracy; during the coronation he made Svante Sture (the head of the clan that was the Vasas' leading rivals), Per

Brahe, and Gustaf Tre Rosor counts (*grevar*), and made barons (*friherrar*) of nine others selected from among the great lords.

Erik had genuine talent for military affairs although, as Strindberg's major sources say or imply, he was not a great commander on the field of battle. But he did have ambitions for military glory and for the expansion of his country. In 1561, intervention under his direction won Esthonia for Sweden and laid the foundation for later expansion east of the Baltic. At the same time, the intervention led to difficulties with Poland which were not to end for generations. In 1563, Erik XIV and Fredrik II of Denmark began a seven-years' war between the closely related Danes and Swedes which was to bring little good to either but much misfortune to both. In that war, Erik could glory only in the brilliant naval victories of his great admiral, Klas Horn.

Yet the source of his greatest personal troubles was perhaps his wily and untrustworthy half-brother John, who through his mother Queen Margareta was more closely related than Erik to the most powerful families of the aristocracy. John had not accepted the Articles of Arboga with good grace; he tried to make the people of his duchy swear allegiance to him and through his marriage to Princess Catherine Jagellonica of Poland in 1562—without Erik's final approval—had plans for expanding the territory of his own duchy, partly through the assistance of Poland. When Erik summoned him to Stockholm, John refused to come. Erik consequently sent an army to Finland to capture John, who offered armed resistance in vain. Brought back as a captive along with his consort, John was tried for treason by the estates and sentenced to death. The sentence was commuted to life imprisonment by Erik XIV, and the duke and the duchess spent four years as prisoners in Gripsholm Castle.

Sometime in the middle 1560's, Erik acquired a mistress who was to exercise a good influence on him and to become one of the best-known and even admired figures in Swedish history and literature. The humbly born Karin Månsdotter—seller of flowers on Stockholm streets, according to Strindberg—is generally presented by Strindberg's major sources as the very opposite of Göran Persson; in other words, as King Erik's "good genius."

Erik had always been suspicious of the Stures and the other great families among the aristocracy. As a result of his suspicion, the behavior of Duke John, disappointments in various areas such as his courtships and his military ventures, and defiant talk among the great lords after the imprisonment of John, Erik broke definitely with the powerful lords in 1567, had the most prominent among them imprisoned in Uppsala Castle, and, while in anything but his right mind, either had them or let them be massacred.

Strindberg's major sources say that there was no question that Erik was temporarily insane during most of the period that followed the massacre. Three days after the murders, the king was found wandering in a nearby forest. In lucid intervals, he was overcome by pangs of conscience and tried to become reconciled by confession of guilt, apologies, and payments by way of compensation to the bereaved families. He even freed John. Göran Persson, in the meanwhile, had summoned the estates and had forced through their approval of sentences of death on the murdered lords.

When Erik recovered, he arranged for his marriage to Karin and invited his brothers to the wedding, which took place on July 4, 1568. Karin's coronation was on July 5. Although the estates had approved both the marriage and the recognition of the infant Prince Gustav as heir to the throne in advance, Erik's brothers were present neither at the wedding nor at the coronation.

A few days after the wedding, Dukes John and Charles started a rebellion, agreeing that upon its successful conclusion they would share the throne. The rebellion was quickly over, partly because Erik and Göran Persson made no really effective efforts to put it down. By September the dukes were in Stockholm, where the final resistance took place. On September 29, Erik surrendered. Contrary to his agreement with Charles, John alone ascended the throne. Erik lived on as a prisoner in various castles until 1577, when he died from poison probably given him on the orders of John.

III. The Play

Examination of the four-act *Erik XIV* will reveal that the conflicts between King Erik and his opponents represent essentially a struggle for power. Since the personality traits and the behavior of the king may and do obscure the ideational content, it should be remembered that the king's behavior is usually related to this basic struggle between the king (and Göran Persson) on the one hand and the lords (and the dukes) on the other. Erik does have a political goal and a political program: like his great father he wants to keep Sweden a strong country, politically and otherwise; he hopes, moreover, to expand Sweden and to make it the unquestionably strongest power in northern Europe. Both he and his major adviser see the best prospect for realizing these goals through preventing the ambitious Stures and other lords, and not least the dukes, from becoming the controlling element in the country. It should be noted, moreover, that the problems concerning the king's marriage, the dukes, and the lords—the three matters that Strindberg emphasizes above all others—are major sources of conflict in the struggle for power.

Note Strindberg's introduction of all these problems in Act I, his development of them in Acts II and III, the realistic and calculated action of Göran Persson toward solving all these problems, and King Erik's unintentional thwarting of the effectiveness of Göran's acts until, in Act IV, it becomes clear that the king's unthinking behavior after the massacre of the Stures and some of the other lords makes it possible for the dukes to rise in successful rebellion. Strindberg demonstrates the progress of the struggle for power and indicates that only when Göran for personal reasons and because of Erik's behavior is no longer able to will to act does Erik with his superior political program become a tragic failure as king. Note, too, that the peak of Erik's humiliation is reached in the unforgettable coronation dinner, which, from having been planned as a supreme occasion in the king's life, becomes ghastly much in the manner of the goldmaker's banquet in *To Damascus, II*. Note as well that Duke Charles's final words summarize what Strindberg felt when he considered King Erik and the world in which he had his being:

> JOHN: Where are you going, brother?
> CHARLES: *My* way, which parts from yours here.
> GYLLENSTJERNA: Oh, God, now it's beginning again!
> JOHN: I think the world has gone mad!
> CHARLES: That's what Erik thought, too. Who knows how it is . . .
> MARIA: Isn't it over soon, mama?
> CHARLES (*smiling*): No, my child; the struggles of life are never over!

Strindberg's presentation of Erik XIV is strikingly and deliberately different from that of any of the central characters in the other historical plays. His sources and the historians in general emphasized the close relationship between King Erik and his major adviser and favorite and indicated that the king and his acts as such could be understood adequately only if the two men were considered together. While central characters such as Earl Birger, Engelbrekt, Sten Sture, Master Olof, Gustav Vasa, Gustav Adolf, Christina, Charles XII, and Gustav III had, as all people must to some degree, relied upon and been influenced by others, they were essentially independent individuals primarily engaged in conflict with opponents. Erik XIV is decidedly different, as Strindberg demonstrates again and again. For example:

> GÖRAN: I don't rely on anyone but myself! I wasn't born to wear a crown, but to rule; since I can rule only through my king, he's my sun. When that sun sets, I'll be extinguished, and that will be that!
> MOTHER: Do you like Erik?

GÖRAN: Yes and no. We're bound to each other by invisible bonds;
it's as if we had been born in the same litter and under *one*
constellation. His hate is my hate, his likes are mine, and things
like that bind people to each other.

It is this mutual dependence that Strindberg is clarifying when
Erik says to Karin: "Where's Göran? I long for him every time
you're contrary. Göran alone knows all the secret ways in my soul;
he can say what I think so I hardly need to speak in his presence
. . . he's my brother and my friend; so you hate him." Erik XIV
and Göran Persson are not opponents but allies whose lives and
acts are curiously interwoven and intertwined, largely because Erik
is not self-reliant but needs the friendship, understanding, sympathy,
and realistic help that Göran can give him, and Göran, on the other
hand, needs the authority and support that the king alone can give
him.

Since the development of the relationship between the two men
furnishes one key to the tragedy of Erik both as king and as human
being, further consideration of it is necessary. Both men are not
only men of action but brilliant men of ideas, too; essentially, they
think alike and have the same basic goal: ruling the country for
the benefit of the great masses by curbing the power of the great
lords and, not least, that of the dukes. (That both Erik and Göran
have selfish goals as well is obvious.) How they think through their
ideas for the welfare of the nation and how they put them into
effect must also be emphasized. In matters that concern the state,
Göran thinks clearly and coolly and acts on the basis of rational
thought and calculated ends. Erik thinks clearly and coolly only
in the rare moments when he is not emotionally involved and upset; on other occasions, he acts on the basis of impulse or whim.

The fundamental facts about the practical aspects of the relationship are conveyed in many passages, but of all these none clarifies
it as much as this:

GÖRAN: What have you done, Erik?

ERIK: The stupidest thing in my life!

GÖRAN: Let it be the last.

ERIK: If *you* want to make the other blunders, you may . . . Haven't
you noticed how everything I touch becomes stupid and twisted?

GÖRAN: Not particularly, but you're not fortunate!

ERIK: What about you? Who's to end on the gallows! But you
know so much more than I; that's why you're going to be my
adviser . . .

GÖRAN: If you make me your adviser, Erik, I don't want to serve
as your nominal councillor, who gets all the blame without really
having anything to say. No, give me power and authority so I
can act and be responsible for my acts myself. Make me procurator.

ERIK: Good! You're procurator!

GÖRAN: Pending confirmation of the appointment by the national
council . . .

ERIK: That's unnecessary. *I* am the ruler!

GÖRAN: That's the way to talk!

It is a practical arrangement between the emotionally unbalanced
and mentally unstable king and an adviser whom even Duke John
recognizes as "the only statesman the kingdom has."

As we have seen, King Erik's three major problems (and sources
of conflict) are the problems dealing with his ambitious brothers,
particularly Duke John; dealing with the lords, particularly the
powerful Stures; and the problem of his own marriage. In setting
out to help Erik solve each one of these, Göran Persson proceeds
calmly and realistically and presents solutions that would have done
admirably in sixteenth-century Sweden. On every major occasion,
however, King Erik's behavior thwarts the effective realization of
his brilliant procurator's plans and acts.

The pattern of the king's behavior is illustrated again and again,
both as it relates directly to the three major problems and as it
relates to other matters. Abnormally suspicious of others, Erik shifts

from one mood to another without warning. One moment he can be kind and gentle, the next abnormally insensitive and cruel (note his treatment of Karin); one moment he is gay and lively, the next beside himself with fury; one moment intensely alert, the next passive and dull. Intelligent to the point of brilliance in insight into himself, most others, and his environment, the king lacks the self-control that permits a human being to function fairly consistently according to some appreciably logical pattern of conduct.

In scene after scene Strindberg deals with the nuances of Erik's personality—his abnormal suspicions, his shifts of mood, his insensitivity to the feelings of others (Karin and the crown; the proposal that Gyllenstierna murder the Earl of Leicester), his conviction that he is hated and is being plotted against, his touching affection for his children; his dependence on Karin and Göran; his striking out at anyone without logical reason; his curious forms of getting compensation (Elizabeth, a harlot); and the like.

The progress of the three major problems does suggest that the pattern of Erik's behavior is fairly predictable. In dealing with his brother, favorite of the lords and undoubtedly Erik's most dangerous enemy, Erik in a mood that he calls generous impulsively approves John's marriage to Catherine of Poland. Yet, when Göran Persson plans the realistic solution of the complex problem that results from that marriage, Erik not only thwarts the procurator in the most important point but provides himself with the most serious threat to his own future as king:

> ERIK: And John has seized my messengers, entrenched himself in Åbo, and raised the Finns in rebellion.
>
> GÖRAN: That means the duke has revolted against his king and thereby forfeited both freedom and life.
>
> ERIK: Let's say his freedom . . .
>
> GÖRAN: *And* his life! That depends on the estates that must judge him!
>
> ERIK (*disturbed*): Not his life! Now that I have children, I want nothing to do with the spilling of blood.

GÖRAN: So, while the estates are assembled, the case of treason must be brought up.

ERIK: Yes, but not his life! Then I couldn't sleep at night!

GÖRAN: Your great father, the master who built this nation, always observed the judicial rule of not taking any special regard for relatives, friends, or other associates. First the country, then that crowd!

If all the details that Strindberg gives us about Erik's dealing with John are taken together, the pattern that evolves is one of fury, hasty and impulsive action, remorse, and attempt at setting things right. Compare Erik's behavior about the Stures before, during, and after their assassination, for the massacre itself presents perhaps the most striking illustration of the pattern: his fury with the Stures, his impulsive participation in the massacre while he is still furious, his remorse, and his attempt at reconciliation with the survivors without consulting his procurator.

ERIK: There he is. You came as if I'd sent for you, Göran . . .

GÖRAN: I hope I haven't come too late, though . . .

ERIK: What have you been up to?

GÖRAN: I've been working with the estates in Uppsala, and there's news.

ERIK: Really!

GÖRAN: After your departure from the castle, I found the indictment and the witnesses' depositions. After various efforts, I succeeded in getting the estates together, and then I appeared as prosecutor . . . briefly, with the result that the estates declared the lords guilty . . .

ERIK: No! And I who've begged for forgiveness and sent out a circular throughout the whole country declaring all those who were executed innocent!

GÖRAN (*sinks down on a chair*): My God, then we're lost! Yes, Erik, whatever you put your hand to goes wrong.

ERIK: Can't you straighten this out, Göran?

GÖRAN: No, I can't straighten out your messes any more. Everything I build up, you tear down, you unfortunate soul!

Even his marriage to Karin, advocated by Göran Persson and approved by the estates, leads to fury and to impulsive and unthinking action on Erik's part.

It is only when Göran himself gives up the attempt to accomplish worthwhile things, motivated by his love for an unidentified woman, and returns to his youthful crippling conviction that men are only puppets in the control of higher powers, that Erik's role as king is over:

> GÖRAN: No, I know absolutely nothing, understand nothing, and so I'm done for. There was a time when I dreamt I was a statesman, and thought I had a mission in life: to defend your crown, inherited from your great father, given by the people—not by the lords—and worn by the grace of God. But I must have been mistaken.

Göran's loss of faith in the possibility of doing good in what both he and Erik consider an irrational and basically evil world leads to his resignation to defeat and consequently to the end of the reign of Erik, who, in spite of all his weaknesses, was still, as Gyllenstjerna says, "the good king, the friend of the people, Erik, the people's king!"

The characterization of what Strindberg calls "a characterless character" is amazingly full and credible. Strindberg himself has suggested in his essay on Shakespeare's *Hamlet* (*Open Letters to the Intimate Theater*, 1919 edition, pp. 75 ff.) that he considered Erik XIV a Hamlet:

> Erik XIV is a Hamlet. Stepmother (= stepfather); murders Sture (= murders Polonius); Ophelia = Karin Månsdotter; Erik XIV dies poisoned as Hamlet does; insane or simulating insanity as Hamlet; vacillating; judges and rejects his judgment; his friend Horatio = Erik's friend Göran Persson—faithful unto death; Fortinbras = Dukes John and Charles; Hamlet was loved by the uncivilized masses. Erik, too, a hater of the lords and the people's king.

Strindberg summarizes his concept of Hamlet: "So Hamlet himself is only made up of apparent contradictions, evil and good, hating and loving, cynical and enthusiastic, cruel and lenient, strong and weak; in a word: a human being, different at every moment, as human beings are, of course."

Strindberg's characterization of Erik applies what he had said in the preface to *Lady Julie*: he has presented the "richness of the soul complex" of an exceptional individual in terms of heredity and, particularly, environment. Any serious student who reads *Erik XIV* or sees it on the stage will, I believe, find it an excellent case report illustrating beautifully both the conditioning and the behavior of an unfortunate human being. He will find, to cite several examples, the inadequate adjustment to life, the lack of emotional security, and both emotional and mental instability; the obsession with the ego, the abnormal suspicions of others and their motives; fears, anxiety, brooding, irritability; feelings of inferiority and compensation for them (note Erik's reaction to Queen Elizabeth's rejection of him as a suitor, his rationalization and his acceptance of the compensatory evasion of the truth). Nor are his impulsive lashing out at others in his fury, his thoughtlessness and cruelty on occasion, without interest as contrasted with his tenderness for his children, his affection for Karin, his admiration for Göran, his respect for Göran's mother, his unwillingness to have Duke John executed, his kindness to and thoughtfulness about most humble people, and his own guilt feelings (which reveal that he has his own set of values). The characterization of what Strindberg called his Hamlet is such that it is no wonder Swedish and foreign actors have found it a most rewarding and challenging role.

Nor is the role of King Erik the only rewarding one. That of Göran Persson is almost equally challenging, partly because of his exceptionally close ties with Erik but largely because Strindberg has chosen to make him an intensely interesting character in his own right. Strindberg is quite right in what he says in the note on *Erik XIV* (p. 248): "Göran Persson's biography has been written

by his enemies." The Göran Persson in Strindberg's play is neither
King Erik's "evil genius" nor a devil incarnate. Instead, he is a
highly complex and thoroughly human being who has an ideal goal
toward which he is working and who, with little faith in the goodness of man, is ruthless in his pursuit of that goal. Note such
nuances of his character as his sympathy for the unfortunate, his
clearheaded analysis of situations, his rational—even if frequently
merciless—acts, his affection for his mother, his understanding of
people, and his attempts to do good in a world that he feels may,
but is not likely to, have a purpose behind it. Strindberg's characterization of Göran is of a highly dynamic and complex human
being.

Strindberg also presents Karin Månsdotter, the soldier's daughter
who became queen and the only woman King Erik loved, in a remarkably rich characterization. Seen in turn with Max the young
ensign who loved her, Göran Persson, the king whose "good genius"
she is, her children, the dowager queen, and her father, and finally
as queen, Karin is a young woman whose beauty, charm, and essentially admirable qualities have endeared her to Swedes down
through the centuries. Quickly and economically Strindberg clarifies
and establishes the nuances of a decidedly attractive product of her
heredity and her environment: her guilt feelings about her role as
mistress, her protective and even motherly affection for the king,
her respect for her parents, her tenderness for her children, her
modesty and humility, her kindness and unselfishness, and her basic
loyalty.

Yet all these would be inadequate in a Strindbergian characterization. We get the less favorable nuances, too: Karin's inability to
grasp what it is that King Erik and Göran Persson are trying to
do for Sweden; her seeing only the surface of the struggle; her
relative lack of insight into Erik; her undue respect for the dowager
queen and the Stures—results of her conditioning, to be sure; her
inability to understand and support the king when he needs both
understanding and support most; and her inability to deal with him

effectively at crucial times. Note, for example, her protests against his suspicions and her flight to Hörningsholm. Yet, her weaknesses are not presented by Strindberg unsympathetically, but rather as the credible results of hereditary and especially environmental factors, results which like so many other factors in Erik's life were unfortunate. The beautiful, charming, and essentially good Queen Karin was after all, as Strindberg suggests, placed in a situation which only a shrewd, brilliant, unscrupulous, and mature woman of the world could really have appreciably controlled.

Aside from some servants, soldiers, and other minor characters who remain types, Strindberg presents a gallery of unforgettably individualized secondary and minor characters: Göran Persson's mother, kind, sensible, and practical; Maria, the normal little child without the reticence and inhibitions of the adult world; Agda, her unmarried mother; Duke John, not a little like a fox; Duke Charles, forthright and realistic, able to think clearly and honestly even about the so-called misbehavior of his stepbrother; Dowager Queen Katarina Stenbock, ever conscious of the fact that her family background is very good indeed; the royal children, presented with the tenderness and insight of a man who knew and loved children; the one-eyed soldier, who in a world where evil outweighs good has learned that obedience to superiors pays but that evidence had better be oral, not written; Max, the young idealist who goes to his death rather than sacrifice his ideals to expediency; Måns Knekt, the humble soldier with his strong sense of right and wrong, crude, yet groping for a standard of social behavior beyond him; Nils Gyllenstjerna, the loyal supporter of King Erik who knows, in a world not too far removed from madness, the need for adjustment to reality; and the Stures, good people still but arrogant and rather far removed from the knightly code of conduct of Count Svante's father, the last of the knights.

The play has no doubt won its well-deserved popularity because of its gallery of superb characterizations, its Strindbergian attention to the telling detail, its many-faceted approach to his subject, its modern and realistic dialogue, the highly interesting story it has to tell, and a dramatic structure that gives the effect of lack of compactness but that is really highly appropriate in a play about the unhappy Erik XIV. The primary reason for its popularity on the stage both in Sweden and abroad lies, I suspect, in Strindberg's highly sympathetic and intensely moving interpretation of an essentially tragic character, whose downfall comes inevitably from hereditary and, even more, environmental factors beyond his control.

Erik XIV .   A Play in Four Acts

Characters

KING ERIK XIV
GÖRAN PERSSON, *the king's friend, later procurator*
COUNT SVANTE STURE
LORD NILS STURE *and* LORD ERIK STURE, *his sons*
LORD NILS GYLLENSTJERNA
KARIN MÅNSDOTTER, *King Erik's mistress, later his queen*
GÖRAN PERSSON'S MOTHER
AGDA
MARIA, *Agda's three-year-old daughter*
DUKE JOHN
QUEEN KATARINA STENBOCK, *the widow of King Gustav I Vasa*
DUKE CHARLES
PEDER WELAMSON, *Göran Persson's nephew*
MAX, *an ensign*
THE GUARD *at the bridge*
A COURTIER
MÅNS KNEKT, *a soldier, Karin Månsdotter's father*
LORD LEJONHUVUD
LORD STENBOCK
PRINCE GUSTAV
PRINCESS SIGRID

Settings

ACT I: *The terrace of the royal palace in Stockholm*
ACT II: *A large room in Göran Persson's home*
ACT III: *On the shore of Lake Mälar near Gripsholm; a room in Uppsala Castle*
ACT IV: *The kitchen in Måns Knekt's house; a tower room; a room in the palace at Stockholm*

ACT I

The terrace of the royal palace in Stockholm. At the back a balustrade of Tuscan columns; above them flowers in jars of faïence. Below and beyond them tops of trees and the tops of masts with flags; farthest away: church towers and gabled houses. On the terrace: bushes, benches, chairs, tables. [The same setting as in the fifth act of Gustav Vasa.]

KARIN MÅNSDOTTER *is sitting sewing by a table;* MAX *stands nearby, leaning on his pike.*

KARIN: Don't come any closer! The king's at the window up there spying on us.

MAX:[1] Where?

KARIN: To the right. But, for heaven's sake, don't look!—How long are you on guard duty?

MAX: Half an hour more.

KARIN: Speak, then. Max, kinsman and friend of my youth . . .

MAX: Love of my youth, you used to say, Karin . . .

KARIN: I don't want to think of that—I forfeited your love . . .

MAX: Why did you? You certainly don't love your lover.

KARIN: *Love!* I'm fond of him as if he were my child; I pitied him from the first time I saw him—I called him my blind Paleface for the last doll I ever had—he looked like her. I've thought of our relationship as a duty, for he's calmer and more serious when he's with me. I've flattered myself by believing I could bring out what's best in him, and I've felt his kindly approval has made me a better person. But now—danger's near! For he has the habit of overestimating me. He sees me as his good angel! Wait till he awakens from that dream and discovers how imperfect I am. How he'll despise me, call me hypocritical and false . . . (*sighs*) . . . Max, step aside! He just moved!

MAX (*steps aside*): I met your father and mother yesterday.

KARIN: Did you? What did she say?

MAX: The same as before.

KARIN: She despises the king's—mistress. She is right; I do, too! But all the same it hurts. And father?

MAX: He says he'll push you into the water the next time he meets you on the bridge!

KARIN: But my brothers and sisters? They won't even talk to me! So there's something to be proud of even for the poor and the lowly.

MAX: Give up this shameful life, and come with me.

KARIN: Should my shame become yours?

MAX: No! Through the holy bonds of matrimony I'd blot out your shame . . .

KARIN: And my children?

MAX: Would be mine.

KARIN: You speak so beautifully, I believe you, Max; but . . .

MAX: Sh-h-h! I see a pair of ears behind the hedge, a pair of ears I'd like to see nailed to the gallows . . .

KARIN: That's Göran Persson . . . who's trying to steal back into the king's favor.

MAX: You must prevent that.

KARIN: If I only could! Everyone thinks I can do everything; but I can't do anything.

MAX: Come with me!

KARIN: I can't—Erik says he'd die if I deserted him.

MAX: Let him die!

KARIN: No, no! You mustn't wish that he or anyone else should die,

for that will bring its own punishment. Go away, Max, or Göran
will hear us.

MAX: Will you meet me tonight where we could talk without being
disturbed?

KARIN: No, I don't want to. I can't!

MAX: Karin, you know as well as I do the king intends to get married. Have you thought of what will happen to you then?

KARIN: When that time comes—but not before—I'll know how to
get out of the way.

MAX: When it's too late! Think of Elizabeth's father, Henry VIII
of England. The wives he discarded weren't allowed to live on,
but died on the block. And the daughter of that dog of a Turk's
going to be your queen![2] The very fact you're alive will be a
constant insult she'll know how to get rid of.

KARIN: What you're saying is terrible . . . Go quickly and don't look
up; he has come out on the balcony.

MAX: How can you tell?

KARIN: I have a mirror in my sewing basket. Go; he has seen you
and intends to throw something . . .

(*A shower of big nails rains down on* MAX.)

MAX: He's throwing nails at me! Does he think I'm a troll?

KARIN: Merciful God! He believes in every evil power but not in
any good one.—Go, for the sake of Christ!

MAX: All right. When you need me, Karin, let me know.

KARIN: Go, go quickly, or he'll throw his hammer after the nails!

MAX: Is he crazy?

KARIN: Sh-h—go, go, go!

(MAX *leaves.*)

(GÖRAN PERSSON *enters from behind a bush; the audience has
been able to catch a glimpse of him occasionally.*)

KARIN: What are you looking for?

GÖRAN: I'm looking for you, my lady, and bring great and good
news.

KARIN: Can you bring anything good?

GÖRAN: On rare occasions even I can bring good to others—but never to myself.

KARIN: Speak, but take care that he doesn't see you—the king's standing on the balcony . . . Don't turn around.

GÖRAN: My king's still ungracious to me, but he's wrong—he'll have to search for a more faithful friend . . .

KARIN: When you say so yourself!

GÖRAN: I can't say anything good about myself very often—I know that, of course, and, when it happens, I don't take any credit. My lady, listen to me! The king's courtship in England has failed. That means greater hopes for you and your children, and for the kingdom . . .

KARIN: Are you telling the truth?

GÖRAN: As I live and breathe! But—listen to me!—the king hasn't heard the news yet. Take care you're not the one to tell him! But be at his side when the blow falls, because it will upset him as only a crushed hope can.

KARIN: I hear that you're telling the truth and that you're my friend and the king's.

GÖRAN: But he isn't mine.

(*A steel hammer is thrown at* GÖRAN *from above, but misses him.*)

GÖRAN (*picks up the hammer, kisses it, and puts it on a table*): My life for my king!

KARIN: Go away, or he'll kill you!

GÖRAN: Let him!

KARIN: He's in a bad mood today. Watch out! (*A flower pot is thrown down, but misses* GÖRAN.)

GÖRAN: He's throwing flowers to me! (*Breaks off a flower, smells it, and puts it in a button hole*)

(ERIK XIV *laughs.*)

GÖRAN: He's laughing!

KARIN: I haven't heard him do that for a long time. That's encouraging.

GÖRAN (*calls up*): More—more!

(*A chair is thrown down and breaks into pieces.* GÖRAN *gathers some of the pieces and stuffs them into his pockets.*)

KARIN (*smiles*): This is too crazy!

GÖRAN: Let me be the court fool since Hercules [3] can't make my lord smile any more.

KARIN: Don't walk on the nails, Göran.

GÖRAN (*kicks off his shoes and steps on the nails*): Yes, with my bare feet if it can cheer up my lord!

ERIK (*from above*): Göran.

GÖRAN: Göran's in disfavor.

ERIK (*from above*): Göran! Stop! Wait!

KARIN (*to* GÖRAN): Don't go!

(*An armful of shoes, pillows, cloths is tossed down.*)

ERIK (*laughs uproariously*): Göran! Wait! I'm coming down!

GÖRAN (*to* KARIN): I'll come back when he really wants me.

KARIN: May I never regret this; but I beg you to stay, Göran. Erik's very unhappy, and he'll get even worse when he finds out about his misfortune.

GÖRAN: Erik isn't unhappy—he's bored, and a king mustn't get bored. Then he's dangerous. I'll come and cheer him up, but I have to go on an errand first . . . I have to . . .

KARIN: But be near at hand when the blow falls; otherwise, he'll hit out at us . . .

GÖRAN: I'll take the storm as I used to—he always struck out at me with his sword—when *he* had done something foolish!

KARIN: Göran!—One word more! Did you hear what Ensign Max and I said?

GÖRAN: Every word!

KARIN: I'm afraid of you, but we two must be friends.

GÖRAN: That's the only thing that's certain . . .

KARIN: May I never regret this!

GÖRAN: Bonds that have been tied in the gutter bind us, my lady; those are bonds that will do, you'll see. (*Exits*)

(ERIK *enters from the right; is met by a* COURTIER *who enters from the left.*)

COURTIER: Your Majesty.

ERIK: Speak up.

COURTIER: Nigels the goldsmith humbly requests an audience to show Your Majesty the finished masterpiece.

ERIK: Let him come. (*To* KARIN) Now you're going to see something beautiful, Karin.

(NIGELS *enters with a leather case.*)

ERIK: Good day, Nigels. You're a punctual man, and you have my favor. (*Points to a table*) Put it there.

(NIGELS *puts the case on a table.*)

ERIK: Open it.

(NIGELS *opens the case and takes out a gold crown set with precious stones.*)

ERIK: Ah! (*Claps his hands*) Karin, look at this!

KARIN (*still knitting*): I see it, my friend. Very beautiful.

ERIK: Did you notice the Swedish lion making England's leopard couchant? [4]

KARIN: Erik, Erik!

ERIK: What?

KARIN: Who's going to wear that crown?

ERIK: England's virgin queen and mine! And, when our hands meet across the sea, we'll have Norway and Denmark, and then Europe will be ours! That's the significance of the six crescents that bend together, and of the six precious jewels. (*He takes the crown and wants to put it on* KARIN's *head.*) Try it on to see if it's heavy.

KARIN (*refusing*): It's absolutely too heavy for me!

ERIK: But let me try it. Look! Do as I say!

KARIN: If obedience is all you ask, Erik, I'm always your obedient servant.

ERIK (*puts the crown on her head*): See! It's very attractive on you, Karin. Look in the mirror in your sewing basket, the one that lets you keep an eye on your lord so well . . . Listen: wasn't Göran here? Where did that crazy fellow go?

KARIN: He was afraid of his lord's disfavor.

ERIK: Huh! Disfavor! I don't want to hear about that. Do I bear a grudge? Didn't I let young Sture go courting [5] for me even though he had proved himself a traitor in the Danish war and had been punished for that?

KARIN: May I get rid of the crown now?

ERIK: Don't interrupt me when I'm talking. I suppose there were many people who felt I was unjust to Sture, but, you see, I didn't care about that . . . however . . . (*Becomes thoughtful, seems absentminded, lost in his thoughts, and stares vacantly ahead*)

(DOWAGER QUEEN *strolls past without any apparent reason.*) [6]

ERIK (*comes to*): What would you like, stepmother? Please do your walking in another courtyard. Please!

(DOWAGER QUEEN *scrutinizes* KARIN, *who is embarrassed.*)

ERIK (*snatches the crown off* KARIN): Sweden, Norway, Denmark, England, Scotland, Ireland—six precious jewels!

(NIGELS *withdraws to the background.*)

DOWAGER QUEEN: Erik!

ERIK: King Erik, if you please!

DOWAGER QUEEN: And Queen Karin, perhaps?

ERIK: Queen Elizabeth, if I wish! Or Mary of Scotland, or Renata of Lorraine, or, at the worst, Kristina of Hesse! [7]

DOWAGER QUEEN: You're more pitiable than wicked. Poor Erik! (*Exits*)

ERIK: Don't pay any attention to that woman's talk, Karin. She thinks I'm crazy, because she doesn't know that I have six crowns in my hands . . . yes, I have . . . Sture, who may get here any time, wrote from England that my prospects were more than bright . . . more than bright! Besides, I had a dream the other night. Hm! But, that doesn't matter. You do love me, Karin, don't you—so much that you rejoice over my good fortune? Don't you?

KARIN: I rejoice over your good fortune, but I suffer more than you from your misfortunes, and every one has to be prepared for misfortune.

ERIK: I am. And you haven't any idea of what a nice game I'm playing now. Four trumps in my hand! (*To* NIGELS) You may go, Nigels. I'll see you again.

(DUKE JOHN *appears at the back.*)

ERIK: Come here, Johnny Redbeard, and you'll get something. I'm in a generous mood today.

KARIN (*to* ERIK): Don't hurt him when you don't have to. There's already so much hate here.

(DUKE JOHN *comes forward.*)

ERIK: After mature consideration, I've decided to grant your request, brother. Catherine of Poland shall be yours.[8]

JOHN: My king's gracious approval of a union that is very dear to me can only make me happy and grateful.

ERIK: Even grateful? Then don't forget, when you become related to the emperor and your son inherits the Polish throne, that you have a Vasa to thank for your power. With England I'll secure the north; with Poland you're to secure the south and the east— and after that—you may imagine the rest yourself.

JOHN: My lord brother's statesmanly thoughts are borne on the wings of an eagle. I—poor sparrow—haven't the strength to follow you.

ERIK: Fine! Go in peace, and enjoy the happiness of your greatness, as I go to enjoy mine.

JOHN: Excuse me, lord brother, but an act of such significance usually requires seal and signature.

ERIK: You're just like a bailiff—you always have to have it in black and white. Here's my hand. And the woman I love is witness enough.

JOHN (*kisses* ERIK's *hand, then* KARIN's, *and goes quickly*): Thank you.

ERIK (*to* KARIN): It seems to me he left faster than he came in—and

I can always see a fox's tail dragging behind him.—Don't you think he looks false?

KARIN: No, I don't.

ERIK: Your sympathy for my enemies is certainly obvious.

KARIN: You think all people are your enemies, Erik . . .

ERIK: Yes, because they hate me! But I return their hatred. Listen, Karin, what were you talking to that ensign about?

KARIN: Why, that was Max, one of my relatives!

ERIK: It's not proper to be friendly to a common soldier.

KARIN: What am I—a soldier's daughter—that I should be proud, when I'm a mistress?

ERIK: Yes, but you're the *king's* mistress . . .

KARIN: Erik, Erik!

ERIK: I say it as it is . . .

KARIN: What would you call our children, then?

ERIK: *My* children! That's something else . . .

KARIN: What?

ERIK: Do you want to quarrel? Eh?

KARIN: No, no, no! If I could only speak out about everything . . .

ERIK: Where's Göran? I long for him every time you're contrary. Göran alone knows all the secret ways in my soul; he can say what I think so I hardly need to speak in his presence . . . he's my brother and my friend; so you hate him.

KARIN: I don't hate him, least of all when he can make you happy . . .

ERIK: You don't hate him any more! What has happened? He must have slandered me.

KARIN: Oh, my God, how unfortunate you are! Erik, my poor Erik . . .

ERIK: Poor? Shame!

COURTIER (*enters*): Lord Nils Sture presents his respects and requests an audience.

ERIK: At last!

KARIN (*gets up*): May I go?

ERIK: No, stay. Do you envy your poor king?

KARIN: No, God knows he hasn't anything to be envied for!

ERIK: Your arrogance has passed all bounds! Watch out for arrogance, Karin. There's nothing so displeasing to the gods as arrogance.

(SVANTE STURE *enters, accompanied by* NILS STURE *and* ERIK STURE.)

ERIK: What's this? Is Lord Nils making a triumphal entrance into the royal palace?

SVANTE STURE: With your permission, my king and lord . . .

ERIK: Lord Nils, our royal ambassador, alone may speak. Surely he's no executor, going about with two witnesses.

SVANTE STURE: No, he isn't, but a dear and sad experience, entirely too sad to recall, has taught me, the head of the Sture family, to deal with public matters publicly so that there won't be any chance to twist the plainest acts and words.

ERIK (*stands by the table with the crown on it*): Are you getting revenge, Lord Svante, by poisoning what is probably the most beautiful and greatest moment in my life by reminding me of your son's crime, which I was merciful enough to forgive?

SVANTE STURE: Lord Nils has never committed any crime!

ERIK: God's death! The fellow refused to obey orders in wartime, and that *is* a crime . . .

SVANTE STURE: He refused to commit inhuman acts . . .[9]

ERIK: War is always inhuman, and the man who hasn't the courage to cut down the enemy should sit at home by the fire. Hasn't enough been said about this? Lord Nils, present your report and no more!

NILS STURE: Gracious king, I have no liking for the delivery of the message I have been given . . .

ERIK: Where is the letter?

NILS STURE: No letter was given me; unfortunately, only an oral answer, which I have to convert into decent language so as not to offend your ears or my tongue.

ERIK: Did she say no?

NILS STURE (*after a pause*): Yes.

ERIK: And that pleases you, Satan!

NILS STURE: For heaven's sake, no . . .

ERIK: Yes, you laughed to yourself, you devil!

SVANTE STURE: He didn't laugh!

ERIK: Yes, he laughed to himself on the sly, I said! And you did, too, you old rascal! All three of you laughed—*I* saw it. Karin, didn't *you* see how they grinned?

KARIN: No, by all that's holy . . .

ERIK: You, too! I think all Hell's conspiring. Go, go, go, damn it! Out, you devils! Out! (*He throws the crown over the barrier, picks up the things he has tossed down from the balcony, and throws them after* NILS *and* ERIK STURE, *who exit.*)

SVANTE STURE (*who has stayed*): Pity the country whose king is a madman!

ERIK: Do you call me, your king, a madman, you villain, you son of a bitch!

KARIN: Erik, Erik!

ERIK: Keep your mouth shut!

SVANTE STURE (*goes*): God be gracious to us all!

ERIK: But I won't be gracious to you, you can be sure of that! (*To* KARIN) Now you're happy, eh? Answer me! You don't need to, for I can grasp your feelings, read your thoughts, hear the words you don't dare to utter. How could you be anything but happy when I've been turned down, when your rival has insulted me? Now you're sure you'll have me all to yourself, eh? Now you think I'm down, gone under, so that you can comfort me! You, comfort me! When the mob laughs at my misfortune and the lords have banquets to celebrate my defeat! And your father and mother—if I should see them today, I'd kill them. Imagine how delighted they'll be. And my stepmother! I can see her sitting smiling so her black tooth shows—she has a black upper tooth they say my late father knocked loose—. The whole kingdom will have a good time today, everyone but me! Me! (*Laughs bitterly*)

COURTIER (*enters*) : Lord Nils Gyllenstjerna.

ERIK: Gyllenstjerna! Bless him! He's *my* man, a *man* above every-thing! Carry him in on a chair of gold.

KARIN (*gets up*) : Now I'm going.

ERIK: Yes, go to hell! (*Throws the sewing basket after her*) And gossip afterward!

    (GYLLENSTJERNA *enters.*) [10]

ERIK: There you are, Nils. It's good to see a sane person after hav-ing to listen to madmen. Tell me, Nils, what's the truth about this English matter? Is the woman crazy?

GYLLENSTJERNA: No, Your Majesty, it's simply this: her heart, as they say, is committed to the Earl of Leicester [11]—well, how should I put it?

ERIK (*laughs*) : He's her lover! So she's a whore.

GYLLENSTJERNA: At least she's not a virgin, this virgin queen.

ERIK: And his name's Leicester. Couldn't he be murdered?

GYLLENSTJERNA: Yes, that could no doubt be arranged, if one wanted to pay liberally enough.

ERIK: Will you murder him?

GYLLENSTJERNA: I?

ERIK: Ten thousand *dalers!* Eh?

GYLLENSTJERNA: I? Seriously?

ERIK: Seriously! You'll get them in advance!

GYLLENSTJERNA: I meant if Your Majesty seriously thought I'd hire myself out as a murderer.

ERIK: Would that be insulting?

GYLLENSTJERNA: A Swedish nobleman . . .

ERIK: And a Swedish king! Do you want to teach me mores?

GYLLENSTJERNA: I came about another matter, but, since my king has so little respect for me, I beg to be excused.

ERIK: Traitor! You, too! But you're all traitors, you gang of lords who think you have finer ancestors than Vasa. Go to Hell!

    (GYLLENSTJERNA *shakes his head as he goes.*)

ERIK: Don't shake your head, you, or I'll shake it so you'll see all
four directions in the northwest!

(GYLLENSTJERNA *stops and stares fixedly at* ERIK.)

ERIK: Look at me. I won't burst!

(GYLLENSTJERNA *shakes his head and exits.*)

(ERIK *alone; walks back and forth; kicks various objects remaining on the ground; then he throws himself down on a divan with a tiger skin on it and laughs and weeps alternately.*)

GÖRAN PERSSON (*enters; comes up to* ERIK; *kneels*): My king!

ERIK: So it's you, Göran! I've been angry with you, but I'm not any
more. Sit down and talk.

GÖRAN: Ask me questions instead, Your Majesty.

ERIK: Don't say Your Majesty. Say Erik. Then I can be freer. Have
you heard the news?

GÖRAN: I don't know any news.

ERIK: Well, then. I've dismissed the Englishwoman!

GÖRAN: Why?

ERIK: She's a whore, has a lover . . . so that's over. But what stirs
my gall is that the Stures think she turned me down, and now
they're spreading my shame.

GÖRAN: Really!

ERIK: Göran, what is there about these Stures who always cross the
road the Vasas are to take? [12] Isn't there something fatal about
that clan? But what?

GÖRAN: Hard to say. They've always been good people, a bit heavy,
but they're descendants of Engelbrekt's murderer, Natt-och-
Dag . . .

ERIK: I'd never thought of that. Maybe that blood guilt has kept
them from getting the crown?

GÖRAN: And they have the blood of St. Erik and the Folkungs; [13] in
a word, all the great ones of Sweden have stood by their baptismal
fonts. But why do you fear them? You surely see how destiny or
whatever it's called has chosen Vasa.

ERIK: Why do I hate them? If I only knew! I suppose there's something to this: Svante Sture loved my first stepmother [14] and is related to my second stepmother, and I hate her so I'm fit to be tied!

GÖRAN: My king and friend, you use that word "hate" so often you'll finally imagine yourself the enemy of the human race. Stop using it! The word is the first realization of the creative power. And you'll bewitch yourself with that incantation! Say "love" a little oftener, and you'll persuade yourself you're loved.

ERIK: New tones, Göran. Have you been looking into it?

GÖRAN: Yes, I have.

ERIK: Agda, I suppose?

GÖRAN: No, it's someone ... else.

ERIK: Is she beautiful?

GÖRAN: No, to others she's ugly, but at a certain moment I saw the "idea," as Plato calls it. You know, the revelation of the perfect, the timeless behind the mask of her face, and since then ... hm ... I love her.

ERIK: Strange! When you said the word "love"—and you hesitated to say it—you became really handsome ...

GÖRAN: Am I so terribly ugly?

ERIK: Damnably ugly! Haven't you ever seen yourself in a mirror?

GÖRAN: I avoid mirrors!—But can you imagine anything as crazy as this: she thinks I'm handsome! (*Laughs*)

ERIK: Does she always think so?

GÖRAN: No, not always. Only ... when I'm not mean.

ERIK (*laughs*): When you're good, then.

GÖRAN (*embarrassed*): If you want to put it like that.

ERIK: You're a sorry fellow, Göran, and I don't recognize you.

GÖRAN: *Tant mieux* for my enemies!

ERIK: Do you intend to get married soon?

GÖRAN: Perhaps.

ERIK: Well, tell me whom I should marry.

GÖRAN: Catherine of Poland, of course; then we'd have all the shores of the Baltic, and we'd be related to the emperor himself.

ERIK (*leaps up*): Death and damnation! What a thought! You, Göran, yes, you're a remarkable man; and I said a while ago to Karin that I myself didn't need to think in your presence. But, an urgent message! Hell! (*Strikes his hands together three times*) (COURTIER *enters.*)

ERIK (*beside himself*): Send a messenger to Duke John! Seize him dead or alive . . . strike off his arms and legs if he flees . . . Quick, as thought!

(COURTIER *exits.*)

GÖRAN: What does this mean?

ERIK: That villain fooled me into promising by hand and word he'd get Catherine of Poland!

GÖRAN: That's really bad!

ERIK: Isn't it as if the devil had mixed the cards! *He,* my stepmother's son, kinsman of the Stures, will inherit the Baltic. He, the Jesuit, the papist,[15] will be the kinsman of the emperor . . . He!

GÖRAN: What have you done, Erik? If you had only let me advise you! Think of this: John's descendants will be kings in Poland, which has as many inhabitants as France and extends into Russia! John's grandchildren can become emperors in Austria, and his consort already has rights of inheritance in Naples through the house of Sforza! [16]

ERIK: So the snake must be crushed in the shell . . .

GÖRAN: And then the Catholics will be over us. You know John's sympathy for the Jesuits and the pope's gang. What have you done, Erik?

ERIK: The stupidest thing in my life!

GÖRAN: Let it be the last.

ERIK: If *you* want to make the other blunders, you may . . . Haven't you noticed how everything I touch becomes stupid and twisted?

GÖRAN: Not particularly, but you're not fortunate!

ERIK: What about you? Who's to end on the gallows! But you know

so much more than I; that's why you're going to be my adviser
... Imagine, that's what I get for being generous ...

GÖRAN: If you make me your adviser, Erik, I don't want to serve as
your nominal councillor, who gets all the blame without really
having anything to say. No, give me power and authority so that
I can act and be responsible for my acts myself. Make me procurator.[17]

ERIK: Good! You're procurator!

GÖRAN: Pending confirmation of the appointment by the national
council ...

ERIK: That's unnecessary. *I* am the ruler!

GÖRAN: That's the way to talk!

(COURTIER *enters.*)

ERIK: Speak.

COURTIER: The duke's yacht has already sailed with favorable
wind ...

ERIK: Lost!

GÖRAN: Have him pursued! Right now!

COURTIER: But the noble Lord Nils Gyllenstjerna asked me to deliver
a message that concerns this matter rather closely.

ERIK: Spit it out ... fast!

COURTIER: The fact may be that Duke John ...

ERIK: Göran, Göran!

COURTIER: Duke John is already secretly married to the Polish princess ...

(ERIK *sits down.*)

GÖRAN: Then we're saved; let me direct the game now!

ERIK: I don't understand.

GÖRAN: Through this arbitrary act the duke has broken the Articles
of Arboga [18] and furthermore entered into an alliance with a foreign power. So send the fleet out and make him a prisoner. Then
we'll try him legally! For treason! Will that do?

ERIK: Yes, but what will I get out of it?

GÖRAN: One enemy less, and a dangerous one!

ERIK: The strife between brothers, the game of the Folkungs,[19] isn't over.

GÖRAN: No, as long as Duke John lives, who, through his mother, inherits the Folkung blood from King Valdemar, there'll be no peace in our country. (*To the* COURTIER) Command Admiral Horn to come here at once, and the wild chase will soon be under way!

ERIK: Is it you or I who's king?

GÖRAN: At the moment it seems to be I!

ERIK: You're too strong for me, Göran!

GÖRAN: Not at all. It's you who are too weak!

CURTAIN

ACT II

A large room in GÖRAN PERSSON's *home. In the corner to the right is a fireplace with cooking utensils. Next to the fireplace is a dining room table. In the left corner is* GÖRAN's *desk.*

GÖRAN is sitting at his desk writing.

HIS MOTHER (*is standing by the stove*): Come and eat, son.

GÖRAN: I can't, mother.

MOTHER: Then the food will be spoiled again.

GÖRAN: It'll get cold—I doubt if that will spoil it. Don't say anything for a little while, please. (*Writes*)

MOTHER (*comes up to* GÖRAN): Göran, is it true you're working for the king again?

GÖRAN: Yes, that's true.

MOTHER: Why haven't you told me?

GÖRAN: Usually I say very little, and I have to keep certain secrets to myself . . .

MOTHER: What do you get for working for the king?

GÖRAN: How much do I get? I haven't asked, and he has forgotten to tell me.

MOTHER: Why would you take a job except for pay?

GÖRAN: Well, mother, that's your point of view, but mine's different.

MOTHER: But I'm the one who has to think in a different way—I have to put food on the table three times a day. Besides, Göran, why do you want to be at court? Weren't you humiliated enough when the old king was alive?

GÖRAN: I was brought up on humiliations, mother, so they don't get under my skin. I serve the king because I consider it a calling or a duty. He's weak and has a gift for making enemies everywhere.

MOTHER: And *you* want to support him, you who can hardly stand on your own feet?

GÖRAN: It looks as if I can . . .

MOTHER: Göran, your good intentions outstrip your abilities too often . . . That's how it was last time, when you helped the deserted Agda and her child.

GÖRAN: They're still provided for, aren't they? Besides, better days are coming—for all of us.

MOTHER: Do you know what thanks you'll get for that good deed?

GÖRAN: I don't want to hear any talk about good deeds, for I don't believe in them, and I don't expect any thanks. An unfortunate woman asked for help, and she got it. That's all there's to it.

MOTHER: But they're saying she's your mistress.

GÖRAN: I can imagine, but that, unfortunately, hurts only her.

MOTHER: Are you sure?

GÖRAN: Sure? Hm!

MOTHER: Besides, Agda could begin thinking you had intentions, and then you'd be blamed for having supported her.

GÖRAN: What haven't I been blamed for, mother? They blamed me for all the crazy things Erik did, even his affair with Karin, which

I tried in vain to prevent. I've learned to understand, though, that she's the only one who can give the king any happiness and inner peace, so I've become Karin's friend . . .

MOTHER: You're getting mixed up in too many things, Göran; you'll burn your fingers!

GÖRAN: No!

MOTHER: Don't rely on princes . . .

GÖRAN: I don't rely on anyone but myself! I wasn't born to wear a crown, but to rule; since I can rule only through my king, he's my sun. When that sun sets, I'll be extinguished, and that will be that!

MOTHER: Do you like Erik?

GÖRAN: Yes and no. We're bound to each other by invisible bonds; it's as if we had been born in the same litter and under *one* constellation. His hate is my hate, his likes are mine, and things like that bind people to each other.

MOTHER: Yes, you'll do as you please, Göran; I can neither follow you nor prevent you . . . Sh! There's Agda!

AGDA (*enters with her three-year-old daughter*): Hello, aunt; hello, Göran.

GÖRAN: Welcome, children. Come and say hello, Maria.

MARIA (*approaches his desk and pokes about in his papers*): Hello, uncle.

GÖRAN (*in a friendly fashion*): You little, little rascal, are you going to mix up my papers? If you only had an idea of what you're doing!

MARIA: Why are you always writing, uncle?

GÖRAN: Well, if I only could say!—If you're hungry, we'll eat.

AGDA: Thank you, Göran; you share your bread with the hungry, and . . .

GÖRAN: Huh! You mustn't say that! How often I've sat at other people's tables!

MOTHER: And he doesn't eat anything himself.

GÖRAN: That's absolutely untrue, for when I let myself go in the evening I'm a glutton, and among carousers, I'm certainly not the least. Go ahead—eat.

(*All sit down at the table. Someone knocks on the door.* GÖRAN *gets up; puts a partition screen before the dining table so that the two women and the child will not be seen.*)

MARIA (*covers her eyes with her hands*): Is it the bogeyman who's knocking? I'm afraid, mama!

AGDA: Don't be silly, Maria; there isn't any bogeyman!

MARIA: Yes, there is; Anna said so; and I'm afraid of him!

SVANTE STURE (*enters, haughtily*): Would you grant me a short conference, Mr. Secretary?

GÖRAN: A long one, lord councillor . . .

SVANTE: Count, if you please. Perhaps you don't know that I am a count?

GÖRAN: Goodness, yes! . . . You see, I made you a count!

SVANTE: Have you no shame?

GÖRAN: Easy, not that tone! I was the king's councillor for the coronation, and on my recommendation alone you were named Sweden's first count.

SVANTE: The devil! That my elevation should have come thanks to a jailbird!

GÖRAN: Easy, lord count! As a wild young fellow, I had to sleep off a spree in the tower, and that isn't too disgraceful, but you ought to sleep for the rest of your life in the tower as a rebel and traitor.

SVANTE: Huh! I can imagine!

GÖRAN (*covers the papers on his desk*): Only your great services in the late King Gustav's time have saved you from a well-deserved punishment. Watch out now!

SVANTE: For you, you priest's bastard! [20]

GÖRAN: My mother's sitting behind that screen. Keep that in mind!

SVANTE: And the bastard, too!

GÖRAN: Shame, Lord Svante! A little while ago I spoke well of you to the king; I said the Stures have always been good people,[21] and I still want to believe that; but you do everything to ruin yourself, with your unreasonable arrogance. You are a nobleman, but what is a nobleman? A horse with a man on its back! You don't know how to govern the kingdom, and you want to learn nothing but stable duties and soldiers' ways; you despise the man with the pen, but the pen has created this new age that has passed you by and that you don't understand. Human rights and human dignity, respect for the unfortunate and forgiveness of sin—these are new ideas that are not yet recorded on your escutcheons. I could be a count, *but* I don't want to be, because my destiny commands me to remain down below among the humble and the lowly, with whom I belong by birth . . .

SVANTE: Are scribblers and bookworms to stand between the king and the lords of the realm?

GÖRAN: The lord of the realm must be one, and one only, and no lords shall stand between the king and the people! The history of our country teaches us that, from King Ingjald,[22] whom you call "the Bad," because he burned the little kings alive; through Earl Birger and the Folkungs all the way to Christian the Tyrant, who executed the little kings. "The king and the people" ought to be the inscription on the national coat of arms, and perhaps the time will come when it will be . . .

SVANTE: When you paint the inscription?

GÖRAN: Who knows?

SVANTE (*growls*): Will you ask me to sit down, or am I to stand?

MARIA (*back of the screen*): Why does the old man shout so, mama?

AGDA: Sh-h, child!

GÖRAN: Stand or sit, my lord; I'm without all rank and a little above . . .

SVANTE: What the devil!

GÖRAN: Don't swear, count; there's a child in there and a woman . . .

SVANTE: Reprimanding *me,* I do believe!

GÖRAN: Yes! Why not? In my capacity as chairman of the king's supreme court,[23] I choose to remonstrate first; then we'll have other means to deal with those who won't listen . . .

SVANTE: The king's supreme court?

GÖRAN: Yes, I'm the highest judge in the supreme court . . .

SVANTE: But I'm a national councillor . . .

GÖRAN: You're a councillor, who's listened to but who doesn't have to be obeyed; I'm the king's procurator, who gives the orders and doesn't obey . . . If we're to stand here boasting like horse traders!

SVANTE: Procurator? That's new!

GÖRAN: Absolutely new! Here's my appointment. Along with other papers of great importance.

SVANTE (*somewhat more politely*): Why, this is a revolution . . .

GÖRAN: Yes, and the biggest since Charles VIII's confiscation of property [24] and the reformation of the church . . .

SVANTE: And you think the lords of Sweden and the councillors of the realm will submit to their own deposition?

GÖRAN: I'm sure they will. King Erik has the army, the navy, and the people on his side!

SVANTE: Can't you open a window? It smells horrible in here! . . .

GÖRAN (*angry*): It smells only of the kitchen, and, when you've gone, we'll air out anyway . . . after you! But you ought to go quickly, very quickly! Do you understand?

(SVANTE *going, but the feathers in his beret hit the top of the door frame.*)

GÖRAN: Watch out for your head, Lord Svante!

SVANTE (*comes back*): I forgot my gloves.

GÖRAN (*has taken the gloves with the fire tongs and hands them to* SVANTE STURE *in that way*): There you are.

(SVANTE *goes—deep in thought—while* GÖRAN PERSSON *holds the door open; whereupon* GÖRAN *spits after* SVANTE STURE.)

GÖRAN: To hell with you! And yours! You have touched me and mine, said the serpent.

MARIA: Was the old man terribly angry with Uncle Göran, mama?

GÖRAN (*blithely*): The old man has gone, dear child, and will never come back.

GÖRAN'S MOTHER: Göran, Göran! Is everything you said true? Are you procurator or whatever it's called?

GÖRAN: Of course I am.

MOTHER: Then be generous to your enemies.

GÖRAN: That depends on them and their behavior. And their fate will be decided in a little while by themselves.

MOTHER: By themselves?

GÖRAN: Yes, for Lord Svante will talk about this, but I have spies, and every threatening word the little kings utter will be judged in the king's supreme court. If they conspire, well—then they're lost.

MOTHER: Be generous, Göran . . .

GÖRAN: What the lords begin, I'll continue!

MAX (*enters*): You summoned me, Mr. Secretary.

GÖRAN: Sit down. (*To his* MOTHER) Mother, leave us, please. (*To* MAX *in a friendly but firm fashion*) Listen, Max. I heard every word of your conversation with Lady Karin . . .

MAX: I can imagine!

GÖRAN: Not so sharply, my boy!—I don't doubt the sincerity of your feelings for a second . . .

MAX: What do you want with my feelings?

GÖRAN: I don't want your feelings to disturb a human being who is precious to all of us and to our country. Lady Karin can become queen, if you don't upset her with your feelings, and you don't need to worry about her good name, for the king himself will restore that.

MAX: No, he won't.

GÖRAN: Listen, young man; what I'm telling you is as good as if the king said it. Now I command you—at the risk you can imagine for yourself—not to approach Lady Karin, for a single suspicion on the king's part about Karin's undivided love can bring him to misfortune and ruin her. You say you love her. Fine: then show you want what's best for her.

MAX: No! Not in the way you have in mind!

GÖRAN: Good! Then you'll be sent away. Do you see this? Here's an
order that will take you to Älvsborg Castle [25] . . .

MAX: I won't accept it!

GÖRAN: Don't shout—it will be easy to make you quiet!

MAX: The Uriah letter! [26] Eh?

GÖRAN (*softly*): In this case, you're the one who's tempting Bathsheba, who has never been yours, away from her children's father.
Take my advice and accept the order.

MAX: No!

GÖRAN: Then go and find a priest, for your hours are numbered!

MAX: Who's numbering them?

GÖRAN: I am. Farewell to you, for eternity!

MAX: With what power do you dare to sentence me?

GÖRAN: With that of justice, and the law, which condemns the man
who tempts a betrothed woman! Now you know. And so: done!

(ERIK XIV *enters*.)

(MAX, *frightened, steals out without being seen by* ERIK.)

GÖRAN (*pulls a bell cord; a bell rings*): Excuse me, Your Majesty.

ERIK (*blithely*): Doesn't matter. Are we alone?

GÖRAN: Yes, just about. Mother's sitting in there. But she may certainly listen, especially since there aren't any secrets here.

ERIK (*through the screen*): Good day, Mother Persson. We've become steady now, Göran and I, so you don't need to be afraid.

MOTHER: I know, Your Majesty; I'm not afraid.

ERIK: Fine! Fine! Well, Göran, now I have news.

GÖRAN: Good news?

ERIK: That depends on how you can make use of it.

GÖRAN: Bad news will do, too.

ERIK: Tell me, then, how this can be used.—As you know, John has
already married Catherine . . .

GÖRAN: That means Poland's on our side against Russia.

ERIK: Can't it also mean: that the duke is above the king?

GÖRAN: We'll see!

ERIK: And John has seized my messengers, entrenched himself in Åbo, and raised the Finns in rebellion.[27]

GÖRAN: That means the duke has revolted against his king and thereby forfeited both freedom and life.

ERIK: Let's say his freedom . . .

GÖRAN: *And* his life! That depends on the estates that must judge him.

ERIK (*disturbed*): Not his life! Now that I have children, I want nothing to do with the spilling of blood.

GÖRAN: So, while the estates are assembled, the case of treason must be brought up.

ERIK: Yes, but not his life! Then I couldn't sleep at night!

GÖRAN: Your great father, the master who built this nation, always observed the judicial rule of not taking any special regard for relatives, friends, or other associates. First the country, then that crowd!

ERIK: You're too strong for me, Göran.

GÖRAN: Not at all. But, as long as I can, I'll defend your crown against your enemies.

ERIK: Do I have enemies?

GÖRAN: Yes. The worst one was here a little while ago.

ERIK: That's Sture!

GÖRAN: That's right, and I'm afraid we've overestimated their excellent qualities. Count Svante, who went to the trouble of coming here to insult me, blurted out threats against the government and the supreme court . . .

ERIK: Did he insult you? Why don't you let me ennoble you so you'll be on the same level as the lords?

GÖRAN: No, I don't want that. I don't want to engage in any struggle for rank with the lords and become a little king myself. As long as I represent the little people, I'm justified, and only my merits can ennoble me or degrade me.

ERIK: It irritates me that you're always right, Göran.

GÖRAN: Nonsense!

ERIK: But have you thought of this: John's related to the lords, and clay and straw stick together?

GÖRAN: That was the first thing I thought of, naturally, and that's why they'll be caught in the same net.

ERIK: Think of it, I can never feel I'm related to John or the higher nobility; but that's my German blood,[28] I suppose. And that's probably what prevents the fulfillment of my big plans for getting married.

GÖRAN: Why, you are married, Erik.

ERIK: I am, and I'm not. You know, sometimes it seems to me—it's fine the way it is.

GÖRAN: Yes-s. Maybe we'll come to the wedding soon?

ERIK: What would the lords say about that?

GÖRAN: But how they'd feel about it! Think of that.

ERIK (*rubs his hands*): It would really burn them up! (*Laughs*) But you mayn't interfere in that matter. Tell me one thing, though: how is your wedding coming?

GÖRAN: *You* mayn't interfere in that matter!

ERIK (*laughs*): I don't know, but I like you better since Cupid caught you, and I rely on you more than I used to. Mayn't I see the "idea" sometime?

GÖRAN: I'll ask you not to joke about what must be sacred to every man of honor . . .

ERIK: You're a beast, Göran!

GÖRAN: I was, but I'm not any more. But this I know: if *she* deserted me, then . . . the old Göran would come back!

ERIK: Old Göran the Devil from the Blue Dove! "To the sound of gold when the game is played . . ."

GÖRAN (*points to the screen*): Sh-h! Don't summon up the evil past . . . I was evil then, very evil, because no one loved me . . .

ERIK: You're emotionally naïve, Göran. Surely you can't believe she loves you!

GÖRAN: What's that? What do you mean? Who said so? Who? Who?

ERIK: There, there! I don't know anything about it. I only said that because that's how it usually is.

GÖRAN: Erik, don't touch that chord, for then the devil will rise from down in my soul, where I've raised a little chapel to the unknown God . . .

ERIK: Hm!

GÖRAN: Yes, it's strange about love—hm—that it's accompanied by memories of one's childhood faith . . .

ERIK: Hm!

GÖRAN: Go ahead, grin.

(*Someone knocks on the door.*)

GÖRAN (*to* ERIK): Shall I open?

ERIK: Of course. There's only one person I don't want to see.

(GÖRAN, *his face a question*)

ERIK: That's Karin's father. The soldier Måns.

GÖRAN (*opens the door; recoils*): Måns!

MÅNS (*comes in unhesitantly; however, without recognizing* KING ERIK *immediately; hands* GÖRAN *a document*): Will you be so kind as to look at this? (*Recognizes* ERIK, *is at first embarrassed, then slowly removes his steel helmet*) The king! I should kneel, but by God in heaven I can't, even if it costs me my head! (*Pause*) Take my head as you've stolen my honor!

ERIK: Your honor, Måns, can be restored . . .

MÅNS: Through marrying her to someone? That's just why I'm here.

ERIK: You're not going to give my betrothed to anyone.[29]

MÅNS: I don't know that my Karin's betrothed! You've ruined her, but there's an honorable man who'll make good the harm you've done.

ERIK (*to* GÖRAN): Think of it! I'm to listen to the like of that from a common soldier.

MÅNS: I wonder which one of us is more common . . .

ERIK (*to* GÖRAN): Tie me up, or I'll kill him.

MÅNS: I'm the grandfather of your children, whether you like it or not. What does that make me to you?

ERIK: You're my Karin's father, so I forgive you. What do you want?

MÅNS: What you never can give me!

GÖRAN: Take your paper and go, man!

MÅNS: Then it will have to be done without a paper, but it's going to be done!

ERIK: What's going to be done? Do you intend to lure Karin away from me and my children?

MÅNS: If we're not agreed on that point, we have the estates of the realm to decide between us.

ERIK: Did you come from Hell?

MÅNS: No, I came from the Lord High Steward, Lord Svante Sture.

ERIK: Always Sture! Måns, you have the upper hand for the moment, because you're right. If you'll be patient, I'll give you justice.

MÅNS: I want only my daughter and my grandchildren, mine, since you don't acknowledge them.

ERIK (*to* GÖRAN): What does the law say about this?

GÖRAN: The law says illegitimate children go with their mother.

MÅNS: That's *that* law, but there's another written in the hearts of abandoned children, and it condemns a dishonorable father to lose the love he thinks he has the right to demand.

GÖRAN (*softly to* ERIK): Bribe him.

ERIK: Måns, I'll make you an ensign . . .

MÅNS: Thank you, but that's not for me. The rich man thinks everything can be bought, and yet . . .

ERIK: Yet he's poorer than the lowliest.

MÅNS: Just about. But, since I didn't come here to beg, I'll have to leave just as poor as I came. (*Pause*) . . . Even a little poorer. (*Goes*)

ERIK: And I have to stand quietly and take the like of that?

GÖRAN: That's a risk one has to take when one embarks on irregularities.

ERIK: What am I going to do?

GÖRAN: Marry her!

ERIK: Shame!

GÖRAN: There's no other way. How would you want to drag John before the estates and at the same time be on trial for adultery yourself?

ERIK: *Diantre!* You're right, as always. Let me go home and think about this. It's Sture, Sture, always Sture! (*Looks about*) You live like a pig, Göran; you'll have to move and set yourself up. (*Points with his thumb behind his back, toward the screen*) What are you up to in there? (*Laughs*)

GÖRAN: Be serious, Erik. Difficult times lie ahead, very difficult.

ERIK: Yes, but I'm too tired to meet them.

GÖRAN: I'll manage everything if you'll let me and if you don't interfere.

ERIK: Manage away, but don't let me feel the reins, for then I'll throw you off. Good-bye, then. And let me see that you set yourself up with a little luxury. (*To the screen*) Good-bye, Mother Persson. (*When she doesn't answer, says to* GÖRAN) Well, you say good-bye to her. (*Goes*)

    (GÖRAN *pulls the bell rope.*)

    (PEDER WELAMSON *enters. He is a tall, one-eyed soldier.*)

GÖRAN: Do you know Max, the ensign in the life guards?

PEDER: Yes, indeed, procurator.

GÖRAN: Take six strong fellows with you and wait for him in the green walk, where he comes on night duty. Tie him up so he won't yell and stuff him into a sack without shedding one drop of blood. Then throw him into the stream and see to it carefully that he drowns.[30]

PEDER: I'll do that, procurator.

GÖRAN: Haven't you any scruples?

PEDER: None!

GÖRAN: That's how a faithful servant should be, and that's how I am as my king's!—God's peace!

(PEDER *goes.*)

GÖRAN (*to the screen*): Do you have a bit of cold food, mother? I'd appreciate it.

MOTHER: Well, did you get any money?

GÖRAN: No, we had other things to talk about.

MOTHER: I don't listen, but I heard some of it . . .

MARIA: Come and eat, uncle.

GÖRAN: Yes, little one, I'm coming.

CURTAIN

ACT III

SCENE I

The background is a Lake Mälar landscape at evening. In the distance can be seen Gripsholm Castle.[31] *Across the center of the stage a bridge; to the right of the bridge a watchman's cottage at the foot of a hill. There are oak trees and hazel bushes on the hill. On the shore a fisherman's cottage, a boat, nets.*

GÖRAN PERSSON *and* NILS GYLLENSTJERNA *enter.*

GÖRAN: Lord Gyllenstjerna, you are the king's friend, aren't you?—in spite of the latest unpleasantness . . .

GYLLENSTJERNA: I'm a Gyllenstjerna, and I'm a friend of the Vasas, but I won't be a hangman!

GÖRAN: It's not a question of that . . . What do you think of Duke John's behavior and his sentence?

GYLLENSTJERNA: Duke John raised Finland and Poland against his country, and the estates sentenced him to death, legally and justly. That King Erik reprieved him is a credit to the king's heart.

GÖRAN: Fine! What should we say, then, when the dowager queen and the lords arrange an ovation to welcome the traitor when he reaches this place?

GYLLENSTJERNA: They make themselves accomplices and thereby incur the same punishment as the condemned man.

GÖRAN: The dowager queen can't be touched, of course, but the Stures and the other lords can. At the first sign that they want to pay homage to the bandit, I'll have them arrested here at the bridgehead, where there's to be a stop. The soldiers already are in the fisherman's cottage, but it's important that you as one of the lords of the realm and as a kinsman of the Stures give our undertaking your personal support.

GYLLENSTJERNA: I'll do my duty, but I won't do anything illegal . . .

GÖRAN: The procedure here will be legal, and the estates will judge the Stures as they have judged Duke John.

GYLLENSTJERNA: In that case, I'm with you; but first I want to see if the lords dare to place themselves beside the traitor against the king. I have my men nearby, and, when you have a shot fired, I'll be here immediately. Farewell for the time being. (*Goes*)

GÖRAN: Listen: yet another word, Lord Gyllenstjerna. (*Follows him*)

WATCHMAN (*comes out of his cottage, accompanied by* PEDER WELAMSON): So far as that goes, I'd rather solve it with a crane saw . . .

WELAMSON: A crane saw!

WATCHMAN: Yes. We'd saw off the bridge girders, and put a guard at the bridgehead. Now, when the lords and ladies come to meet the duke, the guard would say, "Don't go on the bridge!" He doesn't need to say it more than once, and very softly. They'll naturally not bother about what he says, and the bridge'll crash; so they'll lie there through nobody's fault.

WELAMSON: Yes, you could do it like that, too, but it would be a little unsatisfactory, and there are people who can swim. For example, I drowned an ensign by the name of Max in the north channel the other day. We put him in a sack like a kitten and laid eight weights about his feet, but you've never seen the like; he swam like an otter, so we had to club him as you club fish on Twelfth Night.[32]

WATCHMAN: So-o! You were the one who finished off Max . . .

WELAMSON: Oh, yes.

WATCHMAN: That wasn't badly done. Those who disappear don't walk again, and there's no loose talk afterward. But this thing with trials and sentences is pretty bad, for there's always some slip in the proof; and there's such a damnable lot of writing, and, if a person doesn't put it just right, they're likely to declare the biggest rascal innocent. The procurator's a smart fellow, but he always has to write so damned much . . .

WELAMSON: Not always—oh, no; but with the duke there has to be proper forms . . .

WATCHMAN: Is that Polish woman, the duchess, along?

WELAMSON: No, she's coming later, they say . . .

WATCHMAN: Well, Gripsholm is big, and the walls are so thick you can't hear outside what's going on inside.

GÖRAN PERSSON (*enters*): Peder Welamson.

WELAMSON: Procurator.

GÖRAN: Station yourself at the bridgehead and don't let anyone go out on the bridge from this side; the duke's party is coming from the other.

WELAMSON: What you command will be done.

GÖRAN: Watchman. Keep your eyes open to what happens so you can testify afterward.

WATCHMAN: Testify? The others always say the witness on the other side is lying, so that won't do much good . . .

GÖRAN: I'll take care of that. You do your job. Hush, the foretroop's here. To your post! (*Goes to the right toward the back*)

(SVANTE STURE, NILS STURE, ERIK STURE, *with other lords and their followers enter. All are carrying wreaths and bouquets.* NILS STURE *has a large wreath into which has been woven a gilded* J *and a* C *with ducal crowns above them.*)

SVANTE (*to* NILS): Hang the wreath right above the bridge. Then our prince's and our kinsman's way to prison will go through a sort of triumphal arch . . . (*Observes the wreath*) *J* stands for John, and *C* stands for Catherine, but *J* could stand for Jagellony, too.[33] That's courteous!

NILS: And *C* can stand for Duke Charles!

ERIK STURE: Watch your tongue!

SVANTE: Silence, boys! Let the solemnity of the moment plead for peace, when war between brothers rages in the royal castles, and the game of the Folkungs is renewed. Is that Nyköping Castle[34] we can see in the distance?

NILS: No, it's Håtuna.

ERIK STURE (*naïvely*): Why, it's Gripsholm!

NILS: He didn't understand. And he doesn't know Duke John's a descendant of the Folkungs.

SVANTE: Silence, boys!

(NILS *goes with the wreath toward the end of the bridge.*)

WELAMSON (*holds out his spear*): Back!

NILS: Mind your manners, Watchman Cross-eyed!

WELAMSON: Watch out, puppy! If your father had taught you manners when you were small, you wouldn't abuse a man because of his misfortune.

NILS: It wasn't any misfortune you lost one of your peepers. Why not both?

WELAMSON: May misfortune strike you, you flippant pup!

SVANTE: What do you dare to say, soldier?

WELAMSON: As the king's man, I take the liberty of obeying orders, and the one who comes near me, I'll stretch flat on the ground!

SVANTE: That was in a sack before it got into a bag! Think of it: the mob represents the king! The hired help takes precedence over the lords, scribblers over knights! The baseborn over the noble! Our poor country!

LEJONHUVUD (*to* SVANTE STURE): Did you know that soldier's the son of Göran Persson's sister?

SVANTE: No, I didn't, but he looks like it.

STENBOCK: Imagine, that scoundrel Persson has one merit.

LEJONHUVUD: Really! What?

STENBOCK: He has a sister; I didn't think that of him.

LEJONHUVUD: Then he has still another merit. He doesn't practice nepotism.

SVANTE: If you keep this up, you'll end by talking favorably about a rascal.

STENBOCK: To our posts! The duke's here!

(*From the left the following come riding across the bridge three by three: first, three officers fully armed; second,* DUKE JOHN *—handcuffed—between two soldiers; third, three cavalrymen. Following them, foot soldiers*)

SVANTE STURE (*and the other lords strew flowers in the path of the duke;* NILS *has hung his wreath on the road sign*): Long live the duke of Finland! *Vivat!*

ALL: *Vivat! Vivat! Vivat!*

(DUKE JOHN *lifts his hands by way of thanks.*)

(*The procession goes out to the right while the lords stand waving. A shrill whistle is heard, then a shot;* GÖRAN PERSSON *and* NILS GYLLENSTJERNA *enter from the back right; soldiers come out of the fisherman's cottage.*)

GYLLENSTJERNA (*to* SVANTE STURE *and the other lords*): In the name of the king, I arrest you, my lords.

SVANTE: Are you in your right mind?

GYLLENSTJERNA: Yes, I am. Duke John was deposed from his duchy by the estates of the realm. When you, my lords, pay homage to him, you arrogantly challenge the legal judgment and sentence and acknowledge that you are on the traitor's side. Soldiers, do your duty! (*The soldiers take the lords prisoners.*)

SVANTE: Are you a Swedish nobleman and can talk like that?

GYLLENSTJERNA: Yes, and you, a descendant of Kristina Gyllenstjerna and a Sture—never before a traitor to his king! A traitorous subject has been made prisoner, and you place yourselves with flowers in your hands at his side as if you were waiting for a bridegroom!

SVANTE: The duke is not a subject . . .

GYLLENSTJERNA: Excuse me, your memory failed you that time, Lord
Svante! You were along yourself and helped draw up the Articles
of Arboga,[35] in which all the dukes were declared subjects.

SVANTE: That's true. If a person always knew what he's doing!

GYLLENSTJERNA: Go, my lords. Justice awaits you, and the law, before
which we must all bend, commoner and nobleman alike.

SVANTE: Well, the Stures know how to take the bad day as well as
the good, and, if another day comes, we'll find a way.

GYLLENSTJERNA: But, if night comes, you'll be gone! Farewell, my
lords. (*The lords are taken out to the right.*)

GÖRAN: Thanks, Lord Gyllenstjerna. You see, the big and formal
words which must be uttered on occasions such as this I can't
manage; but you have spoken well, so I thank you again. Now
I'm going to Uppsala to act!

GYLLENSTJERNA: Farewell, then, procurator. And don't judge too
harshly.

GÖRAN (*going*): I won't judge at all; I'll leave that to the estates. (*To*
PEDER WELAMSON) Peder Welamson, collect all the flowers and
wreaths.

WELAMSON: Right!

GÖRAN: And then we'll go in to draw up your testimony and the
watchman's, point by point.

WELAMSON: Point by point! But it would be best if it weren't put
into writing.

GÖRAN: Forget you're my nephew, and I'll forget I'm your uncle.

WELAMSON: Even when it comes to promotion?

GÖRAN: Especially then! You see: the nobles demand more of us
commoners than they do of themselves. That's why we try to
reach their high expectations. So far as that goes: stay down in
the valley; it blows less down there than it does on the heights.
And, as far as I'm concerned, I'll see to it they can speak favorably
about this rascal. [*Indicates himself*]

CURTAIN

Scene 2

*A room in Uppsala Castle. The windows at the back, which
face the courtyard, provide a view of the lighted and open windows of the Hall of State.*[36] *Vague shadows of moving figures in
that room can be seen, but only when the curtains are brushed to
the side.*

ERIK (*in his royal mantle; his crown lies on a table; he opens a back
window;* GÖRAN *stands at another window listening*): It's hot this
Pentecost evening . . .

GÖRAN (*points toward the Hall of State*): And it'll get hotter! Not
many lords have come, but the pastors have—in greater numbers.[37]

ERIK: And they don't love me! Were you in the Hall of State?

GÖRAN: I was in there for a minute.

ERIK: How did it feel? Forbidding? I can always feel if I have
friends or enemies before me.

GÖRAN: I always feel I have enemies if two or three are gathered together; that's why I'm always prepared to strike. And I prefer to
strike the first blow . . .

ERIK (*points outside*): Look! I—think—it's John—with his red
beard—over there!

GÖRAN: Oh, no! That's Magnus from Åbo—of course!

ERIK (*puts his hand to his forehead*): Yes, but I saw John! I saw
him! Give me the speech. It's clearly written, I hope?

GÖRAN (*gives* ERIK *a document*): Printed, so a child could read it.

ERIK (*reads part of the document*): That's good.—But have you included all the proof?

GÖRAN: All of it! From Nils Sture's rebellious talk to Lord Svante's homage to the traitor—and only big rascals would be able to acquit those criminals!

ERIK: And the witnesses?

GÖRAN: They're down in the entry. Besides, the written testimony is valid.

ERIK: Can we start soon, do you think?

GÖRAN (*looks through the window*): The speakers of the four estates haven't taken their places, but aside from that it looks as if the great majority's already seated.

ERIK (*comes downstage; places his speech on a chair; then takes the crown and puts it on his head*): This is a terrible heat, and the crown presses the perspiration out of my hair.

KARIN MÅNSDOTTER (*enters*): Excuse me, dear, but the children have an innocent little request.

ERIK (*cheerfully*): Just say it.

KARIN: They said they'd like very much to see the king.

ERIK: But they see me every day . . . Oh, yes, they mean the king with his crown on, the theater king. Well, let them come!

KARIN (*signals toward the door she has left open*): Come, children.
(GUSTAV *and* SIGRID *come in, hand in hand; they are carrying dolls; they come up to* ERIK *and kneel.*)

ERIK: Listen, small fry, don't lie on the floor. (*He bends down and picks them up, one on each arm.*) Look at it now!
(GUSTAV *and* SIGRID *finger the crown.*)

ERIK (*kisses them and puts them down*): You've never been that high, eh?

GUSTAV (*touches the ermine on the mantle*): Look, Sigrid; there are rats on the cape!

SIGRID: No, I don't want to see the wats! (*Goes to the chair on which* ERIK *has laid his speech; and, unnoticed by the others, wraps her doll in it.*)

ERIK (*to* GUSTAV): Well, Gösta, do you want to be king some day?

GUSTAV: Yes, if mother becomes queen.

ERIK: She's already more than a queen, my child.

GUSTAV: Am I more than a prince, then?

ERIK: Yes, you're a little angel!

(COURTIER *enters; whispers to* GÖRAN PERSSON, *who approaches the* KING.)

GÖRAN: Everything's ready! Hurry!

ERIK (*to* KARIN *and the children*): God bless you and keep you! All of you! (*Goes as* GUSTAV *and* SIGRID *throw kisses to him*)

KARIN (*to* GÖRAN): What's going to happen down there?

GÖRAN: The king's going to accuse the lords before the assembled estates.

KARIN: The lords down in the prison?

GÖRAN: Exactly.

KARIN: Should they have been put in prison before they were investigated and judged?

GÖRAN: Yes, if they're caught in the act, they're put in prison, and that's the case here.

KARIN: You're up to a lot that I don't understand . . .

GÖRAN: Yes, the whole system of justice is very complicated, and one has to be accurate and conscientious when a fellow human being's welfare is at stake. (*At the window*) Listen, the king's speaking! And he can be seen from here!

KARIN: Pull the curtains to, Göran. I don't want to see it!

GÖRAN (*pulls the curtains to*): At your service, my lady.

SIGRID: Mama, is that Göran Persson?

KARIN: Sh-h, Sigrid dear.

SIGRID: Is he the one who's so mean?

GÖRAN: Not to good children, only to bad ones.

KARIN: I like you better when you strike than when you caress, Göran.

GÖRAN: Really?

KARIN: And I wouldn't want to have to thank you for anything.

GÖRAN: And just the same . . .

COURTIER (*enters; whispers to* GÖRAN PERSSON, *who, excited, hurries out; then to* KARIN): Her Majesty, the dowager queen, requests an audience.

KARIN (*timidly*): An audience? With me?

DOWAGER QUEEN (*rushes in from the left; kneels abruptly*): Mercy! Mercy for my brother and my kinsmen!

KARIN (*falls to her knees*): Rise, for the sake of heaven and our Saviour! How can you believe I can grant mercy, I who live on mercy myself? Rise, Your Majesty, the noble-born widow of the great King Gustav. I'm too lowly and unworthy for you even to visit me!

DOWAGER QUEEN: Are you Lady Karin, who has the destiny of the realm in your little hand? . . . Rise, lift your hand, and save my kinsmen, for the king is beside himself and is raging!

KARIN: He's raging? Why? I know nothing, and I can do nothing! If I said a word, he'd strike me, just as he wanted to kill me a few days ago.

DOWAGER QUEEN: So it isn't true you're the queen?

KARIN: I? Oh, God, I'm the least among the ladies of the court, if I can even be counted as one of them.

DOWAGER QUEEN: And he mistreats you? Why don't you leave him?

KARIN: Where in the world would I go? My father doesn't want to see me, and my brothers and sisters won't even talk to me. The last friend I had, my kinsman Max, has disappeared, I don't know where.

DOWAGER QUEEN: So you don't know that Ensign Max . . .

KARIN: Tell me!

DOWAGER QUEEN: He isn't alive any more. They've had him killed.

KARIN: So they murder people here? I had thought they did, but I didn't want to believe it.—Now I'm the one who begs for your protection, if you can have compassion for a poor sinner like me!

DOWAGER QUEEN (*thoughtfully*): So that's how it is? . . . Well, then! Come with me to Hörningsholm;[38] that's a fortified castle, and the lords have gathered there to defend themselves against the raging madman who still wears the crown.

KARIN: But my children?

DOWAGER QUEEN: Take the children with you.

KARIN: I have seen so much evil that I find it hard to believe in your generosity.

DOWAGER QUEEN: Don't speak of generosity, but believe what you will about the reasons for my offer. You can't stay here in this murderers' den. But quickly! Pack in a hurry! The king can be here in half an hour, and then the storm will break over you and your children.

KARIN: He has murdered my only friend, the noblest heart, the one who was ready to restore my good name. I forgive him, for he's unfortunate, but I can never see him again. (*Rings*)

(*Maid enters.*)

KARIN: Pack the children's clothes at once, and bring them in here. Take their toys, too, so they won't cry on the way and want to go home.

(*Maid goes out with* GUSTAV *and* SIGRID.)

DOWAGER QUEEN: What lovely children you have! Does their father love them?

KARIN: He idolizes them but would be able to kill them—nowadays he talks only about killing . . .

DOWAGER QUEEN (*slyly*): He'll miss them, then?

KARIN: For a while, yes; and then, not. Poor Erik!

(*Maid enters with children's clothing and toys, which she puts on chairs and tables.*)

DOWAGER QUEEN: I suppose Göran Persson does have a bad influence on Erik?

KARIN: The opposite, rather! Göran is wise, clever, and tries to do right as far as he can . . . but I fear him just the same!

DOWAGER QUEEN: Do you know what they're up to in the Hall of State?

KARIN: It's something about the lords that I don't understand.

DOWAGER QUEEN: The king has vowed they're going to die . . .

KARIN: The Stures, too! The noble Stures the people love?

DOWAGER QUEEN: The very ones who are imprisoned down in the castle cellar. And among them is my own brother, Abraham Stenbock . . .[39]

KARIN: Then I don't want any part of this any more! And my children must not have blood guilt.

(*Noise, cries, murmuring from down in the courtyard*)

DOWAGER QUEEN (*at a window*): Let it all go, and let's flee, quickly! The king's coming; he's so furious he's frothing at the mouth!

KARIN: Follow me; I know the way through the orchard down to the boathouse by the Fyris River. (*Takes some children's garments*) Help me carry these—and now: God protect us! (*Exits with the* DOWAGER QUEEN)

(*Loud noise from the courtyard; clash of weapons; trumpets sound; sound of horses' feet*)

(ERIK *enters; takes the crown off and violently puts it on the table; goes about and looks for something, beside himself with fury.*)

GÖRAN (*enters*): Is the king here? What happened? What in God's name happened?

ERIK (*tears off his mantle, rolls it up, throws it on the floor, and kicks it*): What happened? Nothing happened, for it was done, concocted by Satan!

GÖRAN: Speak so I can understand you; then I'll repair everything.

ERIK: Oh, well! You know I'm no speaker; that's why I had it written. I thought I had my speech in my pocket and opened fire against the traitors impromptu. Then I reached for my speech, but at the same moment I saw the Redbeard grinning at me as only John can. And I couldn't find the paper! Then I got wild, rushed on, mixing up names and figures, and it was as if someone had stirred up everything in my head and picked the mechanism of my tongue to pieces; this someone, whom I hesitate to call Satan, made me say Svante Sture instead of Peder Welamson, and vice versa; I said the lords had decorated the bridge with garlands instead of wreaths, and all the old suspicions of the

Stures that I've suppressed I blurted out, and a lot of accusations
I can't prove. At first they laughed, then they accused me of having given them wrong information about piddling matters, and,
when six of their witnesses testified John was greeted with
bouquets and a wreath instead of garlands, my information was
considered worthless! Think of it! If I had had the lords judged
in the usual legal fashion, they'd have had it at once, since they
were caught in the act, but I was going to be generous, God
knows, since I had the law on my side. Generous! To Hell with
generosity! And the estates voted *for* the villains, the estates pitied
the dastards, and now we're here, we judges stand as defendants
before the traitors! In truth, the one who has the support of Hell
is the one who's right!

GÖRAN: What about the witnesses?

ERIK: They rejected the witnesses! Do you think a bridge watchman
or a soldier may witness *against* lords? But they may witness *for!*
Sture's lackey's words were accepted, against me, the king! Stenbock's old nurse was quoted like Holy Scriptures! Ivarson's [40]
son, who's not of age, was accepted as a witness against law and
justice and was applauded!

GÖRAN: And the result?

ERIK: The lords were acquitted!

GÖRAN: Let me think for a moment! . . . Hm! Hm!—Yes, we'll do
this: The estates will be rejected as the wrong forum, and the
cases of treason will go to the king's supreme court.

ERIK: Fool! We, that is to say, you, as defendant are no longer an
unprejudiced judge.

GÖRAN: Hell! Then I see no other way out than extraordinary judicial procedure. *Fiat justitia!* At any price!

ERIK: Not against law and justice!

GÖRAN: No, *with* law and justice against twisters of arguments and
crooked advocates! The law condemns traitors to death; so, let
them die!

ERIK: Tell me, why did Redbeard grin when I couldn't find my speech? He knew where it was, of course; so he had been involved in stealing it! The speech has to be found, and the one who has it shall die! (*Looks about*) What's this? Am I in the nursery? It looks as if . . . (*Rings*) Göran, I'm afraid the worst has happened. (*Rings*) Why doesn't anyone come? The rooms sound so empty.

(COURTIER *enters.*)

ERIK: Where is Lady . . . Karin?

(COURTIER *remains silent.*)

ERIK: If you don't speak right now, I'll murder you! Where is Lady Karin?

COURTIER: Her Ladyship has left!

ERIK: Left, with the children?

COURTIER: Yes, Your Majesty!

ERIK (*collapses on a bench*): Then *you* may murder *me!*

GÖRAN: Send for them first. They can't have got very far.

COURTIER: The dowager queen has gone with them to Hörningsholm . . .

ERIK: To Hörningsholm, eagle's nest of the Stures . . . always the Stures! Send ten thousand men and storm it! Set fire to it! Starve the defenders to death!

COURTIER: The dowager queen was accompanied by the Södermanland regiment . . .

ERIK: The Södermanland! Ha, that's Duke Charles! [41] I don't dare to touch him, for if I do he'll let out the devil at Gripsholm! . . . So it was the dowager queen, that Sture bitch, who lured my Karin from me. And beautiful Karin went . . . whore, Göran, they're all whores! But they took my children, too, those Stures! That I'll never forgive! (*He draws his dagger and jabs it into the table.*) Never! Never! (*Sheathes his dagger*)

GÖRAN: Did Nils Gyllenstjerna show up in the Hall of State?

ERIK: Yes, at the start I saw him standing near the witnesses' bench, but, when the wind turned, he disappeared. Everyone disappears, but you, Göran.

GÖRAN (*to the* COURTIER): Bring Peder Welamson here. Right away. (COURTIER *exits.*)

GÖRAN: Listen, Erik, if this isn't logic! Common law condemns traitors to death; the Stures are traitors; therefore, the Stures are condemned to death.

ERIK: Fine!

GÖRAN: And this!

NILS GYLLENSTJERNA (*enters*): Excuse me, Your Majesty.

ERIK: See, there's the wretch!

GYLLENSTJERNA: Yes, that's easy to say, but what can one sane person do against a crowd of raving madmen?

ERIK: So! You do consider the Stures guilty?

GYLLENSTJERNA: I certainly have to believe my own eyes and ears, and a crime certainly can be committed even if the estates of the realm aren't present. However—there's a rumor—and that's why I came—that Duke John has escaped!

ERIK (*runs about the room*): Then Hell's broken loose!

GÖRAN: Calm yourself!

GYLLENSTJERNA: But I also have a word to say to you, procurator!

GÖRAN: Speak up!

GYLLENSTJERNA: Preferably in private.

GÖRAN: Nothing's a secret here!

GYLLENSTJERNA (*presses an object into* GÖRAN PERSSON's *hand*): Some-one asked me to give you this object with the message that it has been exchanged for another's!

(GÖRAN *stares at the ring he has just received, throws it over his shoulder out the window. Then he takes a miniature from next to his heart and tramps it under his feet.*)

ERIK (*who has observed everything, laughs*): That was *the* "Idea"! A whore, that one, too! (*Laughs*)

GÖRAN: Now comes Göran as the devil! Think of it: the best life has to give is the worst of all; Hell lies in Paradise; the angels are devils; Satan is a white dove; and the Holy Spirit . . .

ERIK: Stop it!

GÖRAN: Are you religious, you devil? Go, Lord Gyllenstjerna, for we're going to sweep and decorate this place as for a judgment day mass. Go quickly, for distinguished company is coming.

(PEDER WELAMSON *enters.*)

GYLLENSTJERNA (*leaving*): What you're planning to do isn't legal, but it certainly is just. (*Exits*)

GÖRAN (*to* GYLLENSTJERNA): Keep your mouth shut! (*To* WELAMSON) Peder Welamson, there are rats down in the cellars! Go down and kill them!

WELAMSON: Gladly! But . . .

ERIK: Do you hesitate?

WELAMSON: No, not about that. But I want something!

GÖRAN: Everyone wants something, but no one wants to give anything.

ERIK: What do you want? Do you want to be a baron, a count, a national councillor? Speak up! You'll see that that dirt isn't anything to cling to. And you won't be a bit better than those wretches down in the cellar! I can't make kings, but I can make queens! I can make a whore a queen! If you want to be a queen, you may!

WELAMSON: I only want to be a corporal.

ERIK: Corporal! What modesty! I really have better friends than John. Well then, corporal, serve your king.

WELAMSON: It would already have been done, if it hadn't been put into writing. But good enough! (*Goes*)

ERIK (*sits down on a chair*): This is a beautiful Pentecost eve . . . (*laughs*) Green leaves and white lilies . . . now I should have been going down Lake Mälar [42] with Karin and the children . . . The children! Think of it! Those beasts have kidnaped my children . . . And everything they do is right and fine . . . Why may some people do what they want to? Why? And now John's free!

GÖRAN (*has sat down at the writing desk and is doodling*): Why don't you send troops against him?

ERIK: Why don't you?

GÖRAN: I don't know. I can't fight with Satan!

ERIK: Have you lost your courage?

GÖRAN: No, but I don't understand how what has happened could happen. Why, it's against all logic, against all calculation, against all justice. Is there a God who protects rascals, who helps traitors, who makes black white?

ERIK: It looks like it!

GÖRAN: Listen! Someone's singing a psalm down there!

ERIK (*listens*): It's that old wild boar Svante!

GÖRAN: Yes! You can divide the human pack into religious swine and irreligious swine. But they're always swine!

ERIK: Don't you have a religion, Göran?

GÖRAN: I don't know. Until a few minutes ago some bubbles were beginning to rise from the slough of childhood, but they burst and stank!

ERIK (*has reached out and picked up a doll*): Look at this! It's Sigrid's, and her name's blind Paleface . . . I know the names of their dolls, you see! You know, what I've feared above everything else on earth was that my children and Karin would desert me! But reality's never quite what I anticipate, and I'm absolutely cool and calm as I've never been before . . . Might I say it at a happy moment! If only it hadn't been Pentecost eve! That awakens so many memories (*excited*) . . . memories of the children, especially! The best this wretched life gives . . . last year we rowed down Lake Mälar . . . Sigrid and Gustav were wearing bright new summer clothes, and their mother had made wreaths of forget-me-nots which she had put on their curly blond heads. They were in a summer mood, the children, and looked like angels . . . Then they were going to go barefoot on the shore and throw stones . . . Sigrid lifted her little hand, and the stone hit Gustav on the cheek. (*He sobs*) You should have seen how sorry she was . . . how she embraced him and begged for his forgiveness . . . she kissed the sole of his foot to make him laugh . . . Death and damnation! (*Leaps up*) Where are my children? Who

has dared to touch the bear's cubs? The wild boar! Then the
bear will claw the wild boar's offspring! That is logic! (*Draws
his dagger*) God help them!

GÖRAN: Let the corporal take care of that mess. For, if you get involved in it, there'll be a damnable howling!

ERIK: No! I want to take divine justice into my own hands since
the gods are asleep!

GÖRAN: Don't bother about the gods!

ERIK: Exactly! (*Goes out*)

    (GÖRAN *rings.*)

    (*The curtain is lowered for a moment.*)

    (GÖRAN *is still sitting at the desk writing when the curtain goes
up again.*)

ERIK (*enters; excited*): It was a lie, of course, that John had been
released; it's all a lie, the whole world and heaven, too; the
master of the world is also called the father of lies—see the
Gospel of St. Matthew, chapter 8, verses 11 and 12, in the 1541
edition . . . by the way, I wandered from room to room . . . think
of it, those devils hadn't yet made the bed in my bedroom . . .
from room to room without seeing one human being. The whole
castle has been abandoned like a sinking ship, and it was terrible
down in the kitchens; the servant girls had stolen the spices and
the food—the leavings were scattered all over, and the lackeys had
pried wine bottles open . . . However . . .

GÖRAN: Were you down in the cellars, too?

ERIK: Not at all! . . . But see how it looks in here! There's the crown
and there's the mantle, the regalia of the kingdom of Sweden . . .
but look at that little boot; the little foot has worn the heel
crooked . . . that's Sigrid's . . . it's really true that I'm ashamed,
but nobody escapes his fate and I've never escaped mine . . . my
father said I'd end badly! How could he know that if it hadn't
been recorded? And who could have recorded it if not the one
who predetermined it? But the worst was that the corporal cut
out one of Nils's eyes; the corporal is one-eyed, you know, and,

when he cut, he said: "There's for 'Watchman Cross-eyed,' and an eye for an eye!" I concluded that Nils must have taunted the corporal because of his defect. From that we see how everything repeats itself and that Nils, as they say, was struck down because of his own act.

GÖRAN: Are they dead, then?

ERIK: You mustn't ask so many questions, Göran. And then he stuck Svante, the wild boar, and Erik and the other birds . . . Sh-h! This is the worst: when the corporal was going to stick the old fellow, he got brave and declared the estates had acquitted him and asked me to prove my charges. Imagine, that dog wanted me to prove that he had called me a madman to my face, prove that he had thereby committed treason, prove that he had paid homage to the traitor . . . Then I got so furious I ordered him executed . . . but then he cried out: "Don't touch us"—he meant the Stures—"for, if you do, your children will die—they're our hostages!" Hostages? Can you understand what that word said to me? I saw the little ones executed at Hörningsholm; I wanted to recall my order, but it was too late!

GÖRAN: And then?

ERIK: It was a pitiful sight, and there's something sublime about every person at the moment of death. It's as if the mask fell and the butterfly fluttered out. I couldn't stand it . . .

GÖRAN: Yes, but did *you* kill anyone?

ERIK: No—! I only jabbed Nils in the arm,[43] but he didn't die because of that. At any rate, it was terrible, and I wish it had never happened!

GÖRAN: Do you regret you had bandits executed?

ERIK: But the hostages! Think of my children! And the mother of the young Stures! And the dowager queen's brother, Abraham, that they've massacred! She'll never forgive me. Can you straighten this out, Göran?

GÖRAN: No, because I don't understand any of it! Don't you see how the events take place without our being able to do anything

about them? I sit speechless, struck numb; I can't move a finger
and can only wait, asking: What is going to happen next?

ERIK: You haven't any advice to give me any more?

GÖRAN: None!

ERIK: Then I'll go to find the friend I should never have deserted.

GÖRAN: You mean Karin, of course.

ERIK: Yes!

GÖRAN: Go ahead!

ERIK: What's going to happen now?

GÖRAN (*still sitting at the desk, tapping it with his fingers*): If one
only knew!

CURTAIN

ACT IV

SCENE I

The kitchen in the home of MÅNS KNEKT, *the father of* KARIN
MÅNSDOTTER. MÅNS *is sitting by the table. Someone knocks.*

MÅNS: Come in.

(PEDER WELAMSON *enters.*)

MÅNS: Good day, Peder.

WELAMSON: Corporal, if you please!

MÅNS: Really! I hope you've earned your distinction honestly.

WELAMSON (*sits down*): I hope so.

MÅNS: What have you been up to in Uppsala?

WELAMSON: We've executed traitors!

MÅNS: Legally and justly?

WELAMSON: When traitors are executed, it's always just!

MÅNS: Did you have absolute proof?

WELAMSON: I had absolute proof since I saw it myself, so I killed them after the king had sentenced them according to law.

MÅNS: I don't have anything against their thinning out the lords . . . but why did the king go crazy afterward? [44]

WELAMSON: Crazy? He was sorry he had done it; that's not so crazy, is it?

MÅNS: He's been running around in the woods ever since. Isn't that true?

WELAMSON: He was so desperate about his children, whom they had lured away from him, that he went out into the night to find them—that was foolish—got lost in the woods, and had to sleep on the ground in the rain. And he didn't have anything to eat, got sick, and was delirious with fever. What about it?

MÅNS: Is there one spark of good in that man?

WELAMSON: Listen, Måns. I can understand your hating him, but even so you can't deny the king's a human being all the same. Only think of this: the estates had sentenced Duke John to lose his life, but the king reprieved him. And now he has let him out. That's nice, of course, but isn't wise. In his impatience he had the lords who plotted against him killed, but now he's asked their survivors for forgiveness, and has paid them large sums of money. Why, that's nice, too.

MÅNS: Yes, but murder's murder!

WELAMSON: What nonsense is that? He jabbed Nils in the arm, because he was impudent, but he didn't die from that . . .

MÅNS: Yes, but it's the same thing . . .

WELAMSON: Is it the same thing if one murders or doesn't murder? You're a queer fish, a stuck-up, unreasonable old rascal . . .

MÅNS: Don't yell; someone's listening outside the window . . .

WELAMSON: Let him!

MÅNS: Has the king seen Karin?

WELAMSON: I don't know. But I don't think so.

MÅNS: Why did she run away from him?

WELAMSON: The dowager queen frightened her.

MÅNS: What riffraff!

WELAMSON: Riffraff, because they're related to you!

MÅNS: Yes, they certainly could've had better taste! Maybe you think this notoriety gives me honor? The very opposite! Other people can hide their shame, but mine's on a castle spire so the whole country can see it!

WELAMSON: There *is* somebody out there!

(*They turn to the back window, which is partially open; through the opening can be seen the face of* KARIN MÅNSDOTTER *for a moment, pale and wan from suffering.*)

MÅNS: Did you see her, too?

WELAMSON: I saw her—it's Karin! Listen, Måns, you're prouder than the members of the royal family, but it doesn't suit you at all. Be a human being for once!

MÅNS: Give me that stick, over there in the corner.

WELAMSON: I'd let you feel that stick if it weren't for your gray hair!

MÅNS: Off with you before misfortune hits you!

WELAMSON (*going slowly toward the door*): Me? (*Exits and leaves the door open*)

KARIN MÅNSDOTTER (*appears in the doorway*): May I come in?

MÅNS: Are you hungry? Is that why you've come?

KARIN: No, but I'm not happy.

MÅNS: The wages of sin is death!

KARIN: I know, but, before I die, I want to see my brothers and sisters.

MÅNS: I won't let you!

KARIN: That will be the worst punishment I could get—father!

MÅNS (*picks up the stick in the corner and sits down again*): Don't come any closer; if you do, I'll hit you!

KARIN: Forget I was your daughter, and think of me only as a beggar who has tramped about in the woods until her legs will no longer hold her up. May I sit by the door like a beggar or a wanderer?

MÅNS: Get up. And walk, walk until the ground catches fire under your feet . . .

KARIN (*approaches the fireplace*): You can't deny me a drink of water from the pail . . .

MÅNS: Don't dirty the pail with your harlot's lips. If you want food and drink, go out to the pig pen; that's where you belong . . .

KARIN (*approaches him*): Beat me, but let me stay! I'm probably no worse than others.

(MÅNS *lifts the stick.*)

ERIK (*enters*): What are you doing, man?

MÅNS: I was going to punish my child!

ERIK: It's a little late to think of that. Since you've disowned your child, I've taken your place as nearest of kin.

(MÅNS *does not answer.*)

ERIK: If you had been a bit politer, I'd have asked formally for your daughter's hand; now I'll limit myself to inviting you to the wedding.

(MÅNS *says nothing.*)

ERIK: You think I've done wrong, and I admit it; but now I'll make amends for it, but then you're to forgive us, too. Give Karin your hand!

(MÅNS *as before, looks scornfully doubtful.*)

ERIK: You look as if you didn't consider me—sane. Most likely— because you who consider yourself sane are convinced that you wouldn't act as I if you were in my place. All the same, it is as I've said, and you could have got a worse son-in-law than I am.

(MÅNS *as before*)

ERIK: You don't answer me! Has any other king ever been humiliated like this? . . . Don't you understand how highly I value your daughter when I want to raise her to be queen of our country, and when I call on such a crude and proud fellow as you? And such a cruel one! Now I'm going! May I never regret this act which resembles generosity and which will never be understood by you! Come, Karin. Come! (*Takes* KARIN *by the hand; he turns*) I forgive you because I need forgiveness myself! A little while ago I felt I was the worst of all human beings, but now I think I'm a bit better than you!

CURTAIN

SCENE 2

A tower room with a library. DUKE JOHN *is sitting at a desk bent over a folio. Someone knocks.*

JOHN: Come in.

(DUKE CHARLES *enters.*)

JOHN: Have you slept?

CHARLES: I've slept on the matter.

JOHN: And?

CHARLES: It's no misfortune for the realm that the little kings have been destroyed.

JOHN: That seems to be the general opinion . . . But the realm mustn't be ruled by a madman!

CHARLES: There's the touchy point . . . Is he a madman?

JOHN: No doubt of it!

CHARLES: Just a minute! Pangs of conscience, repentance, turning over a new leaf—aren't madness.

JOHN: But his latest acts—which you don't know about yet—are pure madness! You don't know that he, *the king,* has called on Måns Knekt, apologized formally, asked for his daughter's hand, prepared for the wedding, and has already invited me. You'll get your invitation no doubt!

CHARLES (*walks back and forth, deep in thought*): It isn't wise, but it isn't crazy, either.

JOHN: No? Do you think Måns Knekt's grandchildren should sit on the throne of Sweden?

CHARLES: No, I wouldn't be happy to see that, but illegitimate children can't very well become successors to the throne.

JOHN: No? Göran Persson, the cleverest rascal and the only statesman the kingdom has, will get the estates to agree to anything he wants. He got the estates to sentence me to death . . . and he'll probably be able to persuade the estates to adopt the children of the king's mistress and make them legitimate.

CHARLES: Can't one rid the world of him?

JOHN: Try! Or, rather: no Göran without Erik, so . . .

CHARLES: Away with Erik! . . . But he is our brother . . .

JOHN: No! He insists he's not our brother, since we don't have the same mother.

CHARLES: Assume that we two succeeded in overthrowing him . . .

JOHN: And got the estates to approve afterward . . .

CHARLES: John, where have you learned such principles?

JOHN: From my enemies!

CHARLES: A poor school! . . . However, assume that we two bring about a change, what happens then?

JOHN: We two will share the throne! [45] The chair on which Gustav Vasa has sat is surely broad enough for two.

CHARLES: Do you confirm this agreement by word and hand?

JOHN (*shakes* CHARLES's *hand*): Yes, indeed!

CHARLES: I have faith in you, John, since you have what Erik lacks —religion! [46] So we'll say we can't come to the wedding and march to Stockholm instead.

JOHN: Wouldn't it be better to let Erik believe we're coming to the wedding?

CHARLES: Let it depend on circumstances. Why, we don't know what his next move will be yet; so let him reveal his game first.

JOHN: You're almost wiser than I! But I'm afraid of that invitation. He calls us Folkungs because we're descendants of Valdemar; [47] it's too much like the banquet at Nyköping . . . [48]

CHARLES: Or the game at Håtuna.

JOHN: Rather that!

CHARLES: So: let's get in the game. I'll rely on you, John; you know why!

JOHN: Rely on me!

CURTAIN

SCENE 3

A room in the castle. KING ERIK *and* QUEEN KARIN MÅNSDOTTER *enter. They are dressed in royal attire.*

ERIK: Now you're my wife, the mother of our country, and the first lady in the land. I welcome you to the royal palace. Our nuptials weren't brilliant,[49] for the dukes stayed away from the ceremony . . . but they may show up at the banquet. . .

KARIN: Erik, don't let this latest humiliation trouble you; rejoice with me instead over the fact that our children now have parents who are married . . .

ERIK: Everything in my life has been soiled and twisted; even this day when I brought the bride of my youth to the Lord's altar had to be a day of shame! And the children, God's blessing, had to be hidden so that our shame wouldn't be revealed to the world, which knows about it all the same.

KARIN: Don't be ungrateful, Erik. Remember the days and nights of terror when you trembled over your children's fate, because your enemies held them as hostages . . .

ERIK: You're right, and my enemies were more generous than I. They spared the lives of my children when I took the lives of the lords . . . yes, yes, the others are better than I, and I am better off than I deserve. Much better!

KARIN: You should really feel happy to have got out of all dangers as you have . . .

ERIK: I am happy . . . but that makes me uneasy . . . and it makes me feel bad that I had to keep Göran Persson from attending our wedding because of the dukes . . . but that was their condition.

KARIN: Don't feel bad, but be grateful . . .

ERIK: I am grateful . . . although I don't really know why . . . I have done what's right, but still I have to beg for forgiveness!

KARIN: Erik! Erik!

NILS GYLLENSTJERNA (*enters*): Your Majesty, the people want to see the royal bride and hail the queen of our country.

ERIK (*to* KARIN): Do you want to go?

KARIN: Yes, if it's traditional.

ERIK (*to* GYLLENSTJERNA): Let the people come in.

   (GYLLENSTJERNA *lets the people enter.* MÅNS KNEKT, GÖRAN PERSSON's *mother,* AGDA, *and* MARIA *can be seen among the people.*)

KARIN (*to* ERIK): Say a friendly word to father, just one.

ERIK: I don't know, but that man is prouder than I, so I don't need to make a bad thing worse.

MÅNS (*to* KARIN): Now, when everything has been made right, I forgive you.

ERIK (*angry*): What is it he's forgiving you for?

MÅNS: I used to think that Ensign Max would be the one to raise the fallen . . . the two of them were sort of engaged . . . well, well, there wasn't anything really between them, as they say; I mean . . .

KARIN: Father! Father!

ERIK (*to* MÅNS KNEKT): Are you drunk or are you possessed of the devil?—God in heaven, what a wedding! And what a crowd! There's Agda from that whore tavern the Blue Dove, who was Jacob Israel's mistress.[50] A friend of the bride! And that bumpkin is my father-in-law! To hell with it! But it's true I'm to be grateful and glad, and happy. And I'm damnably happy! (*To* NILS GYLLENSTJERNA) Take the riffraff out and feed them. I take it there are half a dozen sisters-in-law who wouldn't say hello to me before, probably a brother-in-law or two who want to borrow money. Drive them out, Gyllenstjerna!

(KARIN *goes out, weeping.*)

ERIK (*to* KARIN *as she goes*): That's how good it was!

(*The people withdraw.*)

ERIK: If I could hear what these wretches think, I'd have cause for hanging all of them . . . except Göran's mother, who should have had sense enough to stay home. Her son did have more sense and stayed away . . .

(GÖRAN PERSSON *enters.*)

ERIK: There he is. You came as if I'd sent for you, Göran . . .

GÖRAN: I hope I haven't come too late, though . . .

ERIK: What have you been up to?

GÖRAN: I've been working with the estates in Uppsala, and there's news.

ERIK: Really!

GÖRAN: After your departure from the castle, I found the indictment and the witnesses' depositions. After various efforts, I succeeded in getting the estates together, and then I appeared as prosecutor . . . briefly, with the result that the estates declared the lords guilty . . .

ERIK: No! And I who've begged for forgiveness and sent out a circular throughout the whole country declaring all those who were executed innocent!

GÖRAN (*sinks down on a chair*): My God, then we're lost! Yes, Erik, whatever you put your hand to, goes wrong.

ERIK: Can't you straighten this out, Göran?

GÖRAN: No, I can't straighten out your messes any more. Everything I build up, you tear down, you unfortunate soul!

ERIK: So that's why the dukes sent their regrets?

GÖRAN: Most likely, but someone warned them, too.

ERIK: Who? Who?

(GÖRAN *does not answer.*)

ERIK: You know who! Tell me!

GÖRAN: It hurts me to have to tell you.

ERIK: So it was Karin!

(GÖRAN *says nothing.*)

ERIK: She! That whore, that false devil! And I who have bound myself to her! So she knew about the estates' judgment—but I didn't! I have to live through the like of that!

(GÖRAN *says nothing.*)

ERIK: That's what I get for being generous. For reprieving John, for making it up to the scoundrels' relatives by means of large sums of money. So I was to be hit right in the heart! By the only person on earth I loved and had faith in—chains about my hands and my feet—the rope about my throat—who is it I'm fighting against?

GÖRAN: Against Satan!

ERIK: I believe it!—If only the dowager queen would come! Then the lords would come—to the banquet.—Think of that witch, Elizabeth of England, when she hears about my marriage! To a private's daughter! That hurts me worst of all. Unspeakably!— (*Laughs*) The king of Sweden celebrates his nuptials with a girl who sells nuts on the streets, a Vasa marries a Månsdotter . . . who has been a soldier's whore! You're the one who drowned him, I suppose. Thanks for that! I got the blame, of course, and had to beg Karin for forgiveness for three days and three nights . . . I always have to beg for forgiveness when others have done dirty deeds . . . Too bad the dukes didn't come; I'd have put powder under their chairs and lit it myself!

(NILS GYLLENSTJERNA *enters.*)

ERIK: Go ahead—bray!

(GYLLENSTJERNA *says nothing.*)

ERIK: More people who've sent their regrets. The dowager queen regrets she can't come!

GYLLENSTJERNA (*shows the* KING *a great many open letters*): Yes, and all the lords regret they can't come.

ERIK: I, the king, honor rascals by inviting them to my wedding, and they don't come! Gyllenstjerna, give the signal to start the banquet. Then call in the riffraff and place them at the tables! All of them! My false jewel's to get the setting she deserves! Send people out on the streets and squares, get the beggar from the gutter and the whore from the tavern!

GYLLENSTJERNA: Are you serious, Your Majesty?

ERIK: Are you joking, you dog? (*Goes and opens the door at the back; signals; fanfares are blown and set tables are carried onto the stage; goes to the left door and waves the people in. They look half drunk and self-conscious.*) To the tables, wretches! There! No false modesty. We won't wait for the bride, for she has just gone into labor! Sit, dogs! If you don't obey, I'll kill you!

(*The people, except for* GÖRAN PERSSON'S MOTHER, *sit down at the tables.*)

(GÖRAN *remains sitting in his chair and looks contemptuously at the spectacle.*)

(GYLLENSTJERNA *lays down his marshal's staff at* ERIK's *feet and starts to leave.*)

ERIK: So—you've had enough now, you plate-licker! Do you consider yourself too good to serve this rabble? Take a look at the king's father-in-law; see how he sticks his fingers in his mouth . . . (*Picks up the staff, breaks it, and throws the pieces after* GYLLENSTJERNA) Go to Hell!

GYLLENSTJERNA: Now your last and only friend is going! (*Exits*)

ERIK (*to* GÖRAN): Think how fine that sounds! And I'm still enough of a child, or enough of a fool, that I'm ready to believe the first rascal who says a kind word!—However . . . (*sits down beside* GÖRAN) Gyllenstjerna wasn't the best nor was he the worst; Lord Back-and-Forth; full of a sense of justice and injustice. Courageous as few and cowardly as none; faithful as a dog and false as a cat . . .

GÖRAN: In other words, a human being!

(*Other people come in.*)

ERIK (*to these people*): Welcome, good people, to the wedding! Sit down at the tables! Eat, drink, and be merry, for tomorrow you'll die! (*To* GÖRAN) It's strange that I've always liked lower-class people. You know, I feel right at home with these characters. But see how the lackeys wrinkle their noses . . . (*Laughs*)

GÖRAN: Do you really think lower-class people are worse than the higher? You know, I've never heard anything in the gutter or the tavern that can compare with the coarseness Svante Sture uttered to me when he visited me.

ERIK: What did he say?

GÖRAN: On his behalf I'm ashamed to repeat the insulting words he uttered in the presence of my mother and the child . . . He didn't stick his knife in his mouth, of course, but that was his greatest merit, too!

ERIK (*to the lackeys who are serving the people at the tables un-willingly*): Be courteous to my guests, or I'll have you whipped! (*To* GÖRAN) What are you thinking about?

GÖRAN: About your destiny—and mine! But I don't understand anything any more. Our saga's almost over, I think. The air's so quiet, and I can hear so much. In one ear I hear the tramping of horses, and in the other the beating of drums of the kind they use at executions. Have you seen my mother lately?

ERIK: She was here a little while ago to look at the bride.

GÖRAN: I don't understand, but I'm longing for her; she talked mostly about money, of course, but she was probably right . . .

ERIK: Göran, I hope you're not angry because I asked you to stay away from the wedding—that was because of the dukes . . .

GÖRAN: Don't you think I understand that? Do you think I'm petty? But I'll ask you to do me one favor.

ERIK: Speak up.

GÖRAN: Don't imagine I had anything immoral to do with Jacob Israel's Agda, because it isn't true. That I helped her out was only one of those whims of . . . hm! . . . generosity that we all get on rare occasions.

ERIK: You really are good, Göran . . .

GÖRAN: Keep still! Forgive me, but I can't bear to have people say anything good about me; it's as if it weren't true or didn't concern me. I suffer from it, in a word.

ERIK: Nonsense . . .

GÖRAN: Do you know what the dukes' staying away means?

ERIK: That they're swine!

GÖRAN: That we're doomed to die! It's that simple and clear, I think.

ERIK: Die? Yes, of course! You're right about that. Do you know what my biggest weakness was?

GÖRAN: No, I know absolutely nothing, understand nothing, and so I'm done for. There was a time when I dreamt I was a statesman, and thought I had a mission in life: to defend your crown, inherited from your great father, given by the people—not by the lords—and worn by the grace of God. But I must have been mistaken.

ERIK: Have you ever noticed, Göran, that there are matters we don't understand, and may not understand?

GÖRAN: Yes. But haven't you often and finally felt yourself a bit better than the others?

ERIK: Yes. And you?

GÖRAN: I have always thought my acts were right . . .

ERIK: I, too; and most likely the others do, too. Who has been wrong, then?

GÖRAN: Who knows? Imagine how little we know! (*Pause*)

ERIK: Göran, will you get Karin?

GÖRAN: Yes, if you forgive her.

ERIK: For what? Oh, for her warning the dukes? That was ugly toward me, but she was probably afraid of getting blood guilt over the children. And on my head!

GÖRAN: She took your powder barrels ahead of time, because she knew her Erik. Forgive her!

ERIK: I already have! But look at them! Now they're beginning to have had enough to eat and are happy and would like to talk . . . Göran, is life more to be laughed at than to be wept over?

GÖRAN: As much the one as the other, I suspect. For me, the whole thing is nonsense, but that doesn't mean there mayn't be a hidden meaning to it. You're depressed, Erik?

ERIK: Yes. The old uneasiness is coming back. But who's making me uneasy? Who? Come with me; I want to see Karin and the children. Can you explain that? I know she isn't much better than I am, but in her presence I feel calmer and less inclined to evil!

GÖRAN: I can't explain anything . . .

ERIK: Sometimes I think I'm her child; sometimes she's mine! . . .
     (*Pause*)

GÖRAN (*listening*): Hush! I hear footsteps on the stairs and in the entrance halls; people are stealing quietly about the doors and . . . they're opening windows . . .

ERIK: You hear that, too?

     (GYLLENSTJERNA *enters.*)

ERIK: There! Nils Göransson Back-and-Forth, born Gyllenstjerna!
     (*Laughs*)

GYLLENSTJERNA: Your Majesty, the palace garrison and the guards have been bribed! [51] The dukes must be much closer than we had thought!

ERIK: Go to the dukes, then!

GYLLENSTJERNA: I'm not that low!

ERIK: What proof do you have for your suspicions?

GYLLENSTJERNA (*shows him a silver coin*): This Judas coin which has been distributed to the garrison and the guards! It's already being called the Blood Penny and was struck from the silver Your Majesty has given in compensation for the Stures and the other lords!

ERIK (*to* GÖRAN): Can you straighten this out? Traitors are executed; I pay compensation; and with the compensation my head's to be bought—and yours! Isn't the world mad? Come with me to Karin.

GÖRAN: I'll go with you as always and wherever you want to go.

ERIK (*to* GYLLENSTJERNA): Go, Gyllenstjerna, and save your life. Thank you for the good you have given me—the rest—we'll erase. Let the people enjoy themselves to the end! They're children whom no one may annoy!

GYLLENSTJERNA (*kneels before* ERIK): God protect and preserve the good king, the friend of the people, the people's king!

ERIK: Do they call me that? Do they say anything good about me?

GYLLENSTJERNA: Yes, and, when Erik comes with grain, the farmer sees St. Erik's broadaxe on the king's staff and says, "God save King Erik!" [52]

ERIK: Hush, madman and blasphemer! We don't believe in saints any more . . .

GÖRAN: And not in devils, either!

(GÖRAN *and* ERIK *go out to the right;* NILS GYLLENSTJERNA *to the left. Pause*)

MÅNS KNEKT (*absolutely sober, but embarrassed, raises a glass*): Good friends, good hospitality has now . . . let us . . . enjoy food . . . good food . . .

MARIA (*loudly and clearly*): I have to go, mama . . .

AGDA: Sh-h, dear!

MÅNS: It isn't I who am the host, of course . . . this coll- . . . colla- . . . this collation . . . is a little queer, to tell the truth. One and another would have liked to have seen the bride and the groom at the table . . .

MARIA: I have to go, mama!

MÅNS: Wait a little, child, and don't drink so much wine . . .

MARIA: I have to go, mama!

MÅNS: Take the brat out, for God's sake . . .

AGDA (*gets up with* MARIA): Come, dear . . . [*They go out; return later.*]

MAN'S VOICE I: What the devil! Can't they do things like that at home? Lackey! Bring the goose again . . .

WOMAN'S VOICE I: No, I was the one who asked first!

MAN'S VOICE II: Hand me the salmon! You!

LACKEY I: Do you know where you are?

MAN'S VOICE II: I'm at *our* home, you goldfinch! It's *our* food, see? We've paid for it!

WOMAN'S VOICE II: Open your belt, Måns dear!

MÅNS KNEKT: Is there anyone who insinuates me . . . about me? You think I'm eating too much?

WOMAN'S VOICE II: No, I said that to little Måns!

MAN'S VOICE III: Lackey, get the trumpets in here! The trumpets!

MÅNS KNEKT: Watch it! No trumpets!

MAN'S VOICE III: I won'er jus' where the fine gen'lemen're eating? Are they sor' of—sor' of too good?

MAN'S VOICE I: The king? Why, he's crazy, you know!

WOMAN'S VOICE II: 'Course he's crazy, or we wouldn't be here!

MÅNS KNEKT: May I . . . (*noise outside*) . . . may I . . . say a word, *one* word!—You wouldn't be sitting here if the king . . . was quite right in his head. He is a little different, and unusual, but now he's shown he's better than a lot of others . . . who don't want to do the right thing by an unlucky girl . . . and the meal he has offered us, poor wretches . . . yes, for we are poor wretches . . . that means he doesn't despise his bride's . . . insignificant origin, one could say. (*Signals are sounded outside from different directions.*) Good friends, these signals, as we soldiers call them, announce that the meal or the collation is over. Let us therefore thank God for the food!

GÖRAN'S MOTHER (*enters*): What sort of spectacle is this?

MÅNS: Well, Mother Persson, there was a king who was going to celebrate his wedding, and he sent his servants to call those who were invited, but they didn't want to come. Then he said to his servants: Go out on the highways and call all those you find to the wedding. And the servants went out and gathered all that they found, both good and evil, and all the places were taken!

GÖRAN'S MOTHER: Where is Göran, my son?

MÅNS: With the king.

MOTHER (*points to the right*): In there?

MÅNS: In there.

(MOTHER *goes to the right.*)

MÅNS: Good friends! When the king comes back, you must all shout with me: King Erik XIV, *Vivat!* Understand? *Vivat! V-i-v-a-t!*

ALL: *Vivat!*

PEDER WELAMSON (*enters, violently*): Is the king here?

MÅNS: No. What's up?

WELAMSON: The castle has been surprised, and the dukes are in the next room!

MÅNS KNEKT (*gets up*): God in heaven, what's going to happen to us?

(*All get up.*)

WELAMSON: To you? What's going to happen to me? It'll be the block, most likely!

MÅNS KNEKT: Nothing's so fickle as fortune, and, when you're really fortunate, misfortune's waiting behind the door! What'll we say? What'll we do?

WELAMSON (*takes a beaker; empties it*): If they only wouldn't torture me, but the duke's a devil!

GÖRAN'S MOTHER (*rushing in*): Good Lord, the king has been taken prisoner! And Göran, my son, my son!

MÅNS: And Karin, my daughter! My daughter!

GÖRAN'S MOTHER: Yes, call her now! She won't go with you . . .

MÅNS: She won't?

GÖRAN'S MOTHER: No, because she has already gone with her husband!

MÅNS: They're crazy, both of them!

(*The doors at the back are opened;* NILS GYLLENSTJERNA *can be seen.*)

GYLLENSTJERNA: The king is coming! (*All withdraw to the sides.*)

MÅNS: But the king's been taken prisoner!

GYLLENSTJERNA: Yes, that one! But not this one! Watch it, people, or it'll be your heads!

(DUKES JOHN *and* CHARLES *enter with their followers.*)

GYLLENSTJERNA: Long live King John III!

ALL: Long live John III!

DUKE JOHN: Thank you! (*To* GYLLENSTJERNA) What sort of crowd is this?

GYLLENSTJERNA: It's King Erik's court!

JOHN (*to* DUKE CHARLES): My sight's none too good, but it seems to me the court looks rather strange . . . Aren't some of them in rags?

CHARLES: Our brother didn't love the little kings, but the little people . . .

JOHN: Yes, that was his weakness . . .

CHARLES (*softly to* JOHN): Or his strength. But yours is not to keep promises!

JOHN: What promises?

CHARLES: Weren't we to share the throne?

JOHN: I've never heard anything about that!

CHARLES: You're a scoundrel!

JOHN: Careful! There are many rooms in Gripsholm Castle . . .

CHARLES: Which you know!

JOHN (*to his followers*): The civil war is over; calm is restored, and we can look forward to a new time with newly awakened hopes for peace . . .

(CHARLES *gestures to his followers and is going.*)

JOHN: Where are you going, brother?

CHARLES: *My* way, which parts from yours here.

GYLLENSTJERNA: Oh, God, now it's beginning again!

JOHN: I think the world has gone mad!

CHARLES: That's what Erik thought, too. Who knows how it is . . .

MARIA: Isn't it over soon, mama?

CHARLES (*smiling*): No, my child; the struggles of life are never over!

CURTAIN

Notes on 'Erik XIV'

Göran Persson (ca. 1530–1568), King Erik's ablest favorite and councillor, has been treated more unfavorably by the popular historians than any of the other outstanding people of his time. Almost invariably he is labeled Erik's "evil genius" and given the primary blame for the cruel and brutal acts committed in the king's name. The earliest accounts were written almost without exception by Persson's enemies. The son of a priest who had turned Lutheran and had married, Göran Persson was exposed to humiliations and hostility throughout his life, for the great masses of people still looked with horror upon the marriage of priests. In the early 1550's, Göran had the opportunity to study at the University of Wittenberg where his brilliance, imagination, articulateness, broad knowledge, and insight into human nature brought him recognition from the professors, including Melanchthon. Göran's aggressiveness, ambition to get ahead, and lack of respect for traditional points of view undoubtedly helped him in Wittenberg as they helped him upon his return to Sweden. There he was in the employ of Gustav I until 1558 when he entered the service of Crown Prince Erik, who found him an adviser quite to his taste. Göran Persson's major goal during King Erik's reign may well have been what Strindberg suggests— the strengthening of the crown at the expense of the lords and to the benefit of both king and commons. As the king's procurator, Göran served both as the chairman of the king's supreme court and as the chief executor of royal directives. In these capacities, he was the object of the lords' hatred; they placed the greatest blame on him not only for their loss of power but for such matters as the humiliation of Nils Sture, the massacre of the lords, and the difficulties between Erik and his brothers and the lords. When the dukes were on the verge of succeeding in their rebellion against Erik, the latter surrendered Göran Persson to the dukes, who had him cross-examined, tortured, and then beheaded and quartered on September 22, 1568. Among other matters not mentioned by Strindberg is the fact that Göran Persson was ennobled early in the 1560's. He was married in 1561 to Anna Andersdotter and was the father of several children, one of whom, Erik Göransson Tegel (died 1636), was in the service of King Charles IX and wrote histories of Gustav Vasa and of Erik XIV.

Queen Karin Månsdotter (*ca.* 1550–1612), the daughter of a soldier in the royal life guards, was, according to the popular and traditional accounts, selling nuts on a Stockholm square when the king saw her for the first time. He brought the unusually beautiful girl to the palace to serve as an attendant to his sister Princess Elisabeth, saw to it that she received the same sort of training as the princess, and soon had her supervise his own illegitimate daughter, Virginia (1559–1633). Apparently, shortly after Virginia's mother Agda Persdotter ceased in the middle 1560's to be Erik's mistress, Karin became his recognized mistress. As early as 1567, Erik secured the national council's approval of their marriage, which possibly took place privately in 1567 but was openly and officially celebrated on July 4, 1568, in Stockholm. Karin was crowned queen the following day. About three months later, John was king, and Karin voluntarily joined her husband in prison. In addition to the two children mentioned in the play—Princess Sigrid and Prince Gustav—there were two other sons, Arnold and Henrik, both of whom were born in prison and died in infancy. From 1573 on Queen Karin was no longer permitted to share her husband's prison but was taken to Åbo in Finland, where adequate means for her support were provided by King John and his successors. In 1575 Prince Gustav was taken away from her. She is remembered in Finland for her kindness and helpfulness. Down through the centuries, the beautiful blond commoner who became queen of Sweden at eighteen has excited the interest of Swedish artists and writers. The Swedish people have been presented with many interpretations of Queen Karin and her place in Swedish history, all agreeing that she had beauty, charm of voice and bearing, and a gentle spirit, a good mind, and common sense; and that she was the finest influence in the unfortunate Erik's life, a good mother, and, in general, an admirable human being, who acquitted herself well in the difficult and far from ordinary situations life had meted out to her.

Queen Katarina Stenbock (1535–1621), Gustav Vasa's third wife, was the niece of her predecessor, Queen Margareta. As a very young girl, she had been officially engaged to Lord Gustav Tre Rosor, the half-brother of Lord Svante Sture. Neither her engagement nor her close relationship to Queen Margareta was allowed to stand in Gustav Vasa's way when he proposed in 1552. The marriage of the young girl and the middle-aged king was apparently successful, although they had no children. Queen Katarina is remembered as an attractive and intelligent woman who, both as queen and as dowager queen, concentrated much of her activity on helping the poor. Queen Katarina, it should be remembered, was two years younger than her oldest stepson, Erik XIV.

Duke John (Johan, 1537–1592), the favorite son of Gustav Vasa and his second queen, was made hereditary duke of Finland in 1556. Secretive and untrustworthy, he worked for his own selfish gains both in the closing years of his father's reign and in his brother's. Although he had signed the Articles of Arboga, he married Princess Catherine Jagellonica of Poland (died 1583) without King Erik's final approval and knowledge and, without consulting Erik, made agreements directly with the king of Poland. As has already been noted, he refused to obey Erik's resultant summons to Stockholm, set up armed resistance to the king, and was finally taken prisoner. Tried before the estates for treason, he was sentenced to lose his life, property, and special privileges and rank. King Erik reprieved him but kept him prisoner at Gripsholm Castle from 1563 to 1567. In spite of his promise to share the throne with Charles, John became the sole ruler in 1568. Suspicious, sensitive, violent, pro-Catholic, and apparently sincerely religious, John played with the idea of restoring Catholicism. As ruler he proved himself the least competent of Gustav Vasa's three sons who in turn occupied the Swedish throne. His greatest monuments are the castles and churches he either built or had restored or rebuilt; he had a genuine interest in art and architecture. With his first queen, Catherine of Poland, he had two children, Sigismund and Anna, and with his second, Lady Gunilla

Bielke, the ill-fated Duke John of Östergötland (see *Gustav Adolf* [Seattle and New York: University of Washington Press and American-Scandinavian Foundation, 1957]).

Lord Nils Gyllenstjerna (*ca.* 1526–1601), closely related to many of the great aristocratic families and a loyal supporter of Erik XIV, was educated at both Wittenberg and Rostock. Upon the accession of Erik in 1560, Lord Nils entered the king's service; he held many positions including those of chancellor, national councillor, marshal, and diplomat. On at least two occasions (1560, 1562), he headed missions to England, primarily designed to secure the engagement and marriage of Elizabeth and Erik. As long as Erik was on the throne, he served that king both faithfully and well, and, after John ascended the throne, Gyllenstjerna served him as a diplomat. The sources agree that Gyllenstjerna was a learned and wise man of experience who, as Strindberg suggests, could adjust himself realistically to the turbulent events of his time.

Count Svante Sture (1517–1567) was the son of Regent Sten Sture and Lady Kristina Gyllenstjerna Sture whom Strindberg presents in *The Last of the Knights* (see Strindberg's *The Last of the Knights, The Regent, Earl Birger of Bjälbo* [Seattle: University of Washington Press, 1956]). Educated abroad, Lord Svante became one of King Gustav's loyal supporters, refusing on occasion to let either the Lübeckers or Swedish malcontents use either him or his name to dethrone Gustav. Even when the king sued for the hand of and married Lady Margareta Lejonhuvud, the woman Sture loved and who loved him, the latter did not join the opposition to the king. He served the king in various capacities, among others that of national councillor. Happily married to Queen Margareta's sister Märta, he became the father of several children, two of whom, Nils and Erik, are characters in Strindberg's play. In 1561, King Erik XIV made him the first count (*greve*) in Sweden, but the relations between the king and the head of the Sture clan became increasingly difficult, culminating in the massacre of the Stures and other lords in Uppsala Castle in 1567. The difficulties are no doubt traceable primarily to King Erik's extreme suspicion about and hatred of the Stures, close relatives of Princes John and Charles, but some of the sources agree with Strindberg in suggesting that the Stures' expressed preference for John, and their pride, ambition for power, and tactlessness may have contributed as well.

Lord Nils Sture (1543–1567), son of Count Svante and Lady Märta Sture, was a highly intelligent, carefully educated, handsome and popular young nobleman who became the special object of King Erik's suspicion and distrust because of his very blond hair; as we have seen, the king was very much influenced by astrologers, one of whom had prophesied that a man with fair hair would ultimately bring Erik to disaster (see, for example, Fryxell, III, 228). Nevertheless, Erik entrusted both important military tasks and diplomatic missions to Lord Nils. In 1561 and again in 1566, he had been sent abroad to secure a marriage agreement for King Erik. In 1566, he had refused to obey the king's order to massacre fleeing Danish soldiers and to lay waste an area in Västergötland where the inhabitants had not given their enthusiastic support to the king. Lord Nils apparently served King Erik well; his rewards were public humiliation in Stockholm in 1566 and assassination in 1567. His younger brother Lord Erik Sture had also served the king.

Duke Charles (Carl or Karl, 1550–1611), the youngest half-brother of Erik XIV and, from 1604 to 1611, Charles IX, was probably the ablest of Gustav Vasa's sons. Although he was only eighteen at the time, Charles is usually credited with the success of the rebellion in 1568 that placed Erik in prison and Duke John on the throne as John III. From 1568 on, as the hereditary duke of the duchy his father had willed him in 1560, Charles was one of the most powerful men in the kingdom. The Articles of Arboga were rescinded shortly after John came to the throne. A suspicious and vengeful ruler, Charles did not ordinarily hesitate to strengthen the central government by liquidating his enemies; hence, the nickname "the Bloody" which has sometimes been applied to him. The father of Gustav II Adolf and the grandfather of Queen Christina, Charles is remembered as a highly effective monarch, an enthusiastic student of theology, and a defender of the reformation.

Prince Gustav (January 28, 1568–1607), the oldest son of Erik XIV and Karin Månsdotter, may have been the legal heir to the throne if, as some of the sources say, his parents were secretly married in 1567. The actions of King John suggest as much: in 1573, Prince Gustav was taken to Finland with his mother; in 1575 he was taken away from her and sent abroad to be educated in Catholic schools. In 1596 he was permitted to see his mother in Reval. During the 1590's and the early years of the seventeenth century, he visited the courts of Emperor Rudolf, King Sigismund of Poland, and Czar Boris Godunov. When the last wanted to use him as a political pawn and offered him his daughter in marriage, Prince Gustav refused and was imprisoned. Released from prison and banished to a small and distant town, Gustav lived in want until his death in 1607. The sources agree that he was a highly intelligent dreamer, a devout Catholic, and a loyal son of Sweden who shared with many others of his time an enthusiastic interest in alchemy.

Princess Sigrid (1566–1633), the daughter of Erik XIV and Karin Månsdotter, was brought up by her mother in Finland, was a frequent guest of the Stures at Hörningsholm, and was for a short time at the Polish court of her cousin King Sigismund. Married first to Lord Henrik Tott, she became the mother of Åke Tott (see Strindberg's *Gustav Adolf*). In 1609, after the death of Henrik Tott, she married Lord Nils Nilsson Natt-och-Dag.

ACT I

1. Strindberg's major sources agree that Max (or Maximilian) was an army ensign who had fallen in love with Karin and who urged her to marry him even after she became the king's mistress; that, upon discovering Max's interest in Karin, King Erik ordered Max to join the army then in Norway; and that, when Max attempted to see Karin before he left, he was seized and, on Göran Persson's orders, disposed of as Strindberg says later on in the play. Fryxell (p. 212) says that according to some older accounts Max and Karin may have been engaged.

2. Erik XIV's extended and expensive courtship of Elizabeth began some time before he ascended the throne (1560) and before she became queen (1558). Before King Gustav I Vasa's death, one mission after the other had been sent to England to secure a marriage agreement; these were headed by Erik's tutor and favorite Dionysius Burreus, Lord Sten Lejonhuvud, Lord Gustav Roos, and Duke John. In September, 1560, Erik was about to sail to England himself but had to return to Stockholm because of the death of his father on September 29. In December, 1559, Lord Nils Gyllenstjerna and Burreus were sent to London on the same errand, and shortly thereafter Lord Nils Sture was sent. When

none of his ambassadors succeeded in securing a favorable reply from the wily English queen (Strindberg calls her queen of Britain), Erik decided to propose in person. In September, 1561, a fleet of fourteen Swedish ships sailed, but had to return to harbor on the second day because of a violent storm. While Erik undoubtedly hoped to increase both his power and prestige by marriage to Elizabeth, there seems to be no doubt either that she dealt with Erik playfully for her own purposes as she did with her other suitors. Duke John was not the only member of the Swedish royal family who knew Elizabeth personally; his sister and King Erik's half-sister, the beautiful and temperamental Princess Cecilia (1540–1627), by then the wife of Kristoffer of Baden, was Elizabeth's guest from 1565 to 1566. See *Queen Elizabeth and a Swedish Princess: Being an Account of the Journey of Princess Cecilia of Sweden to Queen Elizabeth* (edited from the contemporary manuscript of James Bell by Ethel Seaton, 1926).

3. The practice of having a court fool or jester continued beyond Erik's day. A most attractive literary work in which Erik's ironically named court fool Hercules is mentioned is Gustaf Fröding's "En visa om mig och narren Herkules" ("A Song about Me [i.e., Erik] and the Fool Hercules") in "Ur Kung Eriks visor" ("From King Erik's Songs").

4. See *The Sweden Year-book* or an encyclopedia for information about and pictures of the Swedish coat of arms.

5. See the note on Nils Sture above.

6. See the note on Queen Katarina Stenbock above.

7. Erik's courtships of Mary of Scotland, Renata of Lorraine, and Kristina of Hesse were no more logically pursued than that of Elizabeth; frequently, he was courting two or more of them at the same time. Kristina finally married the duke of Holstein; their daughter Kristina married Erik's brother Charles and became the mother of Gustav II Adolf.

8. Although King Erik consented to John's marriage to Catherine of Poland, the king changed his mind for personal and political reasons after John had already hurriedly left for Poland. In spite of the fact that Erik's quickly dispatched messenger caught up with John in good time, John nevertheless married Catherine—against King Erik's orders—on October 4, 1562.

9. See the note on Nils Sture above.

10. Lord Nils Gyllenstjerna, one of the ablest and most loyal of

Erik's advisers, was *överste hovmästare*, i.e., chancellor of the realm and what would have been called later minister for foreign affairs.

11. Gyllenstjerna would have had personal opportunity to observe the relationship of Queen Elizabeth and Robert Dudley, Earl of Leicester, in London since he had already served as Erik's ambassador there. Fryxell (III, 191) says: "Elizabeth seemed to become less inclined toward him [Erik], and Gyllenstjerna said in his letters, that the primary reason for this was Elizabeth's favorite, the young and handsome earl of Leicester. Erik became violently furious with him; first, he challenged him to a duel, and, when that could not take place, he commanded Gyllenstjerna to hire someone in London to murder the earl; Erik promised that the assassin would get both security and rich rewards in Sweden, but threatened Gyllenstjerna with his disfavor if he did not want to carry out the command." Gyllenstjerna, as Strindberg says, refused to obey this order.

12. See Strindberg's *The Last of the Knights, The Regent, Earl Birger of Bjälbo* for information about the relationship between the two great families the Stures and the Vasas, information about the Natt-och-Dag who assassinated the fifteenth-century leader Engelbrekt, and about the Folkung dynasty and its bloody record. St. Erik, the patron saint of Sweden, was a twelfth-century king.

13. The allusion to the Folkungs is particularly apt since the struggles for the throne among various members of that dynasty are strikingly parallel to the struggles among the sons of Gustav Vasa—Erik, John, and Charles. See Strindberg's *The Saga of the Folkungs* and the volume referred to in note 12.

14. Margareta Lejonhuvud, Gustav Vasa's second queen, probably was engaged to young Svante Sture (see *The Regent*) when Gustav Vasa asked for her hand in marriage; at any rate, the sources agree that Svante Sture and Margareta were in love, and they also agree that the marriage of Gustav and Margareta was an unusually successful one. A year after Queen Margareta's death in 1551, King Gustav married Lady Katarina Stenbock, the daugher of Queen Margareta's sister Brita and secretly the fiancée of Lord Gustav Tre Rosor, the half-brother of Svante Sture. The second husband of Svante's mother, Lady Kristina Gyllenstjerna Sture, was Lord Gustav's father; her first was "the last of the knights." See the first two plays referred to in note 12.

15. Duke John was very much interested in theology; as Strindberg suggests here and states in *Gustav Vasa,* he was a Catholic by faith and would have liked to restore Catholicism in Sweden. His consort, Catherine, was a Roman Catholic, of course, and his son Sigismund was reared as a Catholic.

16. In 1572, ten years after John's marriage to Catherine Jagellonica, the last of the Jagellonian kings of Poland died, and, after an interregnum, Prince Sigismund of Sweden was elected king of Poland in 1587; upon John's death in 1592, Sigismund became king of Sweden also. Sigismund was married in turn to two Hapsburg princesses and through them and his mother had claims to rights of inheritance in the Italian house of Sforza.

17. Göran Persson's official title was procurator; his powers were those indicated by Strindberg.

18. In April, 1561, the estates meeting at Arboga officially approved the so-called Articles of Arboga, which provided that the dukes—John, Magnus, and Charles—were the king's subjects, that the inhabitants of their duchies should take the oath of allegiance to the king and not to the particular duke, and that bishops and the legal officials in the duchies could be appointed only by the king. The articles were designed by King Erik and his advisers, among them Göran Persson and Svante Sture, to prevent the dukes from becoming in practical terms independent of the king and the central government.

19. See notes 12 and 13.

ACT II

20. Strindberg has based his account of the humiliation of Göran Persson by Svante Sture and others on ample details in all the major sources. Not only was Göran Persson a commoner who was supplanting the aristocrats in power, but he was the offspring of a Catholic monk who had become a Lutheran pastor and had married the daughter of another former Catholic priest. Although such marriages were legal, they were in popular opinion sinful. Hence, the term applied to Göran Persson and his like, *prästkläpp,* here translated "priest's bastard."

21. See *Gustav Vasa* and *The Regent.*

22. Tradition says that in the seventh century Svealand consisted of

small kingdoms, the center of one of which was Old Uppsala. The king, Ingjald, extended his dominions considerably by inviting six neighboring kings to a banquet. When the guests were asleep, Ingjald gave orders to have the hall in which they were sleeping burned to the ground. Ingjald as a result extended his kingdom and was given the nickname *Illråde* (freely translated, "the Wicked"). For information about Christian the Tyrant, see *The Last of the Knights, The Regent, Earl Birger of Bjälbo.*

23. *Konungens nämnd* or the king's supreme court was set up early in Erik's reign to judge cases appealed from lower courts and to exercise original jurisdiction in such matters as treason. Unfortunately, the supreme court was used on many occasions for arbitrary actions.

24. In 1454, King Charles VIII secured the confiscation of much of the land that had come into the possession of the church or its prelates illegally through donations made when the donors were not in good health or of sound mind, or when they exceeded the amount of inherited property beyond that which the law permitted. See *Master Olof* for information about the reformation as a revolution for both church and state.

25. At the mouth of the Göta River in southwestern Sweden.

26. See II Samuel 11:2-27.

27. See note 18. According to the Articles of Arboga Duke John of Finland had committed treason when he allied himself with the Polish king, married Catherine against Erik's specific orders, made the people of his duchy swear allegiance to him rather than to the king, and fortified his castle at Åbo for purposes of defense against the national forces.

28. Erik's mother was German, of course, while the mother of John and Charles belonged to the higher nobility.

29. Betrothal was long considered in many European countries as morally and even legally the beginning of marriage.

30. See note 1.

ACT III

31. Gripsholm Castle, in which Duke John and his duchess were imprisoned, lies near the little city of Mariefred, Södermanland. The original castle was built in the late fourteenth century; the present one

was built during the reign of Gustav Vasa. It has an eighteenth-century theater and famous art and historical collections.

32. *Trettondagen* or Twelfth Night (January 6) marks the end of the Swedish Christmas season. Fish is a standard part of the Christmas menu.

33. Strindberg's point is that the *J* and the *C* could have represented either Dukes John and Charles or John and his consort, Catherine Jagellonica (in Swedish, Catherine was spelled with either a *C* or a *K*).

34. In 1306, Dukes Erik and Valdemar took their brother King Birger and his queen prisoners at the royal estate of Håtuna (now Håtunaholm) and brought them to Nyköping Castle. In 1317, King Birger imprisoned the dukes after a banquet of reconciliation at Nyköping and later destroyed the prison keys and, according to several sources, let his brothers die of hunger.

35. See notes 18 and 27.

36. *Rikssalen,* or the Hall of State, was a large room in Uppsala Castle in which the estates met on occasion.

37. Until 1866, the *Riksdag* or parliament was divided into four houses or estates: the lords, the clergy, the burghers, and the yeomen (farmers). Each estate had a speaker.

38. Hörningsholm, the landed estate in Södermanland, was then the home of Svante Sture and his immediate family.

39. Lord Abraham Stenbock, dowager queen Katarina's brother, was forced to sign a letter later used as evidence against the imprisoned lords, but was nevertheless imprisoned and executed.

40. Lord Ivar Ivarsson was accused—along with Nils Sture, Klas Tott, Abraham Stenbock, and a German nobleman Josua Genewitz—of conspiring to depose and assassinate King Erik. Most of the king's witnesses against the suspected conspirators were commoners, and consequently not considered acceptable as witnesses by the lords. Ivarsson was executed.

41. Prince Charles, the youngest of Gustav Vasa's sons, was the duke of Södermanland, Värmland, and Närke, so the Södermanland regiment was under his control.

42. The sources agree that King Erik not only loved Karin and their children but enjoyed outings with them of the kind Strindberg mentions.

43. The account Strindberg gives of the assassination of the Stures

and the other lords agrees in most details with the accounts in his three major sources. King Erik stabbed Nils Sture in the arm, but aside from that act left the killings to Peder Welamson (Göran Persson's nephew) and others.

44. Afzelius (II, 191) says: "In the meanwhile, the insane king ran about in the woods near Alsike, where Dionysius Burreus first found him. When he saw his unworthy tutor, the man who had led him to do much that is evil, he ordered the same soldier, who had murdered Nils Sture, to kill Dionysius. This took place west of the village by a spring, which is still called Dionysius' spring." Erik's temporary insanity, his suffering from pangs of conscience, his recovery under Karin's care, and his attempts at compensating the survivors of the assassinated lords are all emphasized in the sources.

45. Fryxell (III, 256) says that John and Charles agreed when their rebellion began that if it was successful they would govern the kingdom jointly. John broke that promise, and Charles had to wait until 1604 before he could ascend the throne.

46. John was probably sincerely religious; ever pro-Catholic, interested in theology, and opposed to strife about faith, John tried ineffectively to provide means for the reconciliation of Protestants and Catholics. His religious faith did not imply a high standard of moral conduct, however.

47. See Strindberg's *Earl Birger of Bjälbo* for information about the descendants of King Valdemar and his sister-in-law Judith.

48. See note 34.

49. The wedding of Erik and Karin on July 4, 1568, was really a double wedding, for Princess Elizabeth, Erik's half-sister, and Duke Magnus of Saxony were also married then. The dukes did not attend, largely, perhaps, because Karin had warned them that their lives would be endangered. It should be emphasized that both the dukes as well as the estates had approved Erik's marriage to Karin and the acceptance of their children as heirs to the Swedish throne. Queen Karin was crowned on July 5.

50. See *Gustav Vasa*.

51. Apparently neither King Erik nor Göran Persson acted quickly and effectively to end the revolt of the dukes. The sources give many specific illustrations of the unwise and tardy behavior of the king and his

procurator between the time of the royal wedding and the actual imprisonment and deposal of King Erik on September 29, 1568.

52. The commoners considered Erik XIV their friend. Not only did he usually treat them well and, at times, familiarly, but on many occasions he protected them from the lords' oppression.